PRAISE FOR THE B

"Anne Hanson's beautifully written memoir mystery is full of interesting characters, intrigue, and surprises. It's a page-turner that will captivate readers from beginning to end. A great read!"
—Elaine Tyler May, Author of *Homeward Bound: American Families in the Cold War Era*

"Hanson interweaves her engaging personal account ... with fictionalized vignettes from various times in her grandparents' lives, which give the memoir a novelistic dimension ... it's an intriguing journey through the world of genealogical sleuthing."
—Kirkus Reviews

"I find Anne Hanson's *Buried Secrets* a rich journey through one family's history. While details differ, however, I think all families share the complexities of past relationships that have come through generations and, without explanation, have given each generation its peculiar character. Buried Secrets brings to life past family members and the process of discovery with clarity.

This book does not easily fit into any neat category. It is concurrently a mystery story, a social history, and an examination of family complexities, for starters. Perhaps the core of this story, the glue that holds it together, is the narrator's reflection "I have learned that the price of a deep and profound love is an equally deep pain upon its loss." Its celebration of love even in difficult circumstances is powerful. "
—Tom Woodward, Retired English teacher of forty-four years at Westtown Friends School

"What a pleasure to read a book of discovery that moves forward like a true mystery whodunnit. It was hard to put down, so eager was I to find out what happened."
—David Rowland, President, Old York Road Historical Society

BURIED SECRETS

LOOKING FOR FRANK AND IDA

ANNE HANSON

Buried Secrets: Looking for Frank and Ida
Published by New England Books, LLC
Brookline, Massachusetts

ISBN: 979-8-218-02527-4
BIOGRAPHY & AUTOBIOGRAPHY / Personal
TRUE CRIME / Con Artists, Hoaxes & Deceptions

Publisher's Cataloging-in-Publication data

Names: Hanson, Anne, author.

Title: Buried secrets : looking for Frank and Ida / Anne Hanson.
Description: Brookline, MA: Anne Hanson, 2022.
Identifiers: ISBN: 979-8-218-02527-4
Subjects: LCSH Hanson, Frank. | Hanson, Ida. | Hanson, Anne--Family. | Family secrets. | BISAC BIOGRAPHY & AUTOBIOGRAPHY / Personal Memoirs
Classification: LCC CT274 .H3542 2022 | DDC 929/.2/0973--dc23

Cover and interior design by Victoria Wolf, wolfdesignandmarketing.com. Copyright owned by Anne Hanson.

NEW ENGLAND BOOKS

For my dad.

This is a work of nonfiction. All the research and events presented via the first-person narrative are real. In portraying experiences that occurred many years ago, I have depicted the original as faithfully as memory allows. In some cases, I have condensed scenes and paraphrased conversations.

This book also contains imagined recreations of scenes that occurred but whose exact details are unknown, as well as scenes based on fact but whose details are the product of my imagination. In addition to the Prologue, such recreations occur at the start of Chapters 2, 3, 7, 8, 10, 14, 16, 21 through 26, and 28. These scenes commence with a date and the phrase "Imagining the past," and conclude with a branch.

PROLOGUE

SEPTEMBER 1955 *(Imagining the past)*

"THERE IT IS. Go left."

Frank was already turning the wheel of the green Studebaker before Ida finished her instructions. They continued slowly down the curving suburban lane.

It was a bright September day, a gentle breeze whispering warm echoes of summer, as my grandparents, Frank and Ida Hanson, drove through a neighborhood just like thousands that had sprung up across the United States in the 1950s. Small, tidy ranch houses with compact lawns, new siding, and fresh paint lined both sides of the road in neat configurations. In the backyards, jungle gyms, swings, and children's toys reigned over miniature green landscapes.

Ida clutched a scrap of paper on which she had written an address in precise cursive. Behind rectangular spectacles, her eyes darted back and forth. Her hand fluttered from the camera on her lap to her hair, tucking an imaginary stray wisp back into her gray bun.

The car's front windows were rolled all the way down, allowing the afternoon air to waft through the vehicle. Frank's gaze held steadily to the road ahead, with an occasional glance up at their tranquil surroundings. Although the modest fringe of white hair encircling his mostly bald head signaled the departure of youth, Frank's muscular arms, relaxed as they guided the steering wheel, remained the powerful tools of a working carpenter.

Ida leaned out the window to study the number on each house they passed.

"That's it." Her abrupt voice again broke their silence.

Number 117, a modest blue ranch house with a newly mowed lawn and a clump of orderly shrubs, looked much like every other dwelling in the neighborhood. The shades were drawn and the driveway was empty. Next door, a blond boy circled his tricycle around and around in the driveway, a few feet from a stocky man washing a shiny blue Ford Mainline sedan.

"Daddeeeeey, Daddeeeeey!" The child's high-pitched, happy shriek elicited a grin from the man, whose ruddy features were reflected on the young cyclist's round face. "Look at me, Daddeeeeey!"

"Stop before we're in front of it," Ida said, "Close your window. I don't want anyone to see us."

Whether the window was open or closed made little difference in their visibility, but after three decades of marriage, Frank knew better than to challenge Ida when her curt tone signaled agitation. He rolled up his window.

She inhaled with a quick, sharp gasp. The man next door was looking straight at the Studebaker. Did he recognize them? Probably not. After a long moment, he turned back to his gleaming vehicle, obliterating soapsuds from the fender with quick blasts of the hose.

Frank pulled over to the curb, halfway between the neighbor's house and number 117. Across the street, a young woman in a yellow blouse, pedal pushers, and a headdress of pink curlers wielded an oversized pair of clippers as she pruned the bushes lining her front walk. Frank and Ida sat in the

Studebaker, the windows rolled up, looking at the small blue house. Sweat trickled down their backs as the heat inside the car intensified.

Ida picked up the camera and pointed it at number 117. The click of the shutter echoed within the quiet, motionless vehicle. Within Ida's mind, it felt like the slam of a hollow door.

"Let's go and come back down the street from the other side."

Frank pulled the Studebaker away from the curb, and slowly they wound down the road. After a hundred yards, he made a U-turn and guided the car back up the lane until they were almost in front of number 117 again, this time on the other side of the street. He halted, leaving the motor running. The woman in curlers had progressed to the side of her house, where she continued to steadily snip offending branches. Straightening up, she stared at the car again, clippers dangling from her right hand.

"You take it now," Ida said, handing Frank the camera.

Through his closed window, Frank pointed the camera across the street at number 117 and snapped.

"Oh no, she's watching us. We need to move. Drive down so she can't see us."

Nodding, Frank pulled forward a few yards until the woman was out of sight behind the corner of her house. He stopped in front of a newly planted seedling with a spindly trunk and thin, delicate branches. Twisting around in her seat, Ida stared back at the blue ranch house for a long minute, her jaw clenched. One hand still clutched the now-forgotten scrap of paper with the address.

"I wish she hadn't seen us." Ida's voice broke between shallow breaths.

"It'll be OK, sweetie," Frank whispered, stroking her hair. "It's all right."

He placed the camera in Ida's purse and wrapped his arms around her. Tears streamed down her face, and she began rocking back and forth, her shoulders heaving, the scrap of paper fluttering to the car floor.

Outside the vehicle, Ida's moans dissipated in the swelling afternoon breeze. The seedling tree's slender limbs quivered as the wind gained force, their bobbing shadows writhing in an unearthly waltz on the sidewalk.

Ida's cries gradually subsided. She sat up straight and very still. Finally, she began wiping her wet eyes and cheeks with Frank's handkerchief, while he gently caressed her shoulder.

"OK, let's go," Ida murmured finally in a dull, low tone.

Inside her camera, the rays of light that had beamed through the open shutter during those fractions of a second had done their work, searing hazy images into the undeveloped film. The telltale prints, unseen for the next fifty years, mutely attested to Ida and Frank's path that September day.

CHAPTER 1:
GHOSTS IN A BOX

AUGUST 2002

"COME ON, DAD," I said. "Let me just look in the box. The pictures might have clues."

"No."

"Why not?" I asked.

"I don't want to get it out. It's depressing."

My father, Harley, couldn't face the box containing his parents' photo collection, even though its contents might help solve our baffling family mystery. For decades, a rotating cast of family members had tried, and failed, to trace the family trees of his Brooklyn-born parents, Frank Elmer Hanson and Ida Agnes (Howe) Hanson. Now, a previously unknown trove of photos had the potential to breathe new life into the family project, as my dad had dubbed our investigation into his parents' identities.

If only I could get my hands on those pictures. How frustrating it was that my dad refused to let me look at them, especially since he was the one who, years earlier, had gotten me involved in the family project. Despite his belief in seeking truth and confronting facts, my father, a retired scientist and behavioral psychologist, shrank from this one particular box of evidence.

Until he was sixty-nine, my dad was one of the four Hanson boys, brothers who had grown up during the 1930s and 1940s in a bungalow in North Hill, a working-class neighborhood of Akron, Ohio. Then, in March of 2000, my dad's favorite older brother, Al, died abruptly of cardiac arrest. A month later, his twin brother, Harvey, was diagnosed with liver cancer. By June of 2000 Uncle Harvey was gone too, slowly inhaling one last gulp of air thirty minutes after I arrived at his bedside in a hospice in Dayton, Ohio. My father had paid his final visit a day earlier.

A month after this double blow, a box containing Ida and Frank's photo collection arrived at the doorstep of the ranch house my dad shared with my stepmother, Carol, in an outer-ring suburb north of Philadelphia. Uncle Al's widow, Aunt Betty, had cleaned house, shipping off Hanson memorabilia that had been consigned to the oblivion of storage ever since Frank, my grampa, died in 1982.

As soon as my dad mentioned the box, I began badgering him to let me see its contents. These photos were our last, best chance for a break in the case of our seemingly unsolvable family mystery—genetic ancestry testing being, at the time, in its untried infancy. Yet no matter whether I cajoled my dad on the phone or appealed in person when I came down from Boston, we always ended up at the same impasse.

"Can you get out the box tonight?" I'd say. "You don't have to look at the pictures. I'll go through them for you. I'll just look to see if there's anything that could help us in the research."

"No, I don't want to," he invariably replied. "Maybe next time you come."

His jaw, the strong angles of his youth now gently camouflaged by a layer of flesh, jutted forward. The subject was closed.

It seemed unfathomable that my father could refuse me access to this newly unearthed box of photos. At his request, I had begun my labors in the Hanson and Howe genealogical wilderness during college two decades earlier. For years, he had even insisted on paying me by the hour.

Although I didn't understand why the search for his parents' missing past meant so much to my father, I immediately loved the process of family history investigation.

"I'm more than happy to do the research, but why don't you do it too?" I asked a few times. His reply, "I don't have the required skill set," made no sense, coming from a man whose trade was designing and performing research studies. However, given how much I relished being my dad's detective, I dropped it.

Forever my favorite person in the world to talk to, my dad was willing to entertain almost any topic, with the possible exception of sports, which he regarded with profound indifference. When I was off on my own at boarding school after my parents' divorce, in my midteens, and later at college, he was the one I called, collect from a pay phone, when I was lonely or needed advice.

"Hi, Annieeee!" he'd say after the operator put me through. Just hearing his singsong greeting, his calm voice still echoing the cadence of his hometown of Akron, Ohio, my pulse would slow down, and I'd relax. Wherever I was, whatever jam I had gotten myself into, my father's nonjudgmental insights and comments invariably comforted me and helped me find a way forward.

My dad didn't believe emotions mattered, professionally speaking, yet he would have made an excellent therapist and indeed had counseled many friends over the years. At Merck & Co., Inc., the drug company where he had directed laboratory research using the principles of behavioral psychology, the human resources manager had frequently sent troubled employees to him for guidance.

When it came to his own feelings and painful subjects, however, my father was stubbornly recalcitrant. "He analyzes everyone but himself," my stepmom, Carol, remarked once before clapping her hand over her mouth, as if she had revealed too much. Nowhere was this observation truer than regarding the box of photos. The ghosts of his brothers and parents, lying silently within that container, evoked feelings that my outwardly cool and collected dad just couldn't confront.

The Hanson family odyssey had begun simply enough in 1953, when Uncle Harvey's new bride, Virginia, asked her in-laws if they would answer a few questions about their family trees. While in most families this would be an ordinary request, among the Hansons, it was an unprecedented strike within forbidden territory.

"They're all dead. They died." That was Frank's terse response whenever my dad asked about his family back in Brooklyn.

"Everyone else I knew, the kids I played with, they all had relatives, uncles, cousins," my dad told me. "I never had any."

My dad's scant knowledge of his father's Swedish immigrant family focused on two little sisters, Florence and May, whom Frank had adored.

"My father always talked about how cute Baby Florence was, how she was his favorite," my dad said.

The other small sister, May, died around the time of the 1918 flu pandemic, which had upset Frank terribly. He also mentioned one other sibling, Al, a musician in the US Navy.

Ida always told her sons that she was the only child of a wealthy English couple who had died when she was a young girl. Her father, practically of noble descent back in Sheffield, England, had emigrated to the United States as a young man. After a brief stay in Connecticut, he'd bought a farm in Brooklyn, New York, where he'd lived the life of an English country squire. The city had taken over the land when it created Prospect Park. So substantial was her late papa's "English fortune," according to Ida, that she and Frank could just go to New York to get money that was coming in from England.

When new daughter-in-law Virginia asked Frank and Ida for information about their families, they acquiesced readily, despite their previous refusals to discuss their pasts. In an exchange unprecedented within the Hanson family, they divulged specific details, such as their parents' and grandparents' names, the names and birth order of Frank's eight younger siblings, and even the names of Ida's aunts and uncles back in Sheffield. Frank's parents had emigrated from Skåne, in southern Sweden, he said. Ida also revealed the date and place of her and Frank's wedding: They were married in New York City by a justice of the peace on May 23, 1923.

Armed with this data, Virginia, a diligent and knowledgeable librarian, spent the next three decades attempting to trace Ida's and Frank's family histories. Her research was a complete and utter failure. Virginia could never corroborate a single element of their stories. Nor could she identify even one ancestor who potentially belonged to us.

During Frank's later years, if questioned about his family back in New York, his standard reply was, "I don't remember." Or he'd say something to the effect of, "The past isn't important. You go on and have your own life." Then he'd change the subject. We couldn't ask Ida because she had died in 1960 after a battle with breast cancer.

When my sisters, Uncle Al, and I joined the family investigation in the late 1970s, our endeavors were just as fruitless as Virginia's. Referring to her painstakingly created ancestry charts, with names and dates neatly penciled in, we devoted untold hours to both long-distance and on-site research. We visited dusty archives in locations ranging from New York City and Washington, D.C., to Columbus, Ohio, and Salt Lake City, Utah. We stared at microfilm, scrutinized birth, death, and marriage records, pored over city directories, and examined church registers and land records. While vacationing with her husband in England in the 1980s, my oldest sister, Karen, even scheduled a research detour up north to the city of Sheffield, a former steel industrial powerhouse that drew few tourists. When internet genealogy sites began developing in the late 1990s, I mined every available online source, again to no avail.

Over the decades, this family project of ours mutated into an endless spiral of doomed excursions within a murky, slippery labyrinth. Despite all our digging, the Hanson and Howe investigators failed to unearth even the tiniest speck of evidence that the families of Frank Hanson and Ida Howe had ever existed.

How could a bunch of smart people look so hard and never find a thing? If our genealogical research were a Nancy Drew mystery, its title would be "The Case of the Missing Ancestors."

In August of 2002, I was again visiting my father and stepmother, Carol. As we drove home from dinner, I decided to ask for the pictures yet again. My father was relaxed after enjoying an extra-rare steak along with a few drinks and good conversation. This was the best chance I was going to get.

"Hey, Dad," I said. "Let's get the pictures out tonight."

"No." From the rear seat of the dark car, I could see only the back of his head, but I could envision him pursing his lips as he stared straight ahead.

"You said I could look at them next time I came."

"You did, Harley," Carol chimed in. "You promised. You said you'd let her see them this visit."

"I changed my mind," he said flatly. After a long silence, we exchanged only a handful of words the rest of the way home.

When we got back to the house, he disappeared into his private study, dubbed the "junk room," and closed the door. Something was up. Typically, my dad's first order of business after getting home was to change from his going-out clothes into his comfortable at-home uniform of old slacks and a threadbare but clean short-sleeved button-down shirt.

A few minutes later, he returned, staring straight ahead, clasping a battered brown cardboard box the size of a large hatbox. Avoiding eye contact, with a soft thump he placed the box in front of me on the table of the keeping room, as he and Carol called the all-purpose living area just off their kitchen.

"Don't look at them now. I don't want to talk about it."

Startled, I stared at this long-sought prize, encased in its shell of brown cardboard and packing tape. I longed to tear it open and dive in, but I would have to hold out a little longer.

"OK, that's fine," I said, composing my face into the most neutral expression I could muster. Wordlessly, I bore my treasure down the beige-carpeted hallway to Carol's small study, which doubled as the guest room.

Carol's brown eyes were sparkling when I returned to the keeping room. "I think the answer is going to be in those pictures," she said.

My father and I spent the rest of the evening chatting in the basement den as we half-watched TV, idly flicking between his favorite stations, the History Channel and public TV.

On the floor by the couch were the slippers my father always wore indoors. Until my parents split up when I was fourteen, a similar pair of worn brown leather slippers by the back door promised his return home from long hours at the Merck labs. When I was a toddler, the child of another scientist in his lab had contracted amoebic dysentery from monkey excrement the fellow had unwittingly tracked home on his shoes. Horrified, thereafter my dad had always donned slippers immediately upon entering the house, a practice he had continued after retirement. He never replaced a pair until the leather was cracking and soles splitting. Also typical of my dad was that he didn't tell me and my sisters why he always wore slippers inside. As was his way, he quietly protected us against dangers large and small.

At midnight, leaving my father downstairs still watching TV, I padded down the dimly lit hallway to Carol's study, where the photos awaited me. Finally, after two long years, I was about to enter the hidden world housed in that simple cardboard box.

Frank's family, with siblings listed by birth order

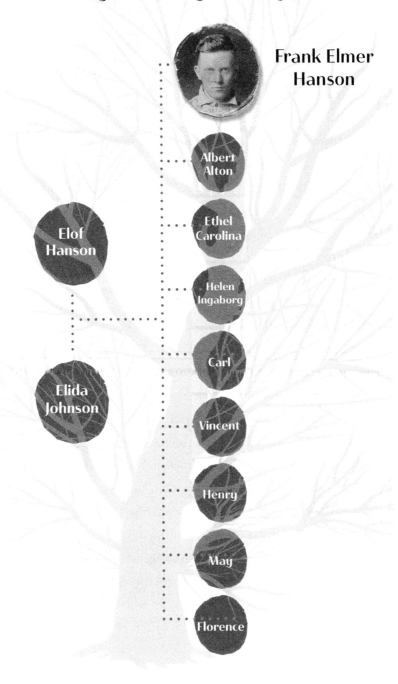

Frank Elmer Hanson

Albert Alton

Elof Hanson

Ethel Carolina

Helen Ingaborg

Carl

Elida Johnson

Vincent

Henry

May

Florence

Ida's family in Sheffield, England

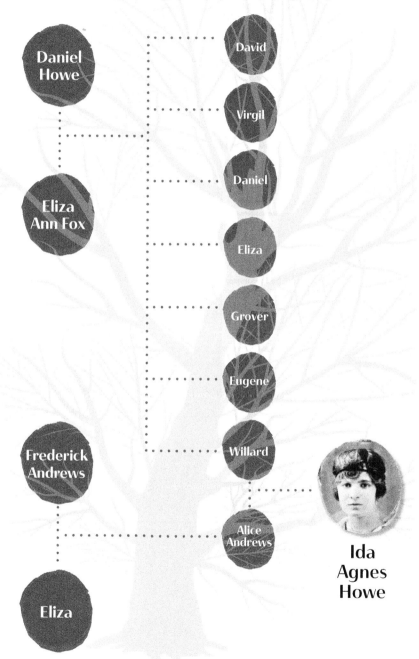

Daniel Howe

Eliza Ann Fox

Frederick Andrews

Eliza

David

Virgil

Daniel

Eliza

Grover

Eugene

Willard

Alice Andrews

Ida Agnes Howe

CHAPTER 2:
YOUNG AND IN LOVE

SUMMER 1923 (*Imagining the past*)

"THAT WAS QUITE A RIDE." Ida laughed and removed her hat, running her hands through her thick brown waves.

"I'll take you on more that are even better," Frank replied.

They spread the blanket on the grass and Ida lay down, stretching her arms with a sigh with contentment. "It's fine today," she said, smiling up at Frank. "Not a cloud in the sky."

They were all by themselves in a small sunny clearing amongst the trees. Frank had parked his Indian motorcycle on a dirt path just within view. Dropping down next to Ida, he leaned on his elbow and looked at her. The distinct lines of her face, with soft skin shimmering in the sun, seemed to contain countless mysteries, yet a promise, too, that she might allow him in.

"I'm so happy," Ida said.

"Me too."

Ida's eyes, always expressive, enveloped Frank in a long, gentle caress. Her bobbed locks tumbled in wild disarray across her forehead and on the blanket. Although Frank had been against her cutting off her long hair, now he loved it.

Leaning over, he gently kissed her mouth and stroked her arm, feeling warm, firm skin beneath her cotton blouse. He propped himself back up again.

"Where d'you think you're going?" She giggled, pulling him toward her.

"Nowhere," he said with a laugh, wrestling with her, pretending to resist. "I'm not going anywhere."

AUGUST 2002

KNEELING ON THE SOFT BEIGE CARPET in Carol's study, scissors in hand, I slashed through the packing tape that sealed the box, yanking it open with a dull ripping noise. The musty odor of old paper and dust wafted up into my nostrils.

Inside I saw an untidy mound of envelopes, photos, and negatives. Some of the photos were stuffed into faded envelopes and tattered paper bags. Others were piled in small containers, while still others were scattered loose. Seating myself at Carol's desk, I began opening yellowed envelopes, scrutinizing their contents under the weak incandescent halo of the small desk lamp.

Carefully I picked up a one-and-one-half-by-three-inch black-and-white image of a young man with a wide smile and a thick shock of wavy hair, who squinted at the camera from his seat on a sandy beach. Grampa! I had seen that long, lean, yet still boyish face before, as well as those improbably luxuriant locks.

Suddenly I was twelve, sitting with Grampa at his gray Formica kitchen table during a summer visit to Akron.

"Do you want to see a picture of me when I was young?" Grampa had asked.

"Oh, yeah." I nodded eagerly. The concept of Grampa having once been young hadn't previously infiltrated my adolescent brain. I definitely wanted to see this.

After disappearing upstairs for a few minutes, Grampa returned to the kitchen with a tiny black-and-white photo. A handsome youth with a long, pale face gazed intently out at me. Frank looked straight at the camera against a dark backdrop, his surprisingly full head of hair combed back in a ripple from his broad rectangular forehead. The photo ended just above his shoulders, revealing the collar of a work shirt buttoned all the way up.

"Is that really you?"

"I wasn't so much older than you when this was taken," Grampa replied, grinning.

Thinking back on that moment, I suspect he was amused to observe my surprise at the contrast between the Grampa I knew, with his partially bald head, white hair, and weathered skin, and this young Frank, whose eyes bored into mine across the decades.

Thirty years later, under the dim light of Carol's desk lamp, the intense young Frank of my mind's eye became one with the smiling, squinting youth at the beach, who beamed happiness at the camera. His wide forehead belonged to my dad and me, as did his broad smile, with his top lip gently curved across his front teeth.

"BR.BCH.BKLN 8-24," Frank had scratched at the bottom of the photo, in his square, spikey printing: Brighton Beach, Brooklyn, New York, August 1924. My grandparents owned an autographic camera, which allowed the photographer to inscribe a short caption into the film below the exposed image, so the information would appear permanently in the border of the printed photograph.

From that same bright patch of Brighton Beach in 1924, a lanky young woman with thick, unruly bobbed hair sits on the boardwalk at a three-quarters angle from the camera. Clad in a one-piece swimsuit that ends in a flounce at the top of her thighs, she stretches her pale, bare, muscular legs out long in front, crossed at the ankle. Although I have no memories of my grandmother, I had seen enough family photos from the 1950s to instantly recognize her strong jawline and slight overbite.

From her faraway youth, Ida gazes calmly beyond the camera, the beginnings of a smile playing on her lips. Later, close to the ocean, Ida stands in full-length side profile to the camera, her rebellious locks contained by a swim cap. I can hear Frank encouraging her poses with gentle prompts: "That's it, tilt your head down, like you're about to dive in." Ida becomes a sleek naiad, poised to plunge beyond the earth into Neptune's roiling waves.

On another outing in the summer of 1924, Ida and Frank frolic about Brooklyn's Prospect Park, in a set of photos inscribed "P.P.BKLN, 8-6-24." Ida, whose fashionable midcalf drop-waist frock entirely hides her figure, stoops to feed a sheep through a wire enclosure. In a playground, they take turns posing at the top of a children's slide.

Were they near the farm of Ida's girlhood? Although she'd never included identifying details, often, during my dad's childhood, she had fondly recalled the splendid farm that the city took over when it created Prospect Park. As a child, Ida had a pet pig, Tug-Tug, of whom she was quite fond. Unfortunately, Tug-Tug eventually wound up on the Howe family dinner table.

"He just disappeared one day," Ida said. "I must've had him for supper and I didn't even know. I was very upset when I found out."

A few days later, on a bright Sunday, the couple photographed each other on a grassy sloping bank overlooking the Hudson River north of New York City. In one shot, Ida thrusts her face close to the camera, sticking her tongue out at Frank.

"So there!" I can hear her giggling.

In these early New York photos, dating from June through October of 1924, Frank and Ida were the only photographers. He was always snapping a picture of Ida by herself, or she was taking one of him. They seemed to be on their own, with no one else in the photos, and no family or friends around to photograph them together.

The absence of family made sense in Ida's case because her English immigrant parents had died when she was in her early teens, followed shortly thereafter by her grandmother. Ida never discussed the exact dates or circumstances of her parents' deaths, aside from one unfortunate incident: "I accidentally barged into the parlor when poor Mama was being embalmed," she told Harley when he was a boy.

After losing her parents and grandmother, Ida had a Jewish guardian who had been her father's lawyer, the story went. Since she had grown up Catholic, this lawyer ensured that she continued to have a Catholic upbringing. After completing high school, Ida attended normal school, as teacher training colleges were called in those days, an accomplishment in which she took great pride.

Ida's guardian approved of her marrying Frank, on the condition that she wait until she was twenty-one.

"After I turned twenty-one, we went together to my guardian's office, and he gave us his blessing to marry," she told young Harley.

In Frank's case, the photos' complete lack of familial faces was odd. During Aunt Virginia's 1953 genealogical interview, he had provided the names of eight younger siblings, as well as of his parents. Why were they nowhere to be found in these New York 1924 photos? Even if his entire family had died by the time Frank returned to Brooklyn to find them, as he'd once claimed during Harley's childhood, could every single family member really have been gone by 1924?

In December of 1924, Frank and Ida took turns photographing each other as they peered out through a porthole of the SS *Kroonland*, the ocean liner in which they voyaged from New York City through the Panama Canal to San Francisco. Ida grips the sides of the porthole with both hands as if trapped, mugging a caricature of panic for the picture. "MEXICO," they scratched into the film. This great journey from New York to San Francisco was a delayed honeymoon a year after she and Frank got married, Ida told her sons. Even third-class passengers like Ida and Frank enjoyed a sumptuous Thanksgiving feast aboard the *Kroonland*, with a menu that included boiled salmon with danoise sauce, braised oxtail à la macédoine, and a stuffed Vermont turkey with cranberry sauce.

Shortly after their arrival in San Francisco, the pair took turns posing atop a cliff overlooking the bay, bundled up in overcoats against the gusting winds. Ida's eyes peeked out beneath the cloche hat, banded with a ribbon and flower, that she had pulled low down her forehead. Just a handful of photos attest to Frank and Ida's two-month sojourn in San Francisco. They lived at 1138 Pine Street, just two blocks from the grand cathedral on Nob Hill, according to the home address Frank printed on the envelope from the pharmacy that developed the film from their trip.

Catching the train east from San Francisco in February of 1925, they finally stopped moving more than 2,500 miles later, in Akron, Ohio, where they remained the rest of their lives. Wedged in among the photos and papers in the box, a worn green bank book from Akron's Citizen's Savings & Loan Company provided the earliest surviving evidence of Frank and Ida settling into the city that became their home. Their first entry, in May of 1925, indicates they opened their account with a deposit of eighty dollars, a princely sum in those days.

A year later, they had saved enough money to buy their first car, a two-door black Model T Ford. In a series of pictures with the date 5/26 scratched at the bottom, the proud pair took turns photographing one another stationed in the driver's seat of their new vehicle, gripping the large steering wheel with both hands. With Ida's lower body concealed by the car door, one cannot see that she was five months pregnant with Frank Elmer Hanson Jr., the first of their four sons.

Countless photos commemorate Frank Jr.'s September 1926 birth, his bright eyes and slight overbite even then resembling Ida's. In 1928 a second infant, Albert Alton, joins toddler Frank in the pictures, the older boy's locks now long sausage curls dangling to his shoulders.

In July of 1929 the photos feature another automobile, this time a brand-new Ford Model A. By October of that year, Frank and Ida's biggest expenditure to date, a bungalow on 1160 Clifton Avenue in North Hill, begins appearing in the photos. A small red Citizens Savings & Loan Co. book documents the couple's commitment to a $2,337 mortgage—equivalent to more than $38,000 in 2022—just six days before "Black Thursday," the first of the three stock market crashes that heralded the Great Depression of the 1930s. Like so many lulled into complacency by the 1920s economic boom, Frank and Ida could scarcely imagine the unprecedented stock market crash and mass unemployment that lay ahead.

When Ida unexpectedly became pregnant again in 1930, she was bound and determined that this time it would be a girl. Instead, a slew of double portraits immortalizes the birth, on March 24, 1931, of my father Harley Myles, a breech baby entering the world feetfirst, followed forty-five minutes later by yet another boy, his twin Harvey Myron.

Beginning their lives during the grimmest period of the Great Depression, Harley and Harvey peer out at the world from the safety of their double baby carriage in photos taken outside 1160 Clifton Avenue. The twins, who were almost always photographed together in their early years, are easily distinguishable. My father's square jaw, high forehead, and curly brown locks, and the blue-gray eyes that from birth seemed full of inquiry, contrasted with Harvey's soft blond waves, generously rounded jowls, and eyes that resembled circular light orbs. Harvey's innocent, almost foolish, expression belied the existence within of a future physicist's keen brain.

The Hanson family saga, as my father knew it, was underway.

When Grampa visited during my early childhood, after eight hours traversing the Pennsylvania Turnpike's tunnels and mountains, he'd snake his Rambler Nash through a 1960s suburban maze of freshly constructed winding lanes and split-level homes before pulling up at our house in the suburbs north of Philadelphia.

"It's Grampa Boy!"

My sisters and I ran out to greet him, yelling his nickname. After his arrival, the first thing Grampa did was give my sisters and me big hugs, shrugging off any discomforts of the four-hundred-mile drive from Akron. As a toddler, I was always hanging on his legs or sitting on his lap, cuddling and playing. Although Frank remained strong and vigorous into his midseventies, my child's brain registered sixtysomething Frank as a man of a different era. Maybe it was the way his black-rimmed glasses cut across his pale features like a dark, heavy bridge. Or perhaps it was his old-fashioned button-down shirts, some with pointy collars, which remained in my frugal Grampa's wardrobe until they were worn out. Grampa might even have been born in 1899, my father told me. I hoped so. Those olden days, of a vanished century, seemed an exotic, distant land.

Even when he was far away in Akron, furniture that Grampa had built echoed his presence every day. A sturdy oak child's chair, its surface smooth and dark, always sat in the corner of our kitchen, ready for use as a footstool. This was one of two identical little chairs that Frank had constructed for the twins from salvaged wood, along with a matching small table, where Harley and Harvey ate when they were small.

When I was in fourth grade, Grampa came to help remodel the quirky, spacious 1906 Craftsman house into which we had just moved. One of his projects was building a closet for my bedroom, whose only storage was a cramped cupboard under the eaves. I'd come home from school in the afternoon and there he'd be up on a ladder in his old maroon shirt, hammering away on my new closet.

At some point in the evening, he posed his favorite question: "What did you learn in school today?"

"I dunno," I remember mumbling, in typical nine-year-old fashion.

I suppose Grampa hoped for a more expansive response, given the financial sacrifices my parents were making for our education. My sisters and I attended expensive private Quaker schools, a decision my parents made during my eldest sister's first year at the local public elementary school, when, having rapidly mastered the curriculum, she began instructing other children. Aside from reflecting Karen's early aptitude for taking charge, this episode sealed my parents' decision to send all three of us to private school.

It was absolutely, positively understood that the Hanson girls were going to college, just like the Hanson boys of a generation earlier. Grampa regularly contributed to education funds for all nine of his grandchildren.

"When you go to college, Grampa will give you a thousand dollars to help with expenses," my father said often.

When our high school and college graduations began in the 1970s, Grampa always came, only giving it up when the devastations of Parkinson's disease rendered him unable to travel.

Although my quiet, gentle grampa never talked much, I felt his love for me. He always was interested in what I said and what I was doing. If I spent an entire Saturday afternoon immersed in my stamp collection, Grampa sat with me at the dining room table.

"What country are those from?" he asked, referring to brilliantly plumed birds on the stamp of a newly independent African nation.

Or he'd point to a rosy pink two-cent stamp featuring George Washington.

"Do you know how old that is?" he asked. "I used to mail lots of letters with that."

One evening Grampa, my dad, and I were hanging out in the kitchen while my dad baked bread, as he did often. I probably was perched on the edge of our tall metal-legged kitchen stool, upholstered in black-and-white houndstooth plastic, while my six-foot-two-and-a-half-inch dad towered over his father, who on a good day was five foot seven.

Our topic of conversation eludes memory, but I recall basking in the attention of Grampa's steady gaze as I chattered away. At that moment I realized—I felt—how much he loved me.

"I think you're his favorite grandchild," my dad confided after that visit.

Around the same time, when I was no longer a little girl but puberty still lay ahead, Grampa stopped hugging and touching me. His love for me was as strong as ever, but physical demonstrations of affection weren't the Hanson way. In a snapshot of us in front of his house a few years later, I stand straight with a satisfied grin, hands clasped in front. Grampa, about a foot to my left, holds exactly the same pose, although his expression is more serious.

As a child I possessed little insight into Grampa's special interest in me, although I intuitively attributed it to our physical resemblance. With my long face and chin, pale skin, and wavy strawberry-blond hair, I took after the Hanson side. Just like Grampa, who was red-haired during his youth, I had highly light-sensitive blue-gray eyes. My sisters, on the other hand, had inherited my mother's brown eyes and dark hair, as well as her cheekbones and even, well-proportioned facial features. In the 1970s, after my mom had dieted herself to thinness and corrected her prominent front teeth with braces, she looked a lot like Jacqueline Kennedy Onassis.

I, on the other hand, didn't look a thing like Jackie O. If not Grampa's spitting image, I came close.

During those first bewitching hours in Carol's study, gazing at the black-and-white images of a young Frank under the pale glow of the desk lamp, I encountered a character strange yet familiar. The carefree young man grinning at Ida that sunny day at Brighton Beach, who looked much like a male version of me at the same age, had lived in a far-off world that I could scarcely fathom. Before Frank was Grampa, before he was even a father, he had been a young man pursuing his destiny in a present as vividly real as my own, yet tangible to me only through these images that echoed a distant past.

As for my grandmother, the statuesque amazon I encountered was a foreign creature. Youthful Ida, the strong angles of her face and body not yet blunted by middle age, seemed a different being altogether than the portly matron my sisters and I knew as our grandmother via our parents' photo albums. In 1950s family pictures, Ida, now thick and dowdy, wore spectacles and frumpy dresses. Her once-unruly brown waves had yielded to a sedate gray braid, which she always wound around the crown of her head into a bun. I never suspected the dramas masked by these seemingly placid images. Ida, a faded stout phantom, was consigned to dormant blocks of black and white within the flat pages of a photograph album.

Among all the surprises in my new box of treasures, one image I knew well. The same photo of Ida in her nurse's uniform had gazed out at me from its prominent place in my parents' photo album when I was a child, as well as from the wall of Grampa's small living room. Proud, unsmiling, and utterly serene, Ida sat for this 1955 studio portrait to commemorate her graduation from the Akron School of Practical Nursing. With her usual plait beneath her stiff nurse's cap, she wore round horn-rimmed spectacles and no detectable makeup. Around her neck was the crucifix necklace that she wears in all of her 1950s photos. The effect is part old-fashioned schoolmarm and part nun: this woman will take excellent care of you, but you better do exactly what she says.

"I never met a woman like her!" Frank often said to my dad.

Despite his loneliness after Ida's death in 1960, he never pursued relationships with other women. Until Parkinson's disease began its onslaught on Frank's health in the mid-1970s, family members occasionally tried to fix him up with eligible widows, but he wanted nothing to do with matchmaking. When my father accompanied Frank to the grocery store during visits, elderly female shoppers were only too happy to chat with him. Although

Frank reciprocated with evident pleasure, he never gave the slightest signal to encourage their obvious interest.

The young couple frolicking on the beach that day in August 1924, who became Grampa and the grandmother I don't remember, had had a secret. The tricky thing about secrets is that, kept too long, they can take on a life, even a personality, of their own.

Over the years, my grandparents' hidden past wove a spell on me. At the beginning, the family project was a puzzle that I dipped into from time to time before flitting off onto the next big activity of my young life. As the years passed, however, our continuing research failures fueled my determination to pry open the door to the past.

By the time I finally got my hands on Frank and Ida's photo collection, my investigation had metamorphosed into a quest to penetrate the deceptions that cloaked my grandparents' real histories. Something was off in their story, and I wanted to know what it was.

That night in Carol's study, I traveled through time with Frank and Ida until the early hours of the morning. During this first journey, I didn't notice two snapshots of a ranch house on an ordinary suburban road that were taken from inside a car, as evinced by the slice of car door at the bottom of the photo. The whispered message of these simple pictures, taken during my grandparents' 1955 vacation road trip, was initially overshadowed by the clamor of more overtly startling images.

In the twenty years since Grampa's death, the ghosts of the past had been resting, mute, concealed in dusty envelopes and paper bags. Released from their hiding place, they spoke volumes once I finally decoded their messages.

Ida at Brighton Beach, Brooklyn, August 1924.

Frank at Brighton Beach, Brooklyn, August 1924.

Ida on swing in Prospect Park, Brooklyn, summer 1924.

Frank feeds a sheep in Prospect Park,
Brooklyn, October 1924.

Ida stands on a cliff that overlooks San Francisco Bay, December 1924.

Ida with Al (left), in ringlets, and Frank Jr. in Akron, circa 1930.

Harley (left) and Harvey in the baby buggy, with
Frank Jr., Al, and Ida (left to right), circa April 1931.

Harley (left) and Harvey, circa 1933.

Ida in 1955 portrait commemorating her graduation
from the Akron School of Practical Nursing.

Ida holds baby Anne, Frank holds Alex, and
Karen stands in front in this 1958 photo.

Anne with Grampa, summer 1960.

Harley with Alex (left) and Anne, early 1960s.

Anne, three, with Joyce.

Karen, Anne, and Alex (left to right) with Grampa,
mid-1960s. In the Hanson household, bookshelves
always lined the living room walls.

Anne with Harley, December 1968.

Anne with Grampa at Karen's college graduation, 1976.

CHAPTER 3:
THE VANISHING FARM

1902 *(Imagining the past)*

"**NEJ RARING, STANNA, STANNA**, *du får inte gå dit!*" (No, sweetie, stop, stop, you can't go there!)

Elida, her waves of long blond hair escaping hairpins and cascading across the white shoulders of her cotton shirtwaist, abandoned her large metal tub full of sodden laundry to chase three-year-old Frank as quickly as the drowsing toddler in her arms and her heavily pregnant belly would allow. Frank, his red-gold waves glinting in the sun as if a halo, had begun scampering at top speed toward the street immediately after she set him down in the sparse patch of yard outside their apartment. All of Frank's senses propelled him toward the screeching, clattering trolley that was changing tracks just a few feet away.

Scooping up the wriggling child in her free arm, her soft cheeks flushed pink from heat and exertion, Elida swayed back and forth, holding Frank and his two-year-old brother, Al, close against her chest and atop her protruding stomach.

"*Du får inte springa rätt ut i gatan, lillpojken min,* älskade *lille Frank.*" (You can't go into the street, my boy, my darling Frankie!)

Elida rubbed the boy's plump cheek with her nose, kissing him with noisy smacks of her lips. "*Vi vill ju inte att du ska hamna framför spårvagnen!*" (We don't want you running into that trolley!)

Carefully lowering herself to her knees, Elida placed both boys on a patch of scraggly grass. Al's body remained limp as he drowsed, his eyes half-closed below a big, square, pale forehead.

Elida pulled a length of rope from her apron pocket and looped it around Frank's squirming torso as he struggled to break free and waved chubby arms toward that wondrous squawking trolley.

"*Spårvagn! Spårvagn!*" he cried. "*Mamma, titta spårvagn! Jag vill åka!*" (Trolley, trolley! Mama! Look at trolley! I wanna get trolley!)

"*Älskling, sitt stilla nu.*" (Honey, please stay still.) Giggling, Elida wedged him between her belly and the side of her torso as she knotted the cord at his waist. She clambered back to her feet and paused, panting, holding the small of her back with one hand. Stepping over to the single tree that had defied the lot's dirt and weeds to straggle upwards, Elida knotted the other end of Frank's rope around the trunk.

"*Så, nu* är *du trygg. Såja, gullebarn, du* är *trygg där. Nu kan mamma hänga tvätten i lugn och ro.*" (OK, you're safe. There you go, sweetie pie, you're safe. Mama can hang the laundry now.)

She waited as Frank, now tethered to the tree, scrambled back to his feet and trotted forward on chubby bare legs as far as the rope allowed.

Elida adored her boys, but she hadn't wanted to have so many babies so fast. When Al had arrived, Frank was barely a year old and nowhere near ready to be weaned. And now another was coming any day.

"*Nu måste du vara en duktig pojke, Frank. Hör du vad jag säger? Du måste stanna härinne på gården.*" (Be a good boy, Frankie. You hear me? You have to stay in the yard.)

"We speak English now, sweetie. You say in English, 'Jag stanna här.'"

"I stay here, Mama, *jag stanna här*." The boy chuckled.

Turning to the twisted, soggy laundry pile, Elida began peeling off items one by one, giving each a vigorous shake before hanging it on the clothesline with wooden pins. Elof had rigged the line by tying a rope as high as he could reach on the tree trunk and attaching it to a nail protruding from the side of their building.

Having reached the end of his tether, Frank plopped onto the ground in a sitting position and looked back at his mother. Elida's lips curved into a smile, and she began to sing: "*Bä, bä, vita lamm, har du någon ull? Ja, ja, kära barn, jag har säcken full...*" (Baa, baa, white lamb, have you any wool? Yes, yes, dear child, a whole sack full...)

AUGUST 1978

"THIS LOOKS LIKE THE PLACE," I said.

My father and I peered through the windshield of his boxy red Land Cruiser at a boarded-up two-story brick building that occupied the whole of a tiny triangular block directly in front of us. To our left, a row of dilapidated four-story red-brick apartment buildings lined Dean Street as far as we could see. The window keystones and majestic arched entrances of these edifices reflected their construction during the early years of the twentieth century, a prosperous era in the life of this Brooklyn neighborhood.

"Yup, I think you're right," my dad replied.

We had come to see Dean Street, one of my father's few certainties of Grampa's past, for ourselves. The way Frank told it, as a child, he had lived on Dean near the intersection of Fifth and Flatbush Avenues. On the very brief list of items from his past that Frank mentioned during my dad's childhood, Dean Street came in just below Frank's beloved little sisters May and Florence. Dean also was the backdrop of one of the rare childhood anecdotes he ever told Harley.

"When I was little, my ma tied me to a tree in the yard so I wouldn't go running out into the street and get hit by the trolley," Frank said.

Another tidbit from Frank's childhood featured boyish hijinks, whereby Frank and his buddies got into the theater for free by retrieving used tickets from the gutter. These simple tales engraved the legendary Dean Street, located near bustling Flatbush Avenue, first into Harley's youthful brain and a few decades later into mine.

On a hot afternoon in August of 1978, my father was helping me move into an apartment in Park Slope, a Brooklyn neighborhood bordering Prospect Park and located less than a mile from Grampa's childhood home. My nomadic college career was underway. It began and ended at Wesleyan University in Connecticut, where I somehow managed to earn a BA in African Studies in four years, with the aid of a few Advanced Placement credits.

Crammed into those years were a semester off, a stint at New York University, and a summer in West Africa. Originating from seeds planted during an eighth-grade African American history class, my interest in Africa ignited when I took a West African history course at NYU. As I learned about African kingdoms of the Middle Ages and the ancient trans-Saharan trade routes, I felt as if I were discovering rich hidden worlds. Whatever the topic, I've always loved exploring the unknown.

Despite my academic successes and enthusiasm for Africa, college was a lonely, often unhappy, time. My relationships with my father and my grandfather were among the few reassuring constants.

The Brooklyn neighborhood my dad and I surveyed through his windshield that summer afternoon was grimly uninviting. No greenery relieved the battered brick, asphalt, and concrete of our surroundings at Dean and Fifth, even though it was the middle of August. Although the gentrification that would subsequently engulf huge swathes of Brooklyn was underway, all the evidence within our immediate line of vision signaled an unvarnished, low-income district.

After my father parked the Land Cruiser, we disembarked for a short exploratory stroll down the littered sidewalk.

"There isn't enough room for a tree here," I said as we paused at the tiny triangle inhabited by the boarded-up building. I was referring to Frank's story of being tied to a tree as a toddler so he wouldn't go running out onto Flatbush Avenue. "Where would the front yard be?"

"I think maybe he lived over there," my dad replied, gesturing to our right at a plain four-story brick apartment building, devoid of ornamentation, with a retail paint store at street level. We walked over for a closer look, but the brick and asphalt yielded no insights. Frank also could have lived in one of the battered apartment buildings to our left, just west of Fifth, we concluded.

None of the lots had even the tiniest of yards, let alone space for a tree to tether a wandering toddler, but maybe seventy-five years ago the back alleys had allowed for a few tufts of grass and small trees. With busy Flatbush Avenue just a stone's throw away, Frank's story about being tied to a tree so he wouldn't go running out into the traffic and trolleys made sense.

Years later, my dad told me about the chat he had with Frank after our visit to Dean Street.

"Pater, Annie and I went to your old neighborhood in Brooklyn when I was helping her move her stuff," my father said. Pater and Mater, Latin for father and mother, were Frank's and Ida's family nicknames, bestowed by Al when he studied Latin in high school. The whole family, as well as Frank and Ida themselves, had permanently adopted these monikers.

After a pause, Frank replied. "Oh." Despite his deteriorating health, Frank's mental faculties were entirely intact.

"We stood at the top of Dean Street and looked down to where your house would have been. There's a bunch of red-brick buildings and a paint store."

"That's the way it was."

My father plowed on. "The neighborhood's kind of run-down now. What was it like when you were growing up?"

"I don't remember."

Frank's refusal to respond both baffled my dad and raised his suspicions.

"I had the funny feeling that something was off," he told me. "It seemed odd, that I told him we visited his childhood home, and he essentially had nothing to say about it."

"When did you say this farm existed?"

The employee behind the desk at the Brooklyn City Register's office, a handsome light-skinned black man, looked with raised eyebrows at the T-shirt-clad college student standing before him, wearing the huge round glasses that were the unfortunate epitome of late 1970s optical fashion. It probably didn't help that I sported an appallingly bad short, layered haircut, reflecting my habit, astonishing to me now, of avoiding hair salons and instead paying acquaintances a few dollars to hack at my wavy locks.

"Between 1900 and about 1910," I repeated. "My great-grandfather Willard Howe owned a farm, and it was taken over by the city and became part of Prospect Park. Where would the records be?"

"That's impossible," he said flatly. "The park was already here in 1900. There couldn't have been a farm in Prospect Park."

"Could you show me the records from before it was a park?" There must be some mistake, I thought. One of the few facts my dad knew for sure about his parents' missing past was that his mother, born Ida Agnes Howe, had grown up on a splendid farm that her wealthy English immigrant father had bought in Brooklyn, New York, on land the city later took over when it created Prospect Park.

Shooting a colleague an almost imperceptible glance of mingled exasperation and resignation, the staffer disappeared into an archive storage area. Ten minutes later, he returned with a land map showing property owners before the park was established in the 1860s. I studied each faded handwritten name, but none even remotely resembled Willard or Howe.

"He looked at me like I was nuts!" I complained to my father on the phone that night as I related my travails at the land records office.

Irked as I was by the employee's reaction to my request, the real problem was that the supposed facts underlying my query were, indeed, quite impossible.

That Ida and Frank were born the same year, I was reasonably certain. This was one of the few facts from their past lives that they both mentioned to my dad multiple times, and from which they never deviated. Indeed, during Harley's childhood, Ida used to tease Frank about being two weeks older than him. Her birthday was April 25, while his was May 8, so she was an "older woman." Their shared birth year, on the other hand, rolled to and fro across the threshold of the twentieth century like a wayward marble.

"Don't tell anybody, but it's 1903," Ida confided to Harley once, when he was a child. Lowering her voice, she had continued, "You know you never talk about a woman's age. I'm telling you confidentially, so keep it to yourself."

"It's a very easy number to remember, 1899," Frank told Harley a few years later. This was the date Frank ultimately stuck with, although, decades later, he had trouble convincing Social Security. "It's gone. It got burnt," he said of his birth certificate.

As children, Frank and Ida had been elementary school classmates at an establishment whose name, to Harley's ears, had sounded like the Burt or Birke School. One of their classmates, a boy called Woofty Gordon, had smelly feet. Years later, they met again when Frank was looking for a part that had fallen off his Indian motorcycle. He rode with a gang whose members all shaved their heads.

When I later researched the history of Prospect Park, my findings confirmed the absolute impossibility of a family farm existing in the late 1800s on land that became Prospect Park. Acquisition of land for the park was completed in the 1860s and initial construction finished in 1868. A woman born in 1899 or 1903, who gave birth to my father in 1931, could not have grown up on a farm in Brooklyn that later was taken over by Prospect Park.

With my visit to the Brooklyn land records office, the fine farm of my grandmother's childhood was expelled from my mental map of my grand-parents' past. It now hovered over me, placeless, yet one more enigma among the jumble of supposed facts that could not be verified.

Prior to this disconcerting experience, two previous days of investigation had been equally fruitless. At the New York City Municipal Archives, my scrutiny of birth, death, and marriage records failed to unearth any Hansons or Howes who matched mine. An examination of old city directories at the central branch of the Brooklyn Public Library, whose monumental facade symbolizes an open book, also yielded nothing. Existing in the era before phone books, city directories of the late nineteenth and first half of the twentieth century listed the name, address, occupation, and sometimes the employer of all heads of households. Despite the library's extensive collection, my perusal of original Brooklyn and Manhattan directories did not reveal a single individual even remotely matching the names, dates, and locations that Aunt Virginia had collected from Ida and Frank during her genealogical interview.

With a few free weeks before New York University classes started, I had been happy to jump in when my dad suggested I give the family research a go. Both he and I had hoped that doing research on the ground in New York City, using original records, would yield results where Aunt Virginia's long-distance efforts had failed. He insisted on paying me, to the tune of fifteen dollars an hour—excellent money in 1978—although I would gladly have done it for free.

Gray and white heads have predominated at every genealogical repository I ever visited, reflecting the typical young person's view of genealogy as dull and dusty stuff. I, on the other hand, was hooked at the age of twenty. I enjoyed academic research, but this was even better: I got to dig through primary sources and immerse myself in old documents, using the fragments of evidence I unearthed to piece together puzzles from the past, seeking to bring the history of ordinary people to life. The only problem was that the people whose stories I sought to revive were nowhere to be found.

"They could've moved a lot and the city directory missed them," I said to my dad when I called to update him on my progress, or lack thereof, in tracking down our missing ancestors. "Or the birth records could have been lost."

"That's certainly possible," he replied.

The noncommittal neutrality in my father's voice did little to assuage my doubts. It just didn't make sense that my careful perusal of city directories and municipal records had yielded nothing. Some records might have been lost, but not all of them. And even if Grampa's Swedish immigrant family had somehow evaded the notice of all municipal authorities and directory publishers, this didn't explain why Ida's prosperous parents, and especially her property-owning English gentleman father, were nowhere to be found.

"You know, I think maybe Grampa changed his last name," I said.

"You could be right," my dad replied. Trusting the quality of my investigation, and astonished that the farm of his mother's childhood could not have existed on the site of today's Prospect Park, he was open to all possibilities.

"He could have been in trouble, and he was running away from something," I continued. After all, my grandfather, always a strong union man, was working in construction in 1920s New York City, where the mob controlled many unions. "Maybe the Mafia was after him, or he ran up against union busters."

When I visited Grampa in Akron that Thanksgiving, I could have peppered him with questions about his family. I didn't. I don't even remember talking about it. An inveterate journal keeper at the time, I scribbled copiously about my feelings for Grampa and my worries about his declining health, but not a word about my recent Hanson and Howe research flop. Only many years later, during extended family history conversations with my dad, did I learn that Grampa, usually so steady and unperturbed, had been upset when my father told him about my New York City genealogical research.

"His balance is a lot worse. He fell tonight, but he seems in good spirits," I wrote in a typical journal entry from that Thanksgiving visit. "I'm so young and vigorous now. It's hard to believe that someday I won't be. When I talk to Grampa, I try to see him as all of the person he is, the person he has been, the things he has done, and not only as what he is now."

I'm sure I told Grampa that my Brooklyn apartment was close to where he grew up. Did I ask him about Dean Street and the vanished Prospect Park farm, only for him to change the subject? Did he say he didn't remember much about the old neighborhood, or indicate politely that he wasn't interested in the topic? Probably all of the above. I, in turn, would have let the matter drop. After a hard and lonely fall in New York City, I wanted my time with Grampa to be enjoyable. My main goal in visiting was to continue developing our one-on-one relationship and to appreciate our time together. If he didn't want to talk about his long-ago Brooklyn past, I wouldn't have pushed it.

"She's the best thing that ever happened to me," Grampa said of my grandmother. Ida was the one person whom Frank, the most reticent of men, would happily discuss at length. He showed me clear Mason jars packed with red tomatoes that Ida had preserved in the 1950s and that still lined the shelves of his basement stairway two decades after her death. "I'm afraid to eat them now, but I can't throw them away." His tone was stoic, his eyes wistful.

Ida's favorite photo of herself, the same studio portrait in her nurse's uniform that I remembered from my parents' photo album, hung on Grampa's living room wall.

"She was really worried before the test for her license, but she did better than everybody," Grampa told me, pride evident in his matter-of-fact statement, as we stood together looking at the photograph.

As we surveyed the family photos that adorned the dusty-rose wallpaper, we stopped at a dual portrait of Harley and Harvey as toddlers with long curls and solemn expressions. "She really wanted a girl," Grampa said with a grin. "She was so mad, she wouldn't look at them for a couple of days after they were born."

Over time, I've heard variants of this anecdote from multiple family members. However, my skeptical father later commented that Ida had breast-fed both him and his brother, so this tale seems more apocryphal than fact.

Due to Grampa's innate reserve, spending extended one-on-one time with him during these visits could be challenging, especially since the outgoing, sociable part of my nature had not yet fully emerged. We'd be sitting around talking at his gray Formica kitchen table, and after a certain point, sometimes I just couldn't think of anything else to ask him or say. Adding to the strain, I, the most opinionated of young women, never argued if he said something that didn't fit with my worldview.

Once, Grampa referred to the residents of a nearby Akron neighborhood as "negroes," uttering the last word after a pause, in a hesitant tone. I didn't correct or reprove him, even though I disliked his use of this term for Americans with African ancestry. Although the term was standard usage during the early and middle twentieth century, employed even by civil rights icon Martin Luther King Jr. in his famous "I Have a Dream" speech of 1963, the word had become derogatory by the late 1970s.

I also never spoke with Grampa about the pain I suffered during my parents' divorce, and the personal troubles that ensued. Although my parents, working as a team, had given me a stable early childhood full of love and encouragement, I had been deeply disturbed by my mother's acrimony toward my father during their split. At fourteen, I could scarcely understand how the chronic mental illness of her own father, my maternal grandfather, Robert, had tainted her childhood and fueled her emotions. My mom and I subsequently repaired our relationship, but during high school and college, my dad was the one I always turned to. As was typical of him, he hid his feelings during the divorce and never spoke a word against my mother in my presence. I never broached these subjects with Grampa because I thought it would make him uncomfortable, or he just wouldn't understand.

One topic Grampa and I happily returned to time and again was our shared interest in health and natural foods.

"You should eat the white part, the pith," he said when we ate oranges together. "That's good for you. It's fiber."

Grampa bought food and whole grains at a food cooperative—the "hippies' place," he called it. A baker of whole wheat bread since my dad's childhood, now he was continually revising what he called his "health bread" recipes. He carefully tracked his modifications on the back of old unused timecards from the Higley Construction Company, or one of the other companies from his days as a construction superintendent. In meticulous detail, in increasingly shaky block print handwriting, he would note the date, ingredients, and what he had changed from one batch to the next.

"Rise Good, Flavour Good, Texture Good but moist, Yeild [sic] 3 lbs. Next batch—no oil—1 Tasp Molasses," he commented on a typical batch that combined whole wheat flour, rolled oats, rye flour, wheat germ, two kinds of yeast, nonfat milk, peanut oil, molasses, honey, and raisins.

But all the health bread in the world couldn't fix the rapid, and accelerating, physical deterioration Parkinson's disease had inflicted on my grandfather by the late 1970s. Until then, Grampa still worked occasionally, as well as engaging in carpentry projects at his sons' homes. He had been a robust, powerful man: my father remembered that, as a boy, he saw Frank lift the front of the family's Model A Ford, a vehicle weighing some one thousand and two hundred pounds.

Just a few years after the onset of Parkinson's, Grampa's hands shook and trembled, and increasingly, he struggled with simple tasks. During this period, on the envelopes of letters he sent me, he traced straight lines with a pencil and ruler horizontally across the envelope before printing my address in ink. The penciled line helped him focus his wayward hands as he struggled to write legibly.

"Getting old is awful" is how he put it to me. Yet Grampa soldiered on. Even as his once-vigorous body succumbed to the ravages of Parkinson's, his mind, as sharp as ever, continually searched for ways to reverse, or at least stall, his physical decline. He showed me a catalog that featured Earth Shoes, an odd-looking late-1970s brand reputed to strengthen leg muscles and improve circulation and posture due to a sole that was thick under the toe and thin at the heel, which caused the wearer to walk heel downward.

"They could help with my balance," Grampa said.

"Boy is he a Hanson," I wrote in my journal during that Thanksgiving visit. "There is a strong will, a stubbornness in him, that I feel is mine too. I see this will in him in how he is reacting to becoming very old and weak. He observes it, fights it, doesn't want to admit it's happening to him."

When Grampa and I said goodbye at the end of that visit, we didn't hug, or say "I love you." We never did because that wasn't the Hanson way. We just stood there, talking, both of us near tears. I knew he loved me, and he knew I loved him. Within, I was fighting back the painful knowledge that I was going to lose him frighteningly soon.

As we gazed at each other, in his eyes I comprehended something new. I had the sense that I was seeing not only Grampa but Frank, an individual, the young man, now trapped in a body that was failing him. In turn, Frank, with eyes so much like my own, gazed back at me. In his expression I saw love, sadness, and, for a brief moment forever impressed in my memory, a look of startled recognition.

Despite their occasional challenges, my visits with Grampa were a gift, and a respite, during a difficult period of my life. During our time together, the mystery of his and Ida's lives in New York was stashed in a compartment at the back of my mind, of low importance compared to our present relationship.

Looking back now, I see us sitting together at his Formica kitchen table, my nineteen- or twenty-year-old self sometimes grasping for topics of conversation. It never occurred to me that Grampa might have understood more than I could ever imagine about the troubles with which a young person struggles. Neither did I suspect that this kind, quiet, resourceful man had experienced problems and drama aplenty in his own youth, nor that he had deliberately concealed the truth of his past for more than fifty years.

Anne with Grampa during visit to Akron, late 1970s.
Anne's era of bad haircuts was in full swing.

CHAPTER 4:
GUN BY THE BED

"I'LL SHOW YOU WHERE IT IS," Grampa had said. We were standing at the end of the second-floor hallway in his house. He fumbled with the cupboard door and finally pulled it open.

"It's right there," he said, pointing to the floor at the very back. Clasping the side frame, he slowly lowered himself into a kneeling position. Then he maneuvered his shaking hand around the end of two floorboards, tugging up to remove them. Beneath was an empty twelve-by-eighteen-inch compartment.

"If anything ever happens to me, you should come and get anything that's there," he said.

"Uh, OK." Surprised, I mumbled my reply.

Grampa replaced the floorboards, so they looked exactly the same as all the others. I would never have known they hid a compartment.

He didn't tell me what he was going to conceal in that hiding place, which my dad later dubbed the "hidey-hole." What or whom did Frank fear?

Whatever it was, he wasn't saying. Having shown me the hidey-hole, he had no further comment. I, in turn, felt honored that Grampa had chosen me as his confidante. I stowed this episode in my brain's short-term storage, soon to be shared and discussed with my father.

"Maybe he's going to put the pistol there."

That was the first thing my father said when I related this episode. When my dad was a boy, Frank kept a loaded pistol under his and Ida's bed.

"It was a Saturday night special pistol, a revolver," he told me. When the boys grew older, Frank transferred the gun to a locked dresser drawer.

Young Harley almost never saw the gun, because he and his brothers were prohibited from entering their parents' bedroom. However, a rare foray within that sanctum, under Ida's watchful eye, was seared in my dad's memory.

"I can remember my mother unlocking the drawers and pulling the gun out," he told me. Also in the drawer was a box of bullets. As his mother held the weapon, Harley could see a bullet through the hole in its chamber.

"The gun was loaded," he said. "I never heard it fired."

Although the Frank my father and I knew was quiet and kind, he could be tough if needed. As job foreman for construction companies in Akron from 1945 onward, he ran large building projects and always maintained authority, seemingly without effort, over potentially unruly crews.

"He would be running a job with a whole bunch of Mohawk Indian steel raisers, and he got the opportunity to fire them on occasion," my father told me years later. "These are people that are on the loose, they're moving from city to city, oh boy, they're pretty tough. But he never had any problems with anybody on the site, ever."

During college, Harley used to come by his dad's job site in the afternoon for a ride home, thus saving the twelve-cent bus fare.

"Is Frank Hanson around?" he'd ask.

"Well, he's around somewhere," one of the crew would reply. "He's like a bad penny, he always turns up."

If Harley happened to glance up while at the construction site, sometimes he saw Frank high in the sky, loping along the I-beams of the building's skeleton, just like his Mohawk crew.

"There he'd be, five stories up off the ground, running along steel beams," my dad told me. "I could no more do that than fly. He was fearless and I suspect that's why he got along so well with his crews. He never asked someone to do something he wouldn't do himself."

While some might consider it commonplace for a man to possess a loaded pistol in the 1930s and 1940s, Frank was an unlikely candidate. His motorcycle gang days long behind him, this shy, gentle city dweller was a family man with no apparent need for male companionship. He didn't hunt, fish, smoke, drink, swear, play cards, gamble, or follow sports. The strongest language Frank ever used around his sons was when he referred to a lazy fellow as a "jamoke," my dad told me. During his scant free time, Frank read, baked, gardened, and did carpentry around the house. On a typical workday evening during my father's childhood, Frank would fall asleep at the dining room table while reading the *Akron Beacon Journal* newspaper after supper, a sturdy glass beer stein containing skim milk, his beverage of choice, on the table to his right.

Maybe Frank, possessor in middle age of a quiet authority that allowed him to easily maintain order among rough-and-tumble construction crews, had been a bold young man in New York who got into a jam. Could he, a strong union supporter who worked in the building trades during the era of Prohibition, municipal corruption, and labor conflicts, have crossed the wrong person?

My dad told me about his first visit to New York City when he, too, had been a college student. He and Harvey accompanied their parents on a two-week excursion to New York during the Christmas holidays in December of 1949. Beginning with the train ride from Akron to New York, the trip was a grand adventure for a pair of eighteen-year-olds who had never been farther east than Niagara Falls.

"For a boy from Ohio, New York City was pretty wild and crazy," my dad recalled.

They stayed in a Manhattan hotel and zipped around the city via subway, which Ida and Frank effortlessly navigated without guides or maps. The family gazed down at the city's mighty steel-and-stone canyons from the top of the Empire State Building, they performed the obligatory pilgrimage to the historic "Little Church Around the Corner," and they visited multiple museums, where Harley was particularly awed by the giant mastodon and mammoth skeletons at the Museum of Natural History. They circled Manhattan Island on a boat tour, rode the ferry to the Statue of Liberty, and even took the F subway line from Manhattan all the way across Brooklyn to Coney Island, at the southernmost tip of the borough—only to find the amusement park rides closed for the holidays.

Their Brooklyn itinerary did not, however, include a visit to Prospect Park, where Ida had lived as a girl, or a stop at Frank's childhood home on Dean Street, where the streetcar turned around on Flatbush.

"Can we go see your old neighborhood?" Harley asked his mother.

"There's no one to talk to or visit. It burned down. There's nothing there." Frank answered for Ida, a rare event.

Relating this episode to me decades later, my dad's memory of his bewilderment and confusion remained vivid. "I remember thinking that this makes absolutely no sense," he told me. "Here we are in New York, my parents' hometown. Why can't we see where they grew up?"

Apparently Frank did engage in some solo reconnaissance of his old haunts during this visit, once disappearing for an afternoon. "I went to see where my Ma is buried," he told Ida and the boys when he returned. "She lived into her seventies." If during this expedition he had met up with living family members, Frank made no mention of it.

"That trip to New York was when I really began to feel something was off," my father later told me.

Fear of mob or gang retaliation explained the loaded pistol by the bed, as well as Frank fleeing New York and changing his name. Unfortunately, my dad and I could only speculate because Frank, while alive, simply refused to discuss his youthful adventures in New York.

Yet even if strife in the wild and woolly New York City of the 1920s had caused Frank to skip town and assume a new identity, surely these conflicts could not have followed him across the country and persisted for so long. It didn't make sense. My father and I were left with another answerless riddle in the life of Frank Hanson.

When I visited Uncle Harvey and Aunt Virginia in Dayton, Ohio, during college, we spent hours relaxing in their cozy living room, discussing just about everything from politics to, of course, the great Hanson research quest. Uncle Harvey, who was far more interested in national politics than in his family tree, extolled the virtues of Barbara Jordan, a formidable black civil rights advocate and member of Congress, as a potential presidential candidate.

Virginia and I, on the other hand, never tired of discussing the family mystery.

"If we just keep on looking, we'll find them," she said, smiling at me from her cushioned armchair. Unlike my slim and youthful-appearing mother, Virginia, by her midforties, had relaxed comfortably into middle age, with a few extra pounds settling in around her waistline and her graying hair neatly coiffed in stiff waves about her head.

"Records weren't kept as well then as they are now, especially in big cities like New York," Virginia continued in her usual gentle tone. "And we know that people aren't always as careful as they should be."

Harvey didn't have much to say about the family project, during this visit or any other time. Unlike my dad, Harvey never considered his parents' behavior odd. Neither did he wonder about their inexplicably missing past.

"I have all the family I want and need," he commented to my father more than once.

Nonetheless, Harvey loved Virginia and Virginia was devoted to the investigation, so Harvey always supported her. When they visited their son Doug at the University of Utah in Salt Lake City, Harvey pitched in to help Virginia search for our Hansons and Howes at the renowned genealogical library run by the Church of Latter-Day Saints (Mormons).

During my visit to Dayton during college, Virginia, rather than Harvey, provided my first insights into Ida's nature. Virginia, also an Akron native, had known the Hanson family since she was thirteen.

"She had... she had a strong personality." Virginia's soft voice hesitated as she delicately considered the appropriate words to describe her late, beloved mother-in-law. "She was a very forceful person."

This was entirely new information. Why had my father never mentioned it? I didn't think to ask him at the time.

Another fact about my grandmother that Virginia shared was that she had spoken fluent German.

"One day I was with her in a jewelry store in Akron that was run by German immigrants," Virginia told me. "I was so surprised when she began speaking in German with the owners."

Virginia also offered morsels about Frank's background that she had gleaned during decades of close listening to her reticent father-in-law.

"Your grandfather seems to know a lot about Judaism. He must have picked that up in Brooklyn," she said.

Indeed, New York City was home to about 1.6 million Jews in 1920, with a massive population settled in Brooklyn.

Virginia added, "I got the sense that he spoke only Swedish when he was small."

This observation fit with Frank's claim of Swedish heritage. As the first child of Swedish immigrants new to the country, he would have spoken Swedish as his first language.

To Virginia also, Frank expressed the intense sorrow he had felt at the death of his young sister May. "He was very upset," she said. "I believe this was during the 1918 flu epidemic."

Aunt Virginia remained a true believer in the veracity of her in-laws' account of their pasts, even though she, a librarian and careful researcher, had never been able to verify any of the information my grandparents shared with her in 1953. "I'm sure what they told me is true," she said.

After I told my dad about Grampa's hidey-hole, he asked his father what became of the gun. "I took it down to the [Cuyahoga River] gorge and threw it in," Frank replied.

A few years after Frank's death in 1982, when the Clifton Avenue house was being sold, my father checked the hidey-hole for himself. It was empty. But the weapon itself had, in fact, remained among Frank's possessions. It ended up stashed away in Uncle Al's home in Atlanta.

This storied pistol made one more journey, in the year 2000, when it traveled to Pennsylvania along with the box of photos that Aunt Betty sent my father after Uncle Al died. Betty placed the gun in an empty tissue box, swaddled the box in a towel, and deposited the whole thing in a shipping container. Then, with seeming unconcern as to legalities, she sent the weapon on its way to my father via the US Postal Service, along with the photos and other memorabilia. Fortunately for the safety of all involved, the pistol arrived at my dad's house unloaded and unaccompanied by ammunition.

My dad showed me the gun a few years later. Retrieving the weapon from its nest in the tissue box, he picked it up gingerly, holding it with his thumb and index finger as far away from himself as he could. If ever someone looked uncomfortable handling a gun, it was my father.

"You're sure it's not loaded, right?" I said.

"It is not loaded."

He gave the gun to me for closer examination. With a nickel-plated barrel and a black handle, it was slightly less than eight inches long. On the top it said, "National Arms Company, New York, USA." The National Arms Company was a nineteenth-century manufacturer of firearms in Brooklyn.

On the underside of the gun, where the serial number had been, was a neat row of tiny gash marks. The serial number was illegible, having been banged out with a metal instrument.

CHAPTER 5:

I DON'T THINK OUR PARENTS EVER EXISTED

MY LAST VISIT WITH GRAMPA, in the summer of 1981, was different than our previous times together. After graduating from Wesleyan and moving to Washington, D.C., I was far happier. Although I concluded that I wasn't cut out for my intended career in international development, which would have built on my African Studies degree, I found friends and a sense of belonging in my new home. Living with a rotating cast of housemates in a large, dumpy early-twentieth-century rented townhouse in the then-inexpensive Mount Pleasant neighborhood, I belatedly experienced the socializing and comradery many enjoy in college dorms. In my work life, a temp job at the telecommunications company MCI evolved into a professional writing and communications role.

Grampa's life had changed too, but very much for the worse, because the attack on his body by Parkinson's disease was continuing with dreadful speed. No longer the frail yet determinedly positive and self-sufficient man of my college-era visits, Grampa was wheelchair-bound and living in a nursing home outside Dayton near Uncle Harvey. His once-powerful arms lay thin and weak on the armrests of his wheelchair. His days of baking health bread, diligent recordkeeping, and trips to the hippie food store were over.

When a group of family members went out to lunch together during this visit, I sat next to Grampa and attempted to recapture our previous intimacy. Despite trying every possible topic of conversation, I totally struck out. Grampa gave short answers to all my questions, making it clear he didn't want to talk. He seemed angry. Looking back now, I'm sure he was indeed furious at the disease that had robbed him of his strength and autonomy.

Nonetheless, Grampa, in his own way, still made it clear that he loved me. At the nursing home, he gave me a small wooden duck he had carved at the workshop. "Butternut Baby Duck I.L.C. 1980," he had inscribed on the bottom. Butternut is a light walnut wood that carves easily without becoming brittle. I've never figured out what the "I.L.C." stood for. It's the last thing Grampa ever gave me.

When Grampa and I said goodbye at the airport gate at the end of my visit, a few tears silently slid down his cheek.

"I never saw him tear up like that before," Uncle Harvey said as he walked me the final steps up the ramp to the boarding area.

On a hot, muggy Saturday morning in August of 1982, I sat in the number 42 bus as it rumbled down Mount Pleasant Street toward downtown Washington, D.C. I was on my way to the US National Archives to search for Grampa and his family in the 1900 and 1910 Federal Census records. Those records list the name, age, occupation, marital status, sex, place of birth, parents' place of birth and other information for each member of every household. Seventy-two years after the 1910 census was conducted, its records had become public information in 1982.

Grampa had died a month earlier, on July 11. His death, my first experience of losing someone I loved deeply, heralded an unwanted induction into the clouded world of grief and its attendant regrets.

"I think it's time for me to go see Grampa again," I had said to my father a few months before Grampa died.

"I don't think that's a good idea," he replied. "He's not in good shape."

My father wanted to protect me from the pain of seeing Grampa in the final stages of Parkinson's disease, lying in bed, mostly paralyzed, unable to speak. Wrapped up in my own rapidly improving life, I had dropped the matter, with the blithe stupidity of youth. Losing my grampa brought a type of pain I had never before known, which would never totally leave.

My initial motivation for joining the Hanson family research project was the knowledge that it was important to my dad. After Grampa died, investigating his family history also became a way to stay close to him, and to keep him in my life.

"If they're there, I'll find them," I said to myself as I strode into the National Archives, a grand neoclassical multicolumned edifice located twelve blocks from the White House. In my search for Grampa's parents, Elof and Elida, I planned to look not just for Hansons but also for any Swedish-born Elof and Elida, with any last name, who had an eldest child named Frank. Although Grampa might have changed his last name, his telling Aunt Virginia that he was the eldest of nine siblings, in addition to providing their full names and birth order, seemed too specific to be invented.

In this pre-internet era, census returns were available to the public only on microfilm, and researchers had to trek to repositories where the films were stored in order to view them. Today's genealogy apps and websites, where you relax on the couch with a laptop or smartphone, type a name, and tap a search button, were a futuristic fantasy worthy of a *Star Trek* episode.

Armed with paper, pens, and determination, in my visit to the archives that day I was putting my name-change theory to the test for the first time.

But before getting down to business, I first had to figure out which microfilm I needed. In those days, you had to know someone's street address in order to locate the microfilm image of the original census record.

Dean Street, the street off Flatbush in Brooklyn where Grampa had lived as a child, was ground zero in my research. I consulted a microfilmed index of census Enumeration Districts (ED) for 1900 and tried to identify the ED for Grampa's section of Dean Street. Hoping I had chosen the right one, I ordered the film for ED 118, in Brooklyn's Ninth Ward.

When the film came, I threaded it through the spools of the microfilm reader and settled down in my cubby in the darkened room. Slowly at first, I began my march through the census pages in search of Dean Street, perusing filmed images of original handwritten records that were projected through the lens of the reader onto the flat white table surface in front of me.

My pace gradually quickened as I became accustomed to the format. Images of the sheets originally filled out by census enumerators materialized in a beam of light and dissipated just as rapidly, to be replaced by another ghostly image from long ago. In his flowing, old-fashioned cursive script, the enumerator recorded the responses as he went from door to door asking questions. "Who lives here? What are their names? How are they related to you? What are the ages of all household members? What is your occupation? Are you a US citizen? Where were you born?" When the resident responded, the enumerator would have scribbled the answers on the lined sheets as quickly as he could.

Bergen Street, Flatbush Avenue, Atlantic Avenue, Fifth Avenue: these were all near Dean Street. Finally, I found Dean. Slowly and carefully, I trundled up and down the street with the census man, turning the machine handle to advance the film from block to block. Grampa's building would have been somewhere around the 400 or 500 block of Dean Street.

To be safe, I started on the previous block. From 379 to 389 Dean Street, no one born in Sweden. Numbers 387 through 403: no Elof, no Elida, no

Frank. From 403 to 417, also nothing. Whoops, census taker switched streets—I had landed on Pacific. I advanced farther until Dean Street resumed. For numbers 378 through 430, still nothing. Clusters of Swedes here and there, but still no Elof, Elida, or Frank. Page by page I repeated the exercise, examining the faded spidery handwriting, slowly turning the machine lever to advance from one census page to the next as I plodded along with the census man.

Hunched over the desk in the dim room, I trawled the entire length of Dean Street for both 1900 and 1910. Often the enumerator's script was faded, smudged, or just plain illegible. I would scrutinize the page, adjusting the machine's lens to enlarge and sharpen the image so I could inspect it even more closely. For good measure, I scanned the adjoining streets too, but I didn't find a single family that even remotely resembled Grampa's.

When I finally staggered out from the archives into the humid midafternoon heat, my eyes were bleary from hours of squinting at dimly lit images of scratchy handwriting. My piggyback ride with the Brooklyn census enumerators had yielded nothing. I could now say with certainty that if my grandfather's family had lived on Dean Street in 1900 or 1910, the census men had failed to find them.

Dear Ms. Hanson,

I have searched our records from 1897 through 1907 and can find no record of a birth for your grandmother...

That's typical of the responses my sister Alex received when she searched for the Hansons and Howes in the 1980s. Focusing on obtaining my grandparents' marriage certificate, as well as family birth and death certificates, she fired off a barrage of letters, information request forms, and certified checks.

We can find no record in this office for the persons named, a form letter would reply. Alex would move on to the next agency on her list, only to get the same response. No matter whom she contacted—the New York City Clerk, the New York City Department of Health, the Connecticut Department of Health, or the Summit County Probate Court in Ohio—the answer was always the same: *No records were found. The name was not found. No record on file.* Even when Alex hired a professional genealogist in Utah, who had access to the massive genealogical research library maintained by the Church of Latter-Day Saints in Salt Lake City, the researcher was unable to identify a single Hanson or Howe who belonged to us.

During a visit to England in 1988, my sister Karen and her husband, Mac, trekked north to Sheffield to look for Ida's father, Willard Howe, in the Sheffield Archives. A large and well-maintained local history repository, the archives surely would contain some record of our Howe ancestors. But Karen and Mac found no Willard Howe. In fact, the archives did not contain a single Willard.

Mac, who was born in the Caribbean but lived in England as a teenager, was first to pick up on the anomaly.

"Willard isn't an English name," he said.

Ida's father and his siblings were Willard, David, Virgil, Daniel, Eliza, Grover, and Eugene, according to Aunt Virginia's genealogical chart. English boys weren't named Willard, Virgil, Grover, or Eugene in the mid–nineteenth century, Mac pointed out.

"These aren't English names. They're American names." Mac was right, but what were we to do? We couldn't find these siblings in US records either.

Uncle Al, the second oldest of my father's brothers, became our chief Hanson and Howe hunter during the late 1980s and early 1990s. If energy and determination could have solved the puzzle of our family history, Al would have succeeded. A cheerful maverick, Al shared Grampa's upbeat temperament and equanimity, although not the shyness. When my father and his brothers were children, Grampa dubbed Al "King of the Babies," because where Al went, the twins followed, captivated by his enthusiasm and conviction.

From his home in Georgia, Al researched church archives and international ship passenger arrival lists. He wrote to the Social Security Administration, to the US Navy personnel department, and to Swedish genealogical organizations. He contacted everyone he could think of, to no avail.

Finally, in a last-ditch attempt, Al resorted to blunt force. He sent a letter to every single Hanson household listed in the phone books of all five New York City boroughs, plus as many Hansons as he could find in New York state. My sister Karen, who worked in New York City at the time, helped by mailing him photocopies of pages from city phone books that contained Hansons.

"Dear Sir or Madam," Al's letter began. "My brothers and I are trying to locate any of my father's living relatives to notify them of his death on July 11, 1982."

After providing more family details, Al asked the recipient to select one of two checkboxes—"Yes, a connection may exist," or "No, a connection does not exist"—and to return the form to him. He enclosed a self-addressed stamped envelope with each letter.

A few of the Hansons replied. They all checked the box, "No, a connection does not exist." One added the note, "Sorry I can't help. Good luck." We certainly needed the luck.

Al officially conceded defeat in 1992. His conclusion? "I don't think our parents ever existed."

CHAPTER 6:
MINED AND DREDGED

IN THE LATE 1990S, my grandparents' secret took on a life of its own. I'm not sure exactly how or when, but the quest to understand it possessed me and infiltrated my psyche. Crouched behind me, the mystery would tap my shoulder, only to duck out of sight when I twisted around in a vain attempt to grasp it.

My duel with the slippery, wily opponent had resumed on a bright November afternoon in 1994. I approached the young woman sitting at the circulation desk of the Pacific Street branch of the Brooklyn Public Library, a stately turn-of-the-century building a few blocks off Flatbush Avenue. Above, a second-floor balcony curved around a central rotunda.

"I have kind of an odd question for you," I began. "Do you keep records of old library cards? I mean really old, from around 1910."

"Huh?" She stared at me blankly.

Not a good start. I repeated my question.

"No, we don't have anything like that."

"Do you know any way I could find out whether someone had a library card here around 1910?"

"No." The young woman's mouth twitched slightly, the rest of her face a smooth, tan, impassive mask.

"OK, thank you."

Trawling the neighborhoods of Brooklyn in search of an eighty-year-old library card was a long shot, but by 1994, pursuing far-fetched leads had become the fate of the Hanson family researchers. All the typical sources had long since been mined and dredged. I had hoped I just might get lucky at the library. Grampa always said he dropped out of school as soon as he was old enough to get a library card and was self-educated thereafter. "I may not know something, but I know where I can look it up," he said often. Located just two blocks from Grampa's childhood home at Dean and Fifth, the Pacific Street branch was the most likely one for him to have joined.

In the twelve years since my 1982 foray into the 1910 census, Uncle Al, Aunt Virginia, and my sisters had been the main researchers on the family project. My big preoccupation, on the other hand, had been trying to figure out what on earth I wanted to do as a career.

The problem was that I liked, and was good at, a lot of things and just couldn't seem to narrow it down to one path. Discontented with both my job at MCI and my then-boyfriend, in the fall of 1984 I quit both for an extended backpacking trip in Europe. Upon returning, I began graduate studies in geography, which led to a sojourn at the University of Minnesota in Minneapolis. There, I finally faced the fact that I wasn't cut out for academia. Although I loved research and excelled at the written word, I hated writing long academic papers. Having a multitude of interests didn't help either, as I struggled to adopt the "mile-deep and inch-wide" focus essential for completing the required MA thesis.

In a stroke of good luck, at the University of Minnesota I discovered journalism at the *Minnesota Daily*, one of the largest student-written and student-run newspapers in the United States. I loved the fast pace and stimulation of the busy newsroom at the *Daily*, which was the fourth-largest newspaper in Minnesota. I thrived on the cycle of reporting, churning stories out, and moving on to the next one. Most of all, I loved coming up with issue-oriented story ideas and then researching them. Unfortunately for me, the 1990s was a decade of disappearing opportunities for journalists. Lacking a journalism degree and the pivotal newspaper internships, I was condemned to the bush leagues of small-town journalism, with only the faintest possibility that during the next decade I could claw my way up to a major daily newspaper.

When I traded journalism for newsletter and technical writing for Minnesota's 3M Corporation, I discovered that without the investigations and research of journalism, I no longer wanted to write. That, in addition to a series of relationships that didn't work, led me to another big change in November of 1994. Yet again I quit a secure job, this time relocating to Boston, back on my East Coast home turf, with the intention of becoming an executive recruiter. This big, scary move turned out to be the best decision I ever made.

En route to my new home in Boston, I stopped over in New York City for a visit with Melissa Murphy, a friend from the *Minnesota Daily*, who was now living and working in New York. And this was how I happened to be at the Pacific Street branch of the Brooklyn Public Library that day in November 1994.

"How'd it go?"

Melissa, who had been wandering the reference area while I pursued my quixotic errand, turned inquisitive blue eyes and unruly black curls toward me.

"No luck."

While visiting Melissa, I also returned to the Hanson family project, which by this time everyone but my dad and I had written off as a lost cause.

When I was packing up my apartment in Minneapolis, he sent me a fat packet stuffed with all the papers and letters from my sisters' and Uncle Al's fruitless investigations, so I could refer to them during my New York stopover. As of that time, I became keeper of the Hanson research archives.

"They definitely don't have records of old library cards," I continued as Melissa and I resumed our stroll down Pacific Street in the crisp autumn air, dried leaves whirling across the sidewalk. We next paused at an elementary school near Dean and Fifth, where I scribbled the name and address in preparation for a call to the city education department. Earlier that afternoon, Melissa had accompanied me on the obligatory trek to Grampa's boyhood home at Dean Street and Fifth Avenue, that still-unprepossessing intersection that was fast becoming a shrine of the Hanson quest.

"She had no idea what I was talking about," I sighed to Melissa about my exchange with the librarian. "She thought I had a screw loose."

My intermittent stabs at the family project in the late 1990s and early 2000s yielded exactly the same results as all my previous efforts: nothing. I scoured New York City school, cemetery, and probate records. I searched in Brooklyn for an elementary school named Burt or Birke. I contacted carpenters' unions, trying to locate membership rolls from the 1920s. Together, my father and I called the Cunard Archives at the University of Liverpool, where a sympathetic librarian informed us, regretfully, that he was not aware of any existing passenger lists from my grandparents' voyage through the Panama Canal on the SS *Kroonland*.

My grandmother kept a diary documenting her and Frank's voyage from New York through the Panama Canal to California, and finally on to Akron. I scoured the copy that Virginia had digitized and sent to me, but my grandmother's entries, while full of details of food and transportation, offered zero insights into her inner life or family background. Her entry for February 8, 1925, the day she and Frank took the train east from San Francisco, is typical:

Left S. Fran 8 p.m. Took trolley and arrived at station 8:15. Waited until 8:40 Ferry over to Oakland. Train pulled out at 11:00. Went to bed. Berths real comfy. Couldn't sleep. Arose 6:30 dressed ready for breakfast. Arrived at Bakersfield and ate figs, toast, coffee 35 cents. Walked a little at station. Went aboard 8:30. Ate dinner at Bartow Roast Beef sandwich, coffee cake 60 cents...

Another time, I visited a Swedish Lutheran church in Brooklyn located off Flatbush Avenue a few blocks from Dean and Fifth. Given that Swedish immigrants made up its congregation in the early twentieth century, I was hoping that a Swedish family with parents Elof and Elida and eldest son Frank, with any last name, might be among them. The minister, a tall man with dark hair liberally sprinkled with gray, listened attentively to my story and name-change theory.

"Swedish immigrants might Americanize their surnames, but it would be very unusual to totally change their last name," he remarked, his eyebrows raised.

The minister and I pored over the dusty early-twentieth-century record books, to no avail.

When I returned to my car, I had a parking ticket. It figured.

Fortunately, my new life in Boston went far better than the family research. I became involved in the local swing dance scene, where I made friends and learned the Lindy Hop, a dance originated by black Americans in the late 1920s. By pure luck, I landed a tiny, affordable apartment in Harvard Square, the iconic neighborhood in Cambridge just across the Charles River from Boston, which is home to Harvard University. On the career front, two years in high-tech sales having convinced me that I lacked the necessary ruthless streak, I quit my job for a three-month technical training program in client-server computing, which was a hot technology in the mid-1990s. While a sales rep, I had observed enough of the information technology world to think I could make this booming field work for me. Programming is language, after all, and I was good at languages. In January of 1998 I landed my first IT position, at Harvard University, in a career that continues as of this writing, in 2022.

Most fortuitously of all, in Boston I met Marc Springer, the man who would become my husband. Marc became my companion and constant supporter as I pursued my investigation of the great Hanson mystery.

As the twentieth century became the twenty-first, my personal and work lives were on track, yet the family mystery seemed unsolvable. I've often been asked why I didn't just bow to fate and give up.

I've never been entirely sure how to answer that question. Part of it was that my father's cause had become my own—the search was about him, about us, about who we were. Although I didn't yet understand the depth of emotions that made my father continue to encourage my pursuit of this seemingly hopeless cause, I did know that the year 2000 had shaken and saddened him.

First had come Al's sudden death in April. It shouldn't have been a shock, but it was. In precarious health for years due to an autoimmune disease, Al had been in and out of the hospital multiple times, but he always bounced back, full of zest for life, until the April day when a heart attack felled him midsentence. The same month, Harvey had been diagnosed with the liver cancer that ended his life in June 2000.

With the deaths, in rapid succession, of the brothers to whom my father had been closest, he lost not just brothers but the two people who shared his childhood memories and his past. Although Frank Jr., my father's oldest brother, was still alive, the five-year age difference, combined with their dissimilar temperaments and interests, meant that unlike the maverick Al and my father's twin, Harvey, Frank Jr. had figured little in my father's childhood.

In the emptier, lonelier world my dad now inhabited, if my continuing to pursue the family project comforted him, I wanted to do it.

A huge part of it, too, was that even though I was happily ensconced in a stable relationship and steady job, the adventurer in me still had energy requiring a cause. My appetite for quitting jobs and uprooting myself had vanished, but not my desire for exploration and discovery. My career in IT, despite its manifold intellectual and financial merits, could not satisfy the researcher and reporter I remained to my core. I always just loved investigations and digging up truth. I needed something beyond the everyday about which to be passionate.

Or maybe it all came down to persistence, which I possessed in large store. The summer before college, I worked seven days a week as a chambermaid, as cleaners were then quaintly called, at a resort in Upstate New York's Lake George. A few weeks in, the owner called me into his office and fired me. At least he tried to. I sat there arguing with him for a half hour until, with a huge sigh of exasperation and resignation and a bit of grudging respect, he gave up. The supposed grounds for firing me were baseless, as my supervisor later discovered and shamefacedly admitted. Fueling my determination to fight back was the fact that, after having been unhappy during much of high school, I was having a great time after hours with my fellow college student cleaners and dining room staff at the resort. I didn't want to leave.

Two decades later, I still was unwilling to give up on something important if I thought I could, or should, prevail. This seemingly intractable problem of my grandparents' missing past had to have a solution. Somewhere, somehow, I would find a key to open the door.

"I'm sure Grampa changed his last name." That's what I had said to my dad after the Prospect Park farm research fiasco, and by the late 1990s, it became my mantra. "There's no other explanation for the fact that we've researched everything and never found anything."

If Frank were fleeing someone or something in New York and didn't want to be found, Hanson would be an excellent name choice. It maintained Frank's Swedish identity while allowing him to become anonymous. The surname Hanson is almost as common among Americans of Swedish ancestry as Smith is among those with English heritage.

Aunt Virginia, the grand dame instigator of the Hanson research in the 1950s, refused to consider the name-change theory. "I'm sure that's not true," she'd say when we chatted on the phone. "I sat across from Mater and Pater, I asked them questions, and I wrote down what they told me. I'm sure their name was Hanson."

"Well, could you tell me what happened that day?" I asked.

Describing events from 1953, more than four decades earlier, Virginia struggled to recall details of what at the time seemed like the most ordinary of afternoons. But it went something like this.

Virginia and Harvey pulled their 1947 Ford coupe up to the gray cedar-shingled bungalow at 1160 Clifton Avenue, whose well-maintained exterior reflected the many improvements Frank had made since acquiring it on the eve of the Great Depression in 1929. The roof, siding, and paint job were all his handiwork. So also were the sturdy, waterproof redwood storm sashes on all of the windows. Using wood salvaged from a building job, Frank had meticulously measured, built, and fitted each storm sash, constructing them to last indefinitely, as was true with everything he created.

The newlyweds pulled two large laundry bags stuffed with clothes out of the back seat. In a month they were heading to Columbus, Ohio, where Harvey was starting his second year of physics graduate studies. In the meantime, however, their summer sublet did not have a washing machine.

"Hi, Mater, Pater, how are you?" Twenty-two-year-old Virginia, her round glasses framed by shoulder-length brown hair curled at the ends, greeted her in-laws with a smile. She and Harvey entered the white-vinyl-tiled kitchen.

"Hi, Ginny," Ida replied. My grandmother was always assigning special nicknames to family members. Her first grandchild, Frank E. Hanson III, became "Butch," while my sister Karen, for reasons unknown, would be dubbed "Cooper."

For the next few hours, Virginia and Harvey hauled piles of clothes in and out of the basement washing machine and then out to the backyard to dry on a clothesline of thick galvanized wire that Frank had rigged up. Before hanging the clothes, Harvey wiped the wire clean with a damp cloth so the laundry wouldn't be dirtied by the thin film of soot that emanated from the nearby Ohio Edison power plant, which burned southern Ohio bituminous coal and coated everything downwind with a layer of grime. Then the pair hung up the clean, damp clothes with wooden clothespins, dark and shiny after decades of use. Harvey, still round-faced beneath a soft wave of blond hair, limped as he stepped back and forth, his uneven gait a remnant of a childhood bout with Legg-Calvé-Perthes, a degenerative hip disease.

After the last batch of clothes was pinned up on the clothesline, the foursome gathered at the dining room table, Virginia and Harvey on one side, Frank and Ida across from them. Ida was, as usual, drinking coffee, which she took with evaporated milk and sugar in a special white ceramic cup. Despite her admitted addiction to coffee, no one else in the family was permitted to touch it.

"It isn't good for you," she always told the boys.

What exactly spurred Virginia's next move, she could not recall. She probably was anticipating starting her new job at the state library in Columbus in a few weeks, where she planned to consult its extensive genealogy resources.

"I'd like to get some genealogical information on your families," she said to Ida and Frank. "Could I ask you some questions?"

Unassuming Virginia, with her sweet smile and gentle manner, was venturing into territory forbidden to her husband and his brothers.

"OK, sure," my grandparents agreed readily.

Digging in her purse, Virginia found a blue-ink pen and a five-by-seven notebook with unlined white paper, which she used in her job at the Akron Public Library.

"What were your parents' names?" she began.

"My father's name was Willard Howe," Ida replied. "My mother's maiden name was Alice Andrews."

Virginia, sitting across the table from Ida, wrote the names in her notebook. "My father was from Sheffield, England," Ida continued. "He came to the US in his teens. He first lived in Naugatuck, Connecticut, before he moved to Brooklyn and bought the farm."

"When were you and Pater married?" Virginia asked.

"We were married on May twenty-sixth, 1923," Ida replied. "It's easy to remember. We were married in 1923 and our first child was born in 1926. It's all in threes." And with that comment, Ida took another sip of coffee.

Virginia faithfully recorded Ida's and Frank's responses in her notebook as she continued her soft questions. Within an hour, her neat, slanted blue-ink print filled several notebook pages, listing every name, date, and fact that Ida and Frank provided. She was harvesting a cornucopia of previously undisclosed Hanson and Howe data. Before that afternoon, Frank had never told any of his sons his parents' names, or revealed that he had eight younger brothers and sisters, not to mention their first names and birth order. Frank's father was Elof, his mother was Elida and her maiden name was Johnson. Frank's siblings, from second-oldest to youngest, were Albert Alton, Ethel Carolina, Helen Ingaborg, Carl Elof, Vincent, Henry, May, and Florence. Frank even provided the names of his paternal grandparents back in Sweden, Peter Hanson and Inga Bloom, as well as a paternal aunt and uncle, Carrie and William.

Ida, too, divulged a stream of previously secret family data, including the names of her father's six brothers and sisters back in Sheffield, in addition to the names of all four of her grandparents.

"When did your mother die?" Virginia asked.

"September twenty-fourth, 1922," Ida replied. Virginia's blue pen entered that answer in her notebook.

Wait—that date doesn't make sense.

Ida always told her boys that her parents died when she was in her early to midteens, followed a few years later by her grandmother. Regardless of her prevarication as to whether her birth year was 1899, 1903, or sometime in between, Ida was at least nineteen, if not twenty-three, in 1922. She would already have been married to Frank upon her grandmother's death a few years later. No need for a Jewish guardian to ensure her Catholic upbringing, or to approve her marriage to Frank at age twenty-one, as she had always told Harley.

Harvey, the physicist with an innate gift for understanding the most complex of mathematical equations, didn't notice that the dates didn't add up. Unlike Virginia and Harley, he was never intrigued by the curious blankness of his family history, or his parents' refusal to divulge even simple details of their pasts.

After she related the events of that long-ago Sunday afternoon, I asked Virginia about the anomaly of the dates. "I always meant to ask Pater about that," Virginia said. Nonetheless, she stuck with her belief in the veracity of her in-laws' account.

"Records were in very bad shape in New York, and immigrants often were missed," Virginia said when I pointed out that we had never been able to validate any of the information my grandparents gave her. "If we just keep on looking, we'll find them," she added.

I felt we had no option but to entertain the name-change theory. Whole families do not live and die in major cities in twentieth-century North America without some shred of evidence eventually turning up. No matter how poorly the records were kept, sooner or later our exhaustive research would have unearthed at least a smidgen of proof that they existed. When you can't confirm facts that are supposed to be true, sooner or later you have to consider alternative explanations.

It is ironic, if unsurprising, that it took an outsider such as Aunt Virginia to start the probe into the Hanson and Howe family trees. The Hanson boys, young men in 1953, had been trained since early childhood that it was futile to inquire into their parents' past. But the new family member, Virginia, had been raised differently. In collecting this genealogical data that summer afternoon, she created the first crack in the seemingly impregnable wall that Ida and Frank had so carefully erected to conceal their past.

With the emergence of internet genealogy resources in the late 1990s, I spent hours glued to the computer in futile searches of Federal Census records for a Swedish-born Elof, regardless of surname, who lived in New York state between 1900 and 1930. Searches for my grandmother's parents, Willard and Alice Howe, in New York proved just as unsuccessful, as did the rest of my online research.

In July of 2002, two years after the unattainable box of photos arrived at my father's, I took the bus from Boston to New York to run down a final lead. One of the rare snippets Frank had several times shared about his family in Brooklyn was the anguish he felt when a much younger sister, May, died around the time of the 1918 flu pandemic. Given my warm memories of Grampa's kind and loving nature, Frank's story of sadness at the loss of his young sister had the ring of truth.

Submerged within the depths of the New York City Municipal Archives on a hot, humid day, I reviewed the chronological indexes that listed the name, age, and date of every single person whose death was recorded in New York City from 1915 through 1920. I was searching for a child named May, with any surname. If a blunt force expedition through a bog of endless indexes was what it took to find Grampa's beloved little sister, I was game. Once I had May's surname and date of death, this genealogical key would lead me to Grampa's family.

Stationed at the microfilm reader, I scrolled through the death indexes page by page, focusing on first names and ages only, squinting to decipher fuzzy type on blotchy backgrounds. As minutes became hours, I sat up, shook my hunched shoulders, and took a swig from my water bottle. My eyes dried out and I kept blinking, my head becoming heavy and my neck strained, as I reviewed faint text on cloudy microfilm that documented the sad shared fate of persons young and old, of every conceivable ethnicity, who perished in New York City during this five-year period.

"Aha, so that's where they were!" A woman sitting nearby emitted a soft crow of satisfaction every time her hungry eyes retrieved yet another nugget of treasure from the smudged film.

I could only sigh. By the end of the day, my dreary slog through five years of New York City mortality had yielded nothing. As usual. No matter what we tried, that's how it always went for the Hanson and Howe researchers.

Nonetheless, even then, I refused to concede to my invisible foe. A month later, in August of 2002, I finally persuaded my father to turn over his parents' photo collection. Maybe the inhabitants of that battered cardboard container would finally reveal the secrets that had always bobbed and weaved just beyond my reach.

When the ghosts finally stirred, waking ever so slowly from their decades-long slumber, our lives would never be the same.

CHAPTER 7:
PHOTOS DON'T LIE

CIRCA 1978 *(Imagining the past)*

FRANK SAT AT HIS GRAY FORMICA kitchen table in the small house on Clifton Avenue. His hands trembled due to his ever-worsening Parkinson's. On the table in front of him was a large opened box full of packets, envelopes, and small containers. This was his and Ida's photo collection.

Laying the box on its side, Frank began pulling out envelopes and piles of loose photos, stopping to intently review any image that included a very young, fresh-faced Ida. Occasionally he placed a photo on the table apart from the unwieldy mass spilling from the box.

Sometimes he paused, gazing out the window at the cherry blossoms hovering just outside. He had fastened the branch of a cherry tree to the side of the house so he could see the blossoms from the kitchen table. Then he returned to his excavation, until he had extracted twelve images in all. Pushing the rest of the jumbled heap back into the box, he set it upright and shook it gently to resettle the contents.

Picking up the top photo from the pile he had set aside, Frank studied it briefly before laying it on the table. He arranged a wooden ruler across the image, using it to pencil a line across the photo with a tremulous hand. Next, clasping the photo in one hand and a pair of scissors in the other, he cut the photo along the line, yielding two dismembered pieces. He repeated this operation for each photo in the pile. A few times, his hand shook so badly that the scissors veered off the penciled line.

Each time he finished his incision across a photograph, he delicately placed one section of the photo back on the table in another pile. Each of these favored fragments included Ida's face and a portion of her person. The discarded segments, Frank tore into tiny pieces.

A few of the photos had dates written on the back. For these, after completing his incision, he copied the date, in wobbly block printing, onto the portion of the photo he was keeping.

Finally, Frank was done. He carefully gathered up the photo fragments he was saving, now jagged strips and squares featuring Ida, minus the excised portions. He placed the uneven images of Ida in an envelope and back into the box. The torn-up discards, a small mound of gray-and-white shreds, he brushed into a paper bag, which he then placed in the trash under the sink.

AFTER RETURNING HOME to my apartment in Cambridge, Massachusetts, with the box of photos in August of 2002, I plunged into the sea of prints, negatives, and frayed envelopes housed in that battered container. Initially I focused on photos taken before my grandparents arrived in Akron in 1925. In the early twentieth century, photos came in all shapes and sizes, and in hues of black, white, and sepia. Most amateur photos were much smaller than typical printed snapshots today, and their dimensions, shape, and tones varied greatly. In my grandparents' collection, they always had a number stamped in ink on the back, indicating the batch in which they had been printed. Based on the shape and size of the photos and the stamp on the back, I began grouping the early images by roll and approximate time frame. Only a handful of these pictures had dates on them, and even fewer had names.

Among the early photos, particularly puzzling were twelve images of young Ida from which Frank had excised someone or something. Although I don't know if the scene of Frank snipping those photos occurred as I have imagined it, the evidence leaves no doubt that late in life, Grampa cut away sections of twelve photos that portrayed my grandmother in her youth.

On some of the images, I could see the pencil line Grampa drew with a ruler to guide the scissors in his shaking hand, in the same way as he used to trace lines across the envelopes of letters to help him print my address legibly. On the back of some of the photos, a date Ida had originally penciled in with her cursive script was partially eliminated by Grampa's surgery. In these cases, he had faithfully copied out the full date on the back of the remaining portion of the photo in his unsteady yet still decisive square block printing. On a photo where just "28/19" was visible on the back, he had printed "6-28-19."

In the cropped photos, Ida stands on hillsides, leans against a fence, sits on rocks, and kneels in front of a pond. Grampa's incisions created a variety of irregular shapes: some of the remnants were long, thin slivers, while others resembled uneven squares. Always, Ida's face was preserved.

My first thought was that there had been another man in Ida's life before Frank. Had Frank cut him out of the photos so no one would know?

Among the treasure trove of photographs I brought home in 2002, the images with sections cut out weren't the only ones raising questions. The box contained scores of photos whose subjects' clothing and hairstyles dated them prior to the summer of 1924. The more I organized and scrutinized these images from my grandparents' early lives, the less sense they made.

For starters, who were all these people? My grandmother claimed to have been the only child of English immigrants who had left their families behind in Sheffield, yet these photos portrayed a multitude of men, women, and children with Ida, many of whom looked like her. A young woman appearing in several photographs bore a striking resemblance to my sister Alex in the strong square lines of her jaw.

Many of these pictures took the form of card photograph portraits, still common in the early twentieth century, in which a photo taken in a photographer's studio, often with elaborate props, was printed on stiff card stock about the size of a small postcard today.

In one such card photograph, a group of women and children have arranged themselves in an open automobile for an elaborate family portrait. A thirteen- or fourteen-year-old Ida, her wavy hair pulled back in a soft chignon, occupies the driver's seat and holds the wheel with both hands.

A woman in her forties, with deep lines running from the sides of her nostrils to the corners of her mouth, sits in the passenger seat to Ida's right, encased in a high-necked, long-sleeved white dress, her ornaments a small brooch and a hat trimmed with ribbon. Several women and a girl sit in the back. One of them, a sweetly pretty round-faced young woman with Ida's eyes, wears a floppy flower-laden hat and holds a baby in her lap. The child, with round, light eyes, perches at attention.

In another photo, Ida, aged seventeen or eighteen, poses with the same sweet-faced young woman in a series of photos in which they take turns modeling fancy hats—one a broad-brimmed affair arranged at a jaunty angle, the other a sort of exaggerated tam-o'-shanter, with a band hugging the head and the crown jutting up in a triangle.

And the children. They were everywhere. Oblivious infants propped up for solo portraits. Women and babies, women with toddlers, kids playing. A youthful Ida surrounded by groups of children. Youngsters frolicking on a snowy hillside with a sled. Remarkable for a woman who had no family.

One entire roll consisted of photographs of a dark-haired boy of about five or six playing in the snow, and on the porch of a wood house. "March 12,

1924," Ida had penciled on the back of one of the photos in her neat cursive script. Someone must have been very fond of that little boy, I thought.

Another anomaly in these images was their setting. My grandparents always said they were born and raised in Brooklyn. However, based on my visit to the Brooklyn land records office, I already knew that Ida could not have lived on a farm located in today's Prospect Park. As for Frank, I had made multiple pilgrimages to the urban neighborhood at the intersection of Dean Street and Fifth Avenue in Brooklyn, where Grampa claimed he grew up. His family had lived near the Flatbush trolley, as he told it, and as a boy, he retrieved used theater tickets from the gutter. Ida and Frank had lived close enough to each other to attend the same elementary school.

Why, then, did these early photos portray a world of detached wood houses, many with ample yards, in addition to barns, fields, and rolling hillsides? The Brooklyn neighborhoods lining Flatbush Avenue, as well as the streets surrounding Prospect Park, were and still are crammed with turn-of-the-century brownstones, brick and stone townhouses, and apartment buildings, with perhaps the tiniest stamp-sized patches of yard. Wood houses just don't exist there, and neither do snowy hillsides with barns in the background.

"These don't look like any Brooklyn I've ever seen," I told my father when I called to report on my progress.

"You know, at this point I have no idea where those pictures were taken," he replied. My dad had concluded, as had I, that we could not rely on even the most basic information his parents had provided about their past. "You're doing a great job. Keep it up."

One familiar icon from Frank's few tales did turn up among these baffling images: his prized Indian motorcycle and his biker gang. In several photos, groups of young men, including Frank, pose astride or next to their bikes, stern faces signaling their intended tough-guy status, and a few of them sporting shaved heads. Again, the backdrops were wooden sheds, dirt roads, and tree-covered hillsides.

In a close-up of Grampa's motorcycle, the sun reflects off the front license plate, the glare blocking all but the first character, the numeral 1. Could information on this plate be buried somewhere in the New York State Department of Motor Vehicles archives? One visit to the agency website convinced me of the folly of trying to locate a motorcycle registered some eighty years earlier, armed with only the manufacturer and one license digit.

In the evening, magnifying glass in hand, I'd sort through stacks of photos, searching for a clue that might reveal where they were taken and whom they depicted. Ensconced on my forest-green sofa in the tiny living room of my Harvard Square apartment, I'd scrutinize photo after photo from packets I had placed on the glass coffee table in front of me.

Occasionally looking up from the photos, my eyes would rest on the framed prints, vintage advertising posters, and maps covering my walls, collected during trips to Europe. On my bookshelf was the butternut baby duck from Grampa, next to a delicately crocheted white cotton teacup and saucer with blue trim. Ida, while recuperating from her 1956 mastectomy, had begun crocheting these dainty confections for each of her six granddaughters. She did not live to give them to my sisters and me. When Grampa later gave us our teacups during a summer visit to Akron, this ethereal vessel became my grandmother's love for me manifest. Now, although these mementos made me happy, they provided no answers.

"Do you think this looks like Brooklyn?"

When Marc, then my boyfriend, came over, I'd ask his opinion. A native of Brooklyn's Coney Island, he was my resident expert on all things New York and Brooklyn. We'd sit on my couch on Saturday afternoons, Marc watching Boston Red Sox baseball on TV while I sorted through the photos. Despite his New York roots, Marc was a fervent Red Sox fan.

"Hmmm, I don't know," he'd say dubiously, examining the photo I had thrust in front of him. "Maybe back then there was a part of Brooklyn that hadn't been developed yet." I could tell he thought this unlikely, and I had to agree.

Marc had been inducted into the Hanson family conundrum almost immediately when he entered my life in June of 2001. On our second date, after a
Saturday night dinner in Boston's hip South End neighborhood, we had gone for
a drink at the top of the Prudential Center, the city's second-tallest skyscraper.

Perched on barstools high above Boston, we had sipped wine as the lights
of the city below twinkled in the dark night sky. Marc listened attentively
as I told him the story: my grandparents, after growing up in Brooklyn and
marrying in the 1920s, had voyaged via ship through the Panama Canal to
San Francisco, California, where they stayed before ending up in Akron,
Ohio. I explained how we had been researching their family history for years
and could never find a single piece of evidence to validate the few supposed
facts they had provided.

From the start, Marc got it. He understood why the secrets of my grandparents' past gripped me so. The grandson of Jewish immigrants from central
Europe, he was the sort of person who, when strolling the Lower East Side
neighborhood in Manhattan where his parents grew up, would try to imagine what they would have seen, what they would have heard, as they walked
these same streets. He, too, became intrigued by the unanswered questions
of my grandparents' missing past, the supposed facts that made no sense, the
histories that could not be verified.

"How do I figure out where these photos are, if they aren't in Brooklyn?"
That's what I'd ask Marc as we sat on my couch, gazing at the black-and-white
images of nineteenth-century wood houses and rolling hills covered by vege-
tation, searching for some little detail that would reveal their location. When
the twentieth century was new, many areas just a short train ride from New
York City still had the fields and barns depicted in my grandparents' photos.
Large patches of Long Island east of the city were still mostly rural, as were
many areas north and west of the city and even in New Jersey.

Most of the photos with barns and fields featured people who looked like
Ida. Maybe my grandmother had quarreled with her family and fled to New

York City. Women had gained considerable freedoms by the early 1920s, after all. An industrious young woman like Ida would have found many job opportunities in or around the city. Maybe that's when she ran into her elementary school classmate, Frank, with romance soon following. The first recognizably Brooklyn photo features Ida feeding a turkey in Prospect Park, with the autographic camera caption of "P.P.B. 4-6-24" in Frank's distinctive block printing.

Another photo depicts a young man in a sailor's uniform and hat standing on a beach, holding a trombone. Penciled on the back was "To mother from her son Albert." This had to be Grampa's brother Albert, the US Navy musician after whom Uncle Al had been named.

Among all of my grandparents' early photos, only one had both a name and a date. A small child with short blond hair and spiky bangs tilts her head and grins up at the photographer. Wearing a simple cotton frock, she stands among patchy tufts of grass in the yard of a wood-frame house. Another building can be seen immediately adjacent to the house. On the back of the photo, in her neat, unmistakable cursive script, my grandmother had written, "Florence H., 6-21-21, aged 3½."

So, this was Baby Florence, Grampa's beloved little sister. I identified ten additional photos of Florence, dating from toddlerhood up through age five or six. The slight child with the heart-shaped face, trusting smile, and wisps of blond bangs across her broad forehead was unmistakable. One photo captures Florence, age two or three, wearing a frilled sun hat while perched on the knee of a middle-aged man with a large mustache. Behind them, a stretch of patchy uncut grass is bordered by a wood structure. In another, she sits on wood steps outside a house, squeezed between two bigger boys, a kitten in her arms. A year or so older, she stands in front of a woodpile, wearing a sweater and her usual small, shy grin, again cradling a cat. In another photo on the outside steps of a wood structure, she poses with a young man who flashes a wide smile beneath a tilted Panama hat. This could have been a youthful Frank, except the face was too long.

What happened to Baby Florence? If Frank was so fond of her, as my father's recollections and the multiple photos attest, why didn't they remain in touch?

"I went back to find them and they were gone," Frank had replied when, as a boy, Harley asked what happened. "They all died. They're dead."

I was willing to bet that at least some of Frank's siblings, eight in number according to Aunt Virginia's genealogical interview, had enjoyed a normal life span. Florence, being the youngest and female, was my best shot at finding one of them alive. The age and date on the labeled 1921 photo meant she was born at the end of 1917 or early 1918. If Florence was still living in 2002, as I looked at these photos of her, she'd be eighty-four.

"Time is running out," I kept saying to Marc. "She could be this frail old lady in a nursing home somewhere. I've got to find her."

None of the photos of Florence appeared to be taken in Brooklyn. The backdrop of most was a wood structure, simpler than those depicted in other photos, with a small yard bare except for a few skinny trees and stubby clumps of grass. Could the Hanson family have started out on Dean Street and subsequently moved out of Brooklyn? Like so many of the photos, the images of Florence raised many questions and answered none, with one exception: She had definitely existed.

A month or so after I began burrowing through the box, the contents of a crumpled brown paper bag yielded a partial answer to the riddle of the cropped photos. Grampa had not destroyed the negatives. Perhaps because of age and frailty, he had neglected this one detail in his otherwise thorough excision of the past.

Within this bag lay a mass of loose, dusty negatives in a variety of sizes. After attempting to examine the images by holding the negatives up to the light of a lamp, I realized there was a better way. Gently placing the negatives in a large, clean envelope, I walked with my treasure one block down Massachusetts Avenue to Ferranti-Dege, a long-established photo store then in Harvard Square that catered to serious photographers.

"We can print them in our darkroom, but since the negatives are irregular sizes, we'll need to do each by hand," a bearded man told me. At a cost of five or six dollars each for more than one hundred negatives, that was a big chunk of change. I opted for a proof sheet instead, with six to eight negatives per sheet.

"Handle with care! Irreplaceable eighty-year-old family negatives enclosed!" I printed in big bold letters on the order form. I hated handing over these precious, fragile slivers. Even the most conscientious darkroom worker could hardly imagine how much these negatives, their contents hidden until now, meant to my father and me. But printing them up was the best way to reveal the secrets that Grampa had attempted to conceal, even beyond his own death.

A few days later, I picked up my photos and hurried home along Massachusetts Avenue, dodging pedestrians on the ever-crowded brick sidewalk. After hustling up the stairs to my second-floor apartment and locking the door behind me, I stood in my tiny foyer, tore the packet open, and began flipping through the proof sheets, searching for the images with excised sections. Then I stopped.

A young child had been cut out of the pictures.

Striding the few steps into my living room, I plopped on the sofa and quickly scanned through the fifteen or so proof sheets. For nine of my twelve cropped mystery photos, I now had the full original image. In one, young Ida cradles a child of about two against her body as she leans on a wood fence, a grassy field behind her. She wears a loose striped cotton summer dress, and her face is framed by soft wisps of hair that have escaped from her bun. The child in her arms has large, dark eyes, dimples, a happy grin, and is clutching a toy truck. It must be a boy.

"I got the negatives printed. You'll never believe what's in the pictures that were cut up!" Within minutes, I was on the phone with my father.

Ever the good scientist, he avoided jumping to conclusions and kept his mounting emotions in check.

"This is very interesting," he said. "I don't know what it means."

For my dad, the higher the stakes, the more critical it was to remain careful and skeptical. As my excitement grew, he sounded ever calmer, playing the same role he always had in my life. Yet I detected anticipation in the intermittent raised tones of his voice.

There were multiple photos of the dark-eyed baby boy. In one, Ida holds the child upright in her arms, against her hip, while she stands on a grassy, wildflower-covered knoll overlooking a lake. Clad in a long white gown and dark boots, the boy clutches a large, furry stuffed toy as he snuggles toward Ida. The sun, shining directly on the child's gown, imbues the garment with an incandescent shimmer, so the boy resembles a glowing cherub. Ida, a few wavy tendrils again slipping free from her bun, wears a soft white blouse and long skirt. A hint of a smile plays across her lips. Inclining her head toward the child in her arms, Ida gazes somewhere off in the distance to the right of the photographer.

"She looks like a Madonna," said my dad, a totally unreligious man, of this image. With the light streaming across mother and child, Ida's serene expression, and the intimacy of their pose, she did.

Only one of the snipped photos contained the man I had been expecting. Ida, her unexpectedly soft round face looking very young above her womanly figure, sits on a seat in a grassy clearing surrounded by trees. Next to her is a clean-shaven, handsome man in his early twenties attired in a crisp white shirt, suit, and tie, his thick, dark hair cropped short. Ida's hair waves gently around her face, and she wears a long-sleeved, ruffled white shirtwaist—a blouse, in today's parlance—plus a long dark gathered skirt and black beads. After checking a few style history sources, I dated the photo as approximately 1915. Ida must have been born in 1899, rather than 1903, given her appearance and the young man's presence.

Once, in a passing remark, Ida had told my dad that she named him after an old boyfriend, Harley Burgess. Of course, I had searched high and low and found no such person. Now, as I looked at Ida and her apparent beau ensconced in the clearing, I wondered, was this the original Harley? Or could he be the father of the boy excised from the photos?

Maybe my grandmother had been married and had a child who died before she met my grandfather. Of course, given the many other young women resembling Ida in the photos, she also could have been posing with a beloved baby nephew.

Another possible explanation for the child cut from the photos was almost unthinkable, given the strict morals of the mother Harley had known and the social conventions of the era: could she have had a child out of wedlock?

In one of the early photos from Frank and
Ida's collection, Ida, at the steering wheel of an
elaborate prop automobile in a studio portrait,
is surrounded by people who resemble her.

This sweet-faced woman appears many
times in Ida's early photos.

Children play on a snowy hillside, with wood buildings in the background. This photo doesn't look like Brooklyn.

Children in front of a barn. These same youngsters appear in multiple photos.

Photo of a young Ida from which Frank
excised someone or something.

Baby Florence with a cat.

On the back of this photo, Ida wrote,
"Florence H., 6-21-21, aged 3½."

CHAPTER 8:
EDUCATION ABOVE ALL

AKRON, CIRCA 1940 *(Imagining the past)*

"BUD, YOU HAVE TO FINISH one ear before you start another."

Ida grinned at Al, who had been nibbling just the tops of the plump yellow kernels as his mouth rapidly progressed up and down the rows of his corn on the cob. Al was always Bud, unless he was really misbehaving.

Every time they had corn on a cob, the great Hanson corn-eating contest began anew: who could eat the most ears? Al was always trying to figure out a shortcut. Tonight, his strategy had been to just barely kiss the tops of the corn kernels, but Mama wasn't having any of it.

"Ahhh, all right." Al screwed up his face in mock protest and then turned back to his corn.

"Honey, you too." Ida nodded at Harley. "Please clean that ear."

"I am," Harley protested. Dripping with sweat, hands slippery with butter, Harley, clad like his brothers and father in an undershirt and shorts, hunched over his white dinner plate as he crunched each blissful mouthful of salted, buttered corn, which he had picked fresh from the big garden just before dinner.

Ida, her face shiny and pink in the heat, damp hair pinned back from her face, sighed with contentment as she surveyed her family. "I like seeing you boys eat a lot," she said.

"I'll eat as much as you want me to, Mama." Harley looked up from his ear just long enough to speak and then burrowed back amongst the bright yellow rows. After finishing the ear to Ida's satisfaction, Harley jumped up from the kitchen table and grabbed a fresh ear from the steaming pile stacked on a platter on the counter. "Ouch, it's hot!"

Back at the table, he slathered butter all over the kernels and shook the saltshaker vigorously up and down the cob. "Mmmmmm!" he exhaled, biting into the plump, sweet kernels. Pure bliss.

For a few minutes, the only sound at the table was that of six mouths chomping on corn, mixed with occasional grunts of pleasure.

"Uh, I'm stuffed." After consuming six ears, Harley was done. In a few minutes all of the boys had eaten their fill, so only Papa was left munching his last ear of corn.

"That's enough for me," Frank finally said. "Ten'll do it."

"Papa's the winner," Harvey cried.

The boys placed their plates on the kitchen counter, stacking the stripped cobs pyramid-style on the same platter that earlier had held the steaming cooked corn. Ida's cotton dress clung to her back as she stood up to wipe globs of butter and stray kernels from the gray Formica tabletop.

"It's time for sugar tomatoes," she said, placing a large Pyrex bowl on the table. Earlier, she had plunged fresh, ripe garden tomatoes into boiling water for a minute before retrieving them and swiftly slipping off their skins. She had then sliced the bright red orbs and placed them in the Pyrex bowl, sprinkling them generously with sugar and then stirring. The result was a candied fruit that in Harley's opinion was as satisfying as any cake or cookie.

After Ida ladled the fruit onto the boys' and Frank's plates, they quickly gobbled up the sweet red slices.

"Yummm!" Harley groaned with delight.

After finishing his tomatoes, Al reached for the serving bowl.

"It's my turn," he said.

"Uh-uh, you had it last time," Harley retorted. "I get it." The boys were vying for the syrupy, pinkish juice remaining in the bottom of the bowl.

"I believe Junior had it last time." Ida decided the matter after brief consideration. Rights to the coveted nectar rotated amongst the boys in strictly observed order. "It's Buddy's turn."

Al grabbed the bowl and tipped it up over his face, loudly slurping down the juice. "Man, that's good," he sighed.

"Are you full up?" Frank Sr. asked the boys.

"I'm full up to the roof!" Al said.

"I'm full up!" the other three boys echoed.

"Can we go?" Harley asked. He wanted to catch at least part of his favorite radio show, *Jack Armstrong, the All-American Boy*.

After receiving Ida's nod, the boys rinsed their dishes and stacked them on the counter for Frank Jr., whose turn it was to wash. Frank Sr. refilled his glass stein with skim milk and settled in for his nightly session with the *Akron Beacon Journal*. Harley, Harvey, and Al had already grabbed the comics and darted into the living room, where they sprawled on the floor, the only carpeted surface in the house, eagerly listening to the adventures of their idol, Jack Armstrong.

Ida sat in her living room chair, a comfy upholstered seat that only she was permitted to occupy, darning socks.

WHEN MY DAD AND HIS BROTHERS were children, Ida found it hard to let them out of her sight. Every weekday morning, when the boys left the house to walk the one block to Andrew Jackson Elementary School, they'd go about six houses down and stop.

"We'd turn and wave, and there she was, waving. It was actually a little embarrassing," my father told me. They repeated the ritual after they had come home for lunch and were heading back to school in the afternoon.

Memories like these flooded back to my dad when we began an ongoing series of recorded conversations about his childhood a few months after Ida and Frank's photo collection came home with me to Boston. Freed from his anxiety over the vexing box, he was once again his old self, full of enthusiasm for the family project. After his liberation from the ghostly photos, my dad was ready to bring me with him into the living world of his past.

Each time I visited, we set up shop at the keeping room table, light streaming in through the big glass patio doors, exuberant yellow in summer, flat and subdued on cloudy winter days. Beyond the patio, the garden's tall rushes gave way to an expansive backyard, bordered at the far end by a jumble of trees and thickets.

In my father's stories, my grandmother, Ida, for so long consigned to the silence of black-and-white photographs, arose to forceful life. By the mid-1930s, the sleek, long-limbed amphibious creature from Brighton Beach had become commander-in-chief of the Hanson household, running the lives of her four boys with an iron will and certainty that she knew best.

"My mother was a super control freak." That's the first thing my dad said when I asked him to describe his mom's personality. "She didn't want her boys to get out from under her thumb for one minute. She wanted to know where everybody was and what they were doing and every other darn thing. She managed everybody's life."

"Can you give me a few examples?"

"Well, I couldn't choose my own clothes until I was in college. We never were dressed appropriately," my father replied. "All the other boys were wearing neat stuff like overalls, or dungarees. We were still wearing hand-me-down knickers [shorts], knickerbockers. Mama thought they were proper. No one else was wearing them and I always felt sensitive about it. She was absolutely oblivious that it might cause some pain."

Although before World War I boys customarily wore short pants, also called by their English name of knickerbockers, until puberty, by the late 1930s and 1940s these puffy breeches, often fastened below the knee with a buckle or button, were entirely outmoded in working-class Akron, Ohio.

Much later, upon contemplating this story, I realized I had never seen my father in shorts, except for the swim trunks he donned to splash in the lake with my sisters and me during rare family vacations in the Pocono Mountains when I was little. Despite Philadelphia's hot and humid summers, my dad always wore long pants. I remember him marching back and forth across the yard behind the lawnmower, shirtless and hairy-chested above his slacks, a straw hat protecting his bald head from the sun. Perhaps his avoidance of shorts stemmed from childhood memories of acute embarrassment over the dreaded knickerbockers.

Every day after school, Ida kept close tabs on her sons.

"I had these close friends from school, Artie and Paul Smeed," my father continued. "German family—good, honest people. Their dad was a fireman. So, we were allowed to go play for a half hour." Second only to the English, whom Ida revered for her royal Howe pedigree, Germans were her favorite people.

"Let me fix your hair." That's what Ida said to Harley every morning before he left for school, her eyes alighting on his short brown hair, already neatly slicked back. After running water over a comb in the sink, she recombed his wavy locks to her satisfaction.

"She just really wanted to do it," my dad told me. As Harley hit his teens and began shooting up toward his ultimate six-foot-two-and-a-half-inch height, he had to crouch down for her ministrations.

"I don't need you to comb it," Harley said one morning when he was about fifteen.

"It'll only take a minute."

"I don't want you to."

Ida bit her lip. Her outstretched hand, holding the already-wet comb, dropped to her side.

Seeing the hurt in her eyes, Harley fought a feeling of shame. He didn't want to make his mother feel bad. But he was sick of her fussing over him, dictating every little detail of his life, from his embarrassing attire to whom he could play with. In a world where Ida ruled, Harley and his brothers learned to claim small victories where they could.

In the late 1930s, Ida had what in those days people called a nervous breakdown. Now, we would say she suffered from severe clinical depression. One day she went to bed and just didn't get up.

"She was bedridden for I have no idea how long," my dad said. "They actually had a hired girl in to keep the house."

Why was Ida so deeply depressed? The family never discussed it. Harley knew something was wrong, but he didn't know what it was. Indeed, when he first began pursuing psychology at the University of Akron, where the department was strictly Freudian, a desire to understand his mother and his family—in particular, his parents' extreme secrecy about their pasts—was a key driver of his interest, he told me.

Taking cues from his mother's depression, as a boy, Harley kept close tabs on Ida's moods. In a diary he kept for a few months at age twelve, many of the entries conclude with an update on Ida's emotional state: "Momee [sic] isn't feeling well," "Momee is sick today," "Momee is better."

"The diary didn't last," my father added. "I know my mother looked at it."

Until Harley's late teens, Ida hyperventilated when she was overwhelmed by anxiety, sometimes fainting as a result. It was due to her "bad heart," she said, which caused Harley to worry, throughout his childhood, that his mother was going to suddenly die.

Yet beyond his mother's anxiety, beyond her intensely protective control, as a child Harley also felt Ida's abiding, encircling love. On days he didn't feel well, "I'd walk home from school, I'd walk in the door, and there's Mama. She'd just say hello and I felt better. It was instant cheer."

Harley was the only one of the four boys who regularly spent time with Mama in the kitchen. He watched as Ida cooked, listened as she chatted, and helped peel potatoes and chop onions. Decades later, he could reproduce a score of her recipes, such as the family favorite he dubbed meatball spaghetti, Ohio style: the hearty tomato sauce contained beef, celery, and onions, but no garlic. At the dinner table, the family topped their heaping plates with grated cheddar cheese.

"She let you do that?!" That's what my grandfather Frank said, the slightly raised pitch of his quiet voice indicating astonishment, the day he learned that young Harley was Ida's frequent kitchen helper.

By the early 1930s, Akron, formerly a prosperous boomtown built on the rubber industry, had seen its industrial unemployment rate climb to an almost inconceivable sixty percent. For five years, Frank could not find any steady carpentry or construction work. With little cash to purchase food, Ida and Frank began growing almost all their own produce. For a few dollars a year, they rented land for a huge garden a few blocks away on Cuyahoga Avenue. The pair grew corn, tomatoes, spinach, sweet potatoes, bell peppers, kohlrabi, okra, lima beans, onions, squash, leaf lettuce, and cucumbers.

"There is nothing quite like fresh-picked sweet corn, nothing! Or real tomatoes, nothing like it."

More than sixty years later, sitting across from me at his keeping room table, my dad waxed rhapsodic as he recalled the garden-fresh flavors of his childhood. "The first time I had fresh buttered baby green lima beans, fresh-picked right out of the garden, steamed and buttered, I thought I had died and gone to heaven."

Whatever the family didn't consume immediately, Ida preserved in glass jars, putting up countless bushels of tomatoes, peaches, green beans, and something she called piccadilly, with ground-up green tomatoes and onions.

"Are you full up?" That's what Frank asked the boys after every meal. "And yeah, we always were," Harley said.

Despite the lack of work during the first half of the 1930s, Frank always found a way to bring in money. Sometimes he peddled birdhouses he had constructed from the ends of old orange crates or other pieces of scavenged wood.

"He was very creative. The birdhouses were all different," my dad told me. "He sold them at the corner on Main Street downtown, probably for about a dime apiece."

While selling his birdhouses, Frank rubbed shoulders with unemployed men offering apples for five cents each. This was the era of the song "Brother, Can You Spare a Dime?" in which a weary panhandler appeals to passersby by describing how he, now unemployed and hopeless, was once like them, a proud breadwinner and worker.

As difficult as things were, the Hansons escaped the fate suffered by the many who lost their homes due to foreclosure or inability to pay rent. Frank and Ida kept up their thirteen-dollar monthly mortgage payments until 1931, when their savings were completely depleted. Although their mortgage record book shows that they did not resume payments until 1936, the bank did not foreclose, its beneficence motivated perhaps by President Franklin D. Roosevelt's 1933 housing refinance bill, or maybe the bank just couldn't keep up with the torrent of defaulted loans during the Great Depression.

In one of the first photos depicting Frank and Ida together, taken in the mid-1930s, they stand close together outside the Clifton Avenue house, arms encircling one another's waists, squinting into the sun. Still youthful and slim, Ida, free of makeup and clad in a simple white cap-sleeve blouse over an A-line skirt, leans in toward Frank, angling her upper body so that her shoulder nestles within his. Beyond reflecting their affection, this pose also camouflages the fact that Ida is two or three inches taller than Frank. Ida's thick, wavy brown hair is roughly chopped at her jawline, even though the 1920s bob had long since gone out of style. This same blunt cut appears in all the 1930s pictures, suggesting that she economized by cutting not only Frank's and the boys' hair but likely her own as well.

Devoted to their boys and each other, Ida and Frank scavenged, repurposed, and sacrificed to nurture their sons during this bleak period. When I showed my dad the January 1925 photos of his youthful parents posing on the cliffs overlooking San Francisco Bay, bundled up against the wind in long overcoats, his eyes widened and his head jerked up.

"I recognize those coats." Beneath her hat pulled low, the wide fur collar of Ida's overcoat spans her shoulders while the garment sweeps down to midcalf, with sleeves gracefully fluting out at her wrists. "My mother cut them up and sewed them into blankets for our beds when I was a kid. That's a little hard to see."

Harley and his three brothers slept in black walnut beds Frank had built from doorjambs and window sashes salvaged from a home remodeling job. Until they graduated from college, all four boys slept in one ten-by-twelve-foot bedroom, into which were crammed these four beds, along with a dresser. By the time he was eighteen, Harley had reached his ultimate height of six feet, two and a half inches, and his feet stuck way out beyond the foot of the bed if he lay on his back. These beds became family heirlooms, with my oldest sister, Karen, sleeping in my dad's childhood bed, followed later by her own son, Mac, whose feet also hung over the end of the bed when he, like his Grampa Harley, reached six feet two and a half.

On weekends, the Hanson family piled into the Model A for a ride out to the countryside. They usually stopped at an old water-driven mill, where Frank bought a giant sack of unhulled wheat kernels, along with freshly pressed cider for the boys.

"At the mill, they strained the cider through blankets—they'd have these brown blanky things on the line drying out," my dad remembered. "My parents kept a set of aluminum cups in the car so we could all have some cider right after they got it. This was an incredible treat. It was cold. It was dark. It wasn't pasteurized. You had to drink it up in a few days because it would start to ferment."

When he was seven, Harley's twin, Harvey, was diagnosed with Legg-Calvé-Perthes, a degenerative disease of the hip joint that, for three years, imprisoned him in an ankle-to-hip cast. Since Harvey couldn't sit up, Frank built a long, narrow stretcher spanning the Model A's folded-down passenger-side front and back seats, so the whole family could still go together on their countryside excursions. With Frank at the wheel and Harvey lying on the stretcher, Ida wedged herself in the back seat by Harvey's feet while Harley, Al, and Frank Jr. crammed in behind Frank on the other half of the back seat.

Ever the observant child, even as a toddler, Harley saw makeshift settlements during these rides "Hoovervilles," his parents explained—shantytowns of flimsy shacks that the unemployed and homeless had built from discarded scraps of wood, metal, and cardboard. These grim encampments, which existed across the United States, derived their name from the deep anger many felt toward Herbert Hoover, US President from March 1929 until March 1933, whose failure to alleviate mass unemployment resulted in misery for so many.

During the Great Depression, the Hansons never participated in government food distribution programs, unlike so many formerly self-sufficient households, such as my mother's, who took food aid in order to survive. However, Frank gratefully accepted employment created and funded by President Franklin D. Roosevelt's New Deal initiatives, and in 1935, he landed steady construction work through the Works Project Administration (WPA). He subsequently switched to another New Deal program, the Public Works

Administration (PWA), ultimately becoming a field commander for PWA construction projects in Northern Ohio.

In the late 1930s, a professional photographer captured Frank on the construction site of Kent State University's McGilvrey Hall, which was funded by the PWA. Frank's black leather jacket, relined by Ida, dated from his youthful motorcycle gang days. Arm resting on a beam, he gazes calmly at the camera. His expression is that of a man content to be putting in an honest day's work to provide for his family.

"That's how I remember him," my dad said when I showed him the photo.

My grandfather's simple assessment of Roosevelt, repeated many times during Harley's youth, was "He gave us work."

Every Monday afternoon after school, Harley and his brothers had to grind a half pound of the unhulled wheat kernels in the red cast-iron wheat grinder down in the basement. And every Monday evening, Frank made four huge loaves of stirred, yeast-risen whole wheat bread with the flour the boys had ground. All week long, the family ate the bread with eggs for breakfast, and Ida made sandwiches with it for lunches and Sunday night supper. Their typical sandwich filling was what Ida always called goose liver, although it really was an inexpensive mix of offal, pork liver, onions, and maybe the tiniest bit of goose liver, all packed into gray sheep-gut casings. Ida bought it at the grocery store in a big lump, because unsliced was four or five cents cheaper per pound than sliced.

On Sunday evenings, as the family sat at the dining room table munching their ersatz goose liver sandwiches on Frank's whole wheat bread, Gene Autry, the singing cowboy riding a crest of popularity during the 1930s and 1940s, invariably came on the radio. Accompanied by the twang of guitars and fiddles, Autry serenaded the family with his hit song "Back in the Saddle Again," whose lyrics celebrated the independence of the cowboy who, in Autry's imaginary world, had no law to follow but his own.

"It's the goose liver voice!" one of the boys always cried out. After countless Sunday nights eating goose liver to the refrain of Autry's voice, my father's brother Al, with his puckish humor, had rechristened Autry in honor of their meal.

In the world Ida ran, one rule held above all others. Her strictest commandment was that her boys must go to college.

"It wasn't even a question," my dad told me. "We were going to the U, that's the University of Akron. It wasn't a matter of if, but, or maybe."

At the time, the University of Akron, then a city-run commuter school, was the inexpensive college of choice for Akron's working-class youth.

With this great goal in mind, minor illness was no excuse for missing school when Harley was a child.

"It was go to school or die," he told me. "You could feel sick as a dog, but you had to go to school."

Ida pushed her sons through elementary school and they all skipped a grade. When Harvey's Legg Calvé Perthes hip disease confined him in the cast for three years, Ida took over his education and taught him at home, using her prized normal school training. During Harvey's years in the cast, Ida toted him around the house on her back as she did her housework and taught his lessons.

"My mother was a fast study, bright. She loved to teach. She was demanding but very, very good," Harley recalled. "She did an incredible job with my brother. He did a bunch of things better than I ever did because of that early schooling."

Ida made it clear that her sons were to ascend to the elevated sphere that she had inhabited as a girl with her parents, the almost-noble English Howes. She was always trying, with mixed success, to teach all four sons those arts she considered necessary for this educated future: drawing, ballroom dancing, piano, and the inevitable German lessons.

When the Hansons made their annual summer trek up to Lake Erie in the fold-up travel trailer that Frank had constructed from scratch using castoff car parts and salvaged wood, with a canvas top sewn by Ida, she would exhibit yet another talent from her curiously varied portfolio. During the family's nighttime strolls on the wide white sands of Ruggles Beach, they would gaze out at the vast dark lake and sky. Sometimes they saw ships communicating with the lighthouse via lights that flashed Morse code messages, which Ida would decode: "My mother would be translating, they would be saying something like 'We're docking,'" remembered my father. Ida said she learned Morse code while working as a dispatcher in a Western Union office in New York City.

As I sat across from my father in the keeping room, listening to his vivid recollections, one of the pillars of my own childhood family narrative, the tale of the Hanson boys' upward mobility through education, began reshaping itself. The story I had absorbed as a child headlined Grampa, the shy carpenter who had dropped out of elementary school to begin working, and who gave each grandchild one thousand dollars for college. It featured my father and his three brothers, who had performed a single-generation sprint from Akron's working-class North Hill neighborhood to the promised land of higher education and PhDs.

In an era when few North Hill families considered higher education an option, my father's oldest brother, Frank Jr., was the first local kid to graduate from college, and Harley the first to get a PhD. Ultimately, all four Hanson boys graduated from the University of Akron and went on to earn advanced degrees. My father's oldest brother, Frank Jr., taught physics and chemistry before obtaining a master's degree in education and serving as principal of several Akron high schools. Al, who flunked out of the U a few times before finally getting his bachelor's degree at the same time as the twins in 1952, worked for years as a microbiology researcher for the US Centers for Disease Control in Atlanta before obtaining his PhD in bacteriology in the

1970s. Harvey earned a PhD in physics and enjoyed a long, fruitful career as a professor at Wright State University in Dayton, Ohio, where he was one of the founding faculty members of the physics department.

"He must have been a pretty smart carpenter," a high school friend commented after hearing the tale of my grandfather's grade school education and his four sons' collection of advanced degrees.

Absent from my early versions of the Hanson education story was its determined instigator, my grandmother Ida. Until these conversations with my father, decades later, I had never understood her central role in the Hanson education quest.

"All the education, it was at my mother's insistence," my father said firmly. "She's the one who required it. My father supported her, so he supported it. And man, there was no question, we were going."

Beyond education, Ida also focused on the imperative of adhering to strict moral standards.

"My mother was so strait-laced and proper, holier than thou," Harley said. According to Ida, regular churchgoing was necessary for proper moral comportment. After trying out several churches in Akron, she became a devoted member and volunteer at St. Andrews Episcopal Church, a high Episcopal institution, which among Protestant denominations is most similar to the Catholic Church.

"She loved the priest, Father Bruin," my dad said.

Despite her belief in churchgoing as the foundation of proper ethical standards, Ida was forced to make an exception for Frank, who never went. He liked to paraphrase Karl Marx, a founding philosopher of communism, by saying, "Religion is the opiate of the masses," much to Ida's annoyance.

Although Frank was off the religion hook, Harley and his brothers were not. "It's not a matter for discussion," Ida said flatly when Harley whined that he didn't want to go to church. The boys were members of North Hill United Presbyterian Church, which Ida had tried out before finding St. Andrews.

"She made us go, but it didn't stick," my father said. Ida might have found a more receptive audience if she hadn't stuffed her sons into those outmoded knickerbocker suits for church every Sunday. In almost every pre- and post-church photo from the late 1930s through the 1940s, the three youngest boys scowl at the ground, misery writ large across their young faces. Frank Jr., having graduated to long pants, grins more often than not.

Presumably the Episcopal and Presbyterian churches believed that young men and women should meet and date, but not Ida's boys.

"She didn't want me and my brothers even to have girlfriends," my dad told me. "She was always saying, 'Don't mess around with the girls—don't kiss the girls!!'" Any young woman who happened to catch the eye of one of Ida's boys was the enemy.

During high school, Al fell for his North High classmate Lena Testa, whose brown eyes, wavy dark hair, and tan skin reflected her southern Italian ancestry.

"He was totally smitten," my dad told me. "They were a forever thing."

Perceiving mortal danger, Ida launched a campaign of passive aggression to derail the relationship. She must prevent the dreaded early marriage proposal at all costs.

"She's just not the right sort," she kept saying.

One might think that Lena's membership in the Roman Catholic Church would have been a plus, given that during Harley's childhood, Ida said, continuously, that she was raised Catholic. Apparently not. Ida never explained why she abandoned the faith of her girlhood, beyond vague hints that she could not marry Frank in the Catholic Church. She made disparaging remarks about Catholics from time to time: "They take your money. They tell you what to do."

The rest of the family liked Lena, and Al, always the most rebellious of Ida's outwardly obedient sons, continued sneaking around with her behind Ida's back. Nonetheless, Ida did succeed in preventing an early marriage. In

BURIED SECRETS

an era when it was common to propose to one's high school sweetheart before graduation and marry shortly thereafter, especially if the woman was not going to college, Ida persuaded Al to put off asking Lena to marry him. When he entered the University of Akron and continued to delay a commitment, Lena finally ended the relationship.

"I think Lena got tired of waiting," my dad said.

When my dad began dating my mother, Joyce Halfen, a history major whom he met in French class at the University of Akron when their alphabetical surname seat assignments deposited them next to one another, he chose an upwardly striving young woman from a blue-collar family who was determined to improve her life through education. By this time, my mom's mother had effectively become a single parent as well as the family's sole breadwinner. Although neither of her brothers went to college, my mother worked her way through the U, aided only by a four-hundred-dollar scholarship. For a working-class girl from a cash-strapped household to put herself through college might not seem so unusual today, but in the late 1940s and 1950s, young women were supposed to marry as soon as possible and become homemakers. Even when they pursued higher education, it often terminated when they landed the all-important "Mrs." degree.

Despite Ida's and Joyce's shared belief in higher education, their relationship was always strained. The first time Harley brought Joyce home, Ida was barely civil to the petite, dark-haired young woman during that tense introductory visit. So uncomfortable did Ida make Joyce feel that my mom began crying as soon as she and Harley exited the house. It is ironic that my mother, descended from multiple flavors of Germans, happened to belong to Ida's favorite tribe.

"Mater didn't want to let go of *any* of her boys," my mom recalled five decades later, the ire still strong in her voice. She added, "*Everyone* had to know how much she sacrificed for her boys."

Although Ida's intensive nurturing and care came with a heavy dose of control, it enabled her sons to fulfill their potential and pursue any path they chose. Even after the three younger sons left Akron, she sent money and countless personal items, she laundered and mended the dirty clothing they shipped to her in big footlockers, she cut their hair, and she faithfully performed any and all tasks and errands she was forever asking them to assign her.

"You know I will do anything for you," she wrote Harley at graduate school in the fall of 1952. Her solicitude extended to Al's honeybee hive and Harvey's aquarium.

"Did you know I am in the fish and bug business," she wrote of the aquatic menagerie Harvey left behind when he and Virginia moved to Columbus, Ohio. "First it was only feed the fish. Now I have to mix up cereal and yeast and take worms out of one box and put in another and watch them crawl. What horrors."

As for Harley's college romance with Joyce, Ida counseled him to delay marriage until he finished graduate school. "My mother actually gave very good advice. I should have done that," he said as we sat in the keeping room late one night.

Although my dad's and my rambles through the past usually focused on his parents and childhood, occasionally we touched on the life and family he had created with my mom. Over time, his calm statements deepened my understanding of my parents' relationship.

"Why didn't you ever talk about your mom's personality when we were kids?" I asked once. "I never knew that she was so forceful until Aunt Virginia told me, when I was in college."

"I guess I was afraid it would be viewed as a criticism by your mother," my dad replied.

As a result of my father's strategy for keeping the peace and protecting his mother, during my childhood I knew almost nothing about my grandmother's determined, controlling, and intensely loving persona, and her insistence on education. I understand why he made that choice, yet it saddens me that, for so many years, I had no idea of my grandmother's outsize role in determining the destiny of my dad and his brothers.

My mom resented Ida's interfering ways, yet she, too, benefited from Ida's boundless ministrations. Following my parents' wedding in December 1952, they depended on Ida and Frank's financial support for years, my dad told me, especially when my two sisters were born while my father was still in graduate school. My mom's typical response to Ida's intense involvement in Harley's life was to distance herself with subtle snubs, which, in turn, hurt Ida's feelings.

Al's wife, Betty, held a more measured view of Ida. "I didn't like her, but I respected her," she once told me. "I respected what she was able to do with those four boys during the Depression."

All four Hanson daughters-in-law, including my mother, felt real affection for Frank, but Aunt Virginia, Harvey's wife, was the only daughter-in-law who truly loved Ida. No doubt one factor in their intimacy was Virginia's long history with the Hansons. Virginia first met my dad and Harvey when she was thirteen, through her father, the affable insurance collector Milton Albertson, who used to stop by Clifton Avenue every few weeks to pick up a dollar or so on Frank and Ida's insurance policy. Until Frank Jr. brought his bride-to-be, Ruth Surbey, home in the mid-1940s, Mr. Albertson was one of only two non–family members who ever crossed the threshold of the very private, insular Hanson abode. The other was Ida's one friend in the neighborhood, the English-born Mrs. Garforth, whose English origins might have helped her find favor with Ida.

Virginia's tolerant nature, combined with her inclination to find the best in others, no doubt also contributed to the deep bond she formed with Ida as well as Frank.

"Mater and Pater, they both were wonderful to me," Virginia told me.

Wounded by my mom's cold shoulder, and failing to understand the causes, Ida sometimes used Virginia as an example of how Joyce should behave.

"If you are busy Harley with your studies, which is most important right now, maybe Joyce might have a bit of time to write," Ida wrote Harley in 1955, when he was in graduate school at Duke and he and my mother were living in North Carolina. "Virginia writes quite often when Harvey is busy studying."

To circumvent Ida's overwhelming need for control, as well as to prevent her from worrying, all four boys got in the habit of keeping things from her. That they loved their mother went without saying, but this defense mechanism was essential for keeping Ida at a distance, so they could create their own lives as young adults.

"They had a term in the 1950s, 'Smother Love,'" my dad told me. "That was probably accurate. She was overprotective, suffocating, controlling, and it was all done for the best possible reasons."

Through my father's stories, I began to know the complex, indomitable grandmother whom fate had denied me. Whatever her flaws and quirks, she had, with intelligence and resourcefulness, nurtured her four sons during the crucible of the Great Depression, and well beyond.

Now that I possessed my grandparents' photo collection, my quest was to connect the formidable Mater of my dad's stories with the young Ida of that faraway land. Where were these barns, fields, and wood houses? Who were the people, so many resembling Ida, who populated this world? Who was that Madonna and child?

Frank and Ida, mid-1930s.

Frank at McGilvrey Hall construction site
at Kent State University, late 1930s.

The Hanson boys at Ruggles Beach, Lake Erie, late 1930s. Standing (left to right) are Al, Frank Jr., and Harley. Harvey, who couldn't stand due to Legg-Calvé-Perthes disease, reclines on a stretcher that Frank built.

Harley working in the family garden, early 1940s.

Sunday best and knickerbockers (except Al), early
1940s. Al, Harley, Ida, Harvey, and Frank Jr. (left to right).
How did Al get out of church and knickerbockers?

Frank, Ida, Harley, Harvey, Al (left to right)
during country drive, mid-1940s. The twins
again wear the dreaded knickerbockers.

Harvey, Frank, and Harley (left to right) in front of eagle
statue at the Bronx Zoo in New York City, December 1949.

It's Kind Of A Family Affair

HANSON
1%

Graduation is a family affair for the Hansons. Four members of the family slightly more than 1 per cent of the graduating class will receive their degrees at University of

Akron next week. Looking over a textbook in a joint examination cramming session are (left to right) Albert Hanson and his wife, Marian, and his twin brothers, Harley and Harvey.

The *Akron Beacon Journal* featured the Hanson family,
whose members were 1% of the 1952 University
of Akron graduating class. June 3, 1952.

116

Virginia and Harvey, early 1950s.

Harley and Joyce in Frank and Ida's living room, 1955.

Harley with Ida after receiving his Ph.D., 1956.

CHAPTER 9:

MESSAGES FROM
THE GRAVE

BEGINNING IN THE MID-1950S, every summer or fall my grand-parents took road trip vacations, which are amply documented in their photo collection. They visited their sons and grandchildren and toured national parks and historical tourist sites in the northeastern US. During these excursions, they always headed up to New England for Ida's favorite meal, lobster roll.

"I can eat lobster roll for breakfast, lunch, and dinner," Ida told Harley of their New England jaunts. "Your mother loves her travel, but she can't get more than a mile from a coffeepot," Frank added with a smile.

Two road trip snapshots from September 1955, in which a ray of light had registered hazy images of a small ranch house on the film of Ida's camera, whispered dispatches that I strained to decipher. Upon examining these photos with a magnifying glass, I realized they had been taken from inside the Studebaker, with the windows rolled up. Before darting through the camera's open shutter, the light had traversed the glass of a car door window, resulting in a slight warp in the images. A swathe of dark matter stretched in an uneven horizontal along the bottom of the pictures—the top of the car door.

On the exterior of the ranch house, dark shutters framed the front windows above a neat border of small shrubs and plants. In the front yard stood a single sliver of sapling, its spindly branches raised in weak supplication. Inside the house's two front windows, I could just make out the low drape of curtains fastened at the sides. All the shades were drawn exactly halfway, except at the center of a triple pane window, where the shade had been pulled a fraction higher, perhaps to accentuate a small table and lamp just below.

Why had they photographed this tidy but utterly ordinary dwelling, through closed car windows no less?

The ghostly ranch house wasn't the only unusual image from my grandparents' 1950s road trips. Why did they photograph the unadorned late-nineteenth-century triple-decker wood apartment building on a tiny city lot, or the larger, more elaborate wood Victorian homes on substantial plots of land with grass and trees? And what about the snapshots of a simple white 1950s Cape Cod saltbox house? No one would take vacation snapshots of these everyday habitations unless they had personal meaning.

I inspected each image for hidden clues. One of the larger homes, a Folk Victorian fronted by an expansive yard, possessed a third-floor gable but no ornamentation beyond simple wood trim by the door. In the front yard was a small sign, the letters too tiny to decipher. Subjected to the strength of my magnifying glass, it yielded its secret: "Beware of Dog."

Another notable aspect of Ida and Frank's 1950s vacations, as documented by their photo collection, was their penchant for traipsing around graveyards. They frequented one particular cemetery almost every year between 1955 and 1959. It seemed a spacious, bucolic oasis, featuring gently rolling hills and mature deciduous trees, with paved roadways curving through the grounds. In the background of some of the photos, I could see their 1948 Studebaker parked along the lane.

"That graveyard is still there," Marc said. "If we can figure out where it is, that will tell us a lot."

Indeed, if I could identify this graveyard, I could go there, wherever that might be, and find the graves in the photos.

The trick, of course, was to identify the cemetery. Among all twelve grave photos, only two contained headstones with the faintest of visible inscriptions. The first grave seemed to be recent, judging by the multiple bouquets lying at the base. The smooth, thick headstone rose to a gently fluted arch, and I could just see the simple inscription, "PODEN." In the forefront stood a large pot of fresh flowers, as if a sentry at attention. My grandparents captured this image in a photo developed in September of 1959.

Although I researched the unusual name "Poden" for hours, it did not seem to exist as a surname in North America in the mid-twentieth century. I kept coming across the Spanish verb "poder," which means "to be able." I certainly was not able to make any headway with Poden.

The second photo with an inscription, this one from July 1956, was a crooked hillside shot of a grave with a grove of trees in the background and behind the trees a two-story wooden house. Beneath a fuzzy blur of letters, a pot of flowers with wide, spreading leaves obscured the lower half of the headstone. Could this wobbly picture, taken some distance from the grave, be an accident my grandparents had not bothered to discard?

Nevertheless, it could help me figure out the cemetery location. After ordering an enlargement from Ferente-Dege, I could just make out two bits of the inscription. "DAVID STEELE DIED DEC 31, 1877 AGED 51." On a second line, the writing continued, "ELIZA A. HIS WIFE."

This was my first real clue. Logging in to the standard genealogy websites of the time, I carefully searched for any relevant "David Steele" or "Eliza Steele" records. No results.

Other graveyard photos whispered hints that I strained to understand. Year after year, Frank and Ida always visited one particular burial site, which appeared to be graced by neither headstone nor plaque.

September 1955: They take their first photo of this unmarked grave. It is about two feet wide, and two flower arrangements mark its boundaries.

July 1956: They return again. This time, the photo depicts Ida kneeling at the grave, although an unfortunate beam of sun glaring through the middle of the image obscures any details. Again, the spot is flanked by flowers on each side. Could this be the burial site of Ida's little boy?

Two months after that July visit, in September 1956, Ida underwent a radical mastectomy of her right breast. Although she had had breast lesions for years, her doctor did not diagnose the cancer until about 1955. She put off treatment for another year, until Harley and Harvey had earned their PhDs and she had taken her state practical nursing licensure exam.

October 1957: On this visit, Frank takes two photos of Ida at the unmarked grave. In one, my grandmother kneels at the site, arranging a bouquet of flowers. In the other, she simply stands in front of the grave, head bowed, arms at her side.

September 1959: The familiar bouquet of flowers adorns the center of the gravesite, but now two pots with seedling bushes have been placed on both sides. By 1959 Ida's breast cancer had returned and was spreading. She would have known that this was likely to be her last visit.

"That's sacred ground, all right," my father said when I showed him the photos of his mother at this unmarked grave.

I focused my investigation on finding the cemetery and identifying who was in the graves my grandparents photographed. Based on the housing stock and landscapes of the photos, plus the approximate itinerary of my grandparents' road trips, the images could have been captured anywhere in a broad swathe of the eastern US, from Uncle Al's home in the suburbs of Atlanta, Georgia, on up through the Eastern Seaboard and New England. With my grandmother a Catholic turned Episcopal and Grampa having renounced any religious affiliation, an astounding number of graveyards could be home to my elusive quarry.

In the row behind the unmarked grave that my grandparents had visited and photographed every year, a tombstone with the name Williams, carved with intentionally rough, naturalistic curves combining elements of the Art Nouveau and Craftsman styles, was visible in each of their photos. Why couldn't the proprietors of these beautiful stones have had an unusual name, such as Quarrington or Moverley, instead of the ubiquitous Williams? If so, I would have had a better chance of locating this patch of earth so holy to my grandmother.

As 2002 became 2003 and winter yielded to spring, I passed many an evening on my green sofa, bright lamp to my left, magnifying glass in hand, searching for the tiniest of clues in these images of graveyards, trees, houses, and people.

"What are you doing?" Marc asked when he called those evenings we weren't together.

"I'm looking at the grave photos," I replied. "There's got to be something I've missed that will help me find where they are."

Among the thousands of people packed into the apartments, condominiums, dormitories, and houses of Harvard Square, I had to be the only one who spent evenings eyeballing photos of gravesites through a magnifying glass. If I can figure out where the graveyard is, I can find the graves my grandparents photographed, I told myself. I'll walk the whole cemetery if I need to. Once I find the graves, I'll have names and locations of real people. The answer seemed so tantalizingly close, yet just out of reach.

In March of 2003, I began calling cemeteries on my lunch break at Novell, the software company where I worked. I made a list, entitled "Six Feet Under," of every graveyard in the New York City metropolitan area and northern New Jersey. I figured I'd start with the supposed locations of my grandparents' youth and fan out from there if needed.

Come lunchtime, I roamed the office hallways until I found an empty conference room. After closing the door, I plunked myself down at a table, pulled out my cell phone and list, and dove in.

"Hello, I'm trying to find out whether several individuals are interred in your cemetery," I always began. I had quickly learned that no one is buried—interred is the preferred term. "I have a name and date for two of the individuals, but for the other I just have a last name. Do you think you could check for me?"

"OK, I can look it up," a kind person sometimes said. However, occasionally the reception was downright chilly. "We don't look up anything over the phone," barked a particularly gruff staffer at a Queens cemetery. "You have to mail your request. We'll get to it when we can."

A cemetery administrator in Hyde Park, New York, near the Hudson River site of one of my grandparents' summer 1924 outings, went out of his way to help me. "Email me a picture of the Williams grave," he said. "We have stones like that." During an April snowstorm, he tromped through the snow to see if this photo was taken in his cemetery. It wasn't, but I appreciated his kindness.

After two weeks, I was fed up with calling graveyards. Maybe I could hire someone to do this for me. I contacted a few Association of Professional Genealogists members specializing in metropolitan New York, only to be disappointed by their responses. After a promising phone call with one genealogist, it took him a month to follow up and mail me a research contract. Another woman didn't even bother to get back to me.

Then I called Leslie Corn. A full-time genealogical researcher based in Manhattan, she was friendly and professional.

"You don't need to hire me," she said after hearing my story. "You can do this yourself."

If I joined the New York Genealogical & Biographical Society, she explained, I'd gain access to the HeritageQuest online database service, which included census data for the periods in which I was interested. "This subscription is worth its weight in gold," she said, because the indexing was superior to that of the services I had been using. If I found David Steele or the enigmatic Poden in the HeritageQuest census databases, I'd know where they had lived and died, and I could call off my graveyard dragnet.

It was worth a try. I took Corn's suggestion and signed up.

Frank and Ida relaxed at a picnic table during
a 1950s road trip. One of those thermoses
undoubtedly contained coffee for Ida.

The sacred burial site with no marker to which Frank and
Ida returned year after year. The Art Nouveau Williams
gravestone is always visible in the background.

CHAPTER 10:
A SLOW DAY AT THE OFFICE

JULY 1956 *(Imagining the past)*

WITH FRANK AT THE WHEEL and Ida in the front passenger seat, the Studebaker rumbled along a street lined on one side with simple late-nineteenth-century two-story wood houses on small lots. Across the street stretched a rolling expanse of verdant cemetery, spiked with the gray-and-white teeth of tombstones. Turning into the quiet green burial grounds, the Studebaker snaked up a narrow, paved lane to the top of a hill, where Frank braked and turned off the ignition.

"I'll get the flowers," he said, retrieving one of two large potted plants from a box in the back seat. He and Ida, who was clasping her purse and a camera, stepped across the grass to a simple, tall light gray tombstone. Frank deposited the flowers in front of the stone and stepped back.

Ida knelt at the grave, placed purse and camera at her side, and bowed her head. Slowly, she breathed in and out, her eyes closed. "The Lord is my shepherd, I shall not want," she began.

Remaining on her knees after the prayer, Ida retrieved a folded sheet of stationery from her purse. Silently she scanned the brief lines written in her cursive script and then refolded the note multiple times into a small, tight rectangle. After Frank handed her a penknife, she reached into the front of the flowerpot and scratched a narrow hole in the soil, where brown earth met the interior side of the container. She wedged her rectangular missive into the cavity and brushed dirt over it, leaving one tightly rolled end poking out from the soil like an errant, white crocus bulb.

"Here, give me your purse," Frank said. He held Ida's arms, steadying her, as she clambered heavily to her feet. "Oh dear, my knees." She grimaced and leaned over the plant a final time to review her handiwork. "I need to make sure she can find it," Ida said. "OK, it's good."

They began walking away from the grave, Ida leaning on Frank's arm. She halted after several yards. "I forgot, I want to take a picture," she said.

Ida pointed the camera toward the grave, unaware of her crooked stance, or that the viewfinder encompassed not only the headstone and hillside but also, beyond the cemetery border, a stand of trees and a wood dwelling. She depressed the shutter button.

JULY 3, 2003

MY GREEN SUBARU CRUISED smoothly through the normally traffic-clogged streets of Cambridge as I drove out to the Novell office, located in a suburban office park along the Route 128 high-tech corridor. It was

Thursday morning, the day before the 2003 July 4 holiday. I was looking forward not only to a quiet, productive workday, but especially to my lunch break, when I planned to use my newly activated HeritageQuest subscription to research David Steele and his wife Eliza, inhabitants of the crooked hillside grave photo.

After driving the twelve miles to work in record time, I pulled into a prime space in the rooftop parking lot and descended from the bright, hot sunshine into the cool, carpeted building. Clad in my summer work uniform of not-too-short miniskirt, a brightly colored top, and sandals, I carried a light sweater, a necessary defense against aggressive office air-conditioning that left me shivering on the hottest summer days.

As I entered the information technology area where I worked as the lead on one of the company's internal software systems, before me yawned a vast open room with drab off-white walls, a patterned carpet of indeterminate hue, and endless rows of gray cubicles neatly arranged in a variety of configurations. Only a few heads bobbed up and down within the cubicle walls, since almost everyone had taken the day off.

I settled in and worked without interruption for several hours on enhancements we would soon be implementing to a custom financial program. I frowned at the computer screen in front of me. The code I had developed performed as expected ninety-nine percent of the time, which meant I had to figure out the reason for the one percent of failures.

Most people don't realize how similar programming can be to detective work. The programmer spends a lot of time solving mysteries and deciphering puzzles. Why did the code work in one scenario but not another? What variables am I missing? Is there a better way to address the current issue? Creativity, persistence, and willingness to step back and consider alternatives are key. As in conundrums involving human beings, more often than not a solution to the thorniest technological problem lies within reach, if only one perseveres and keeps an open mind.

Usually, a medley of computer beeps and snippets of conversations from neighboring cubicles provided background accompaniment as I looked at my screen, occasionally shifted in my chair, and tapped the keyboard—the visible manifestations of my work. Today the crowded chorus was muted, save for the occasional machine chirp and the stray human voice. The low roar of air-conditioning droned in the empty office. In the cubicle across from me, several mystery computers of indeterminate function buzzed determinedly.

At noon, forgoing lunch, I got down to my real business of the day. After I logged into HeritageQuest, a few clicks brought me to the page where I could look up names in the 1870 US Census. My mystery man, David Steele, had died in 1877 at age fifty-one, according to the inscription on my grandparents' grave photo. If the census takers had been thorough, I should be able to find Mr. Steele in 1870. My first goal was to identify where he had lived, so I could get an idea as to where he had died. From there, I could determine the location of the mysterious graveyard my grandparents had visited so many times.

"Steele, David," I typed into the last and first name search boxes. With another click, I submitted my search data.

Up popped a bunch of David Steeles. One of them, age forty-three, lived in Connecticut. Seemed about right. I clicked a few more times to view an image of the original document. In seconds, my monitor displayed the form that census enumerator Marshall C. Talcott had filled out as he went from house to house on August 3, 1870. In cramped but legible cursive script, he recorded the address, names, ages, marital status, birthplace, occupation, and other details for each person in the household. I enlarged the image and began reviewing last names.

I caught my breath. There he was: David Steele, aged forty-three. His forty-one-year-old wife was Eliza A. Steele. Both names corresponded exactly to my grandparents' crooked grave photo.

David, a farmer, was born in Connecticut, as were his parents before him. He and Eliza were parents to a large brood of children. Quickly reviewing the names of their eight offspring, my eyes froze at the last entry. Their youngest child was a three-year-old boy named Willard. Willard!

Unbelievable. Could David and Eliza Steele's son Willard be the same person as my grandmother's father Willard? I had originally been interested in David Steele because locating him could help me find the unmarked sacred grave to which my grandparents had returned so many times. Now, however, it appeared that David and Eliza Steele might actually be Ida's grandparents, and their grave photo far from an accident she had not bothered to discard.

Until this moment I, and other family members, had toiled mightily and in vain, chasing the phantoms and fables of my grandparents' past. Now, finally, it seemed that enumerator Talcott's neat, faded 1870 census entries were telling a story that somehow could be true. Ida's father, the supposed Willard Howe, who had allegedly bought that fantastical farm in Brooklyn, New York, in reality might be the son of Connecticut native David Steele, owner of a farm in New Britain. Could I finally have found my grandmother's family?

Transfixed, I inhaled every detail of the census page. The first names of David's and Eliza's other children seemed awfully familiar: David, Virgil, Daniel, Eliza, Udella, Grover, Eugene. Later that day, I confirmed that these names were virtually identical to the names of Willard Howe's siblings, as detailed by my grandmother for Aunt Virginia during their genealogical interview fifty years earlier.

The Steele family lived at 435 Farmington Avenue in New Britain. I knew little about New Britain beyond that it was a former manufacturing town now down on its luck, as were so many postindustrial cities that had not been able to reinvent themselves. New Britain was mostly a name I saw on highway exit signs while on Interstates 84 and 91, trying to get through Connecticut as quickly as possible while coming from or going to New York and Philadelphia.

In my office, all continued as before. The air-conditioning hummed, the mystery computers buzzed, and the few coworkers present presumably carried on with their tasks. I, on the other hand, had traveled 133 years back in time, to the world as it had been on August 3, 1870, the hot Wednesday when census taker Talcott visited the Steele home in New Britain. Oblivious to the bland, sterile cubicle landscape around me, it seemed, all of a sudden, that I was going to have a hugely exciting day.

With a few quick taps on the keyboard, I fast-forwarded a decade to the 1880 US Census. If I really had found the David and Eliza A. Steele of my grandparents' grave photo, David would be gone, because he died in 1877.

"Steele, Eliza, New Britain, Connecticut," I typed in the 1880 census lookup boxes. A fifty-two-year-old Eliza Steele of Connecticut popped up in my search results. Clicking through until the original census image came up on my screen, I found Eliza A. Steele, now a widow, living at the same address on Farmington Avenue with four of her children. Willard, her youngest, was now thirteen.

With growing certainty, I bounded ahead another twenty years, to the 1900 census. (Most 1890 census returns were destroyed by a 1921 fire in the Commerce Department building in Washington, D.C.) "Steele, Willard," I typed in the search boxes. "New Britain, Connecticut."

In moments, Willard's census record appeared on my screen. Between 1880 and 1900, he had grown up and married a woman named Alice, with whom he had six children. Still living on Farmington Avenue, he worked as a grinder and polisher. Willard's seventy-two-year-old widowed mother, Eliza A., lived with the family.

In the split second it took me to scan through the names of Willard's and Alice's children, I wavered between certainty and doubt. After so many years of flailing in the genealogical wilderness, I hardly dared believe that I had finally broken through.

There she was.

CHAPTER 11:
SACRED GROUND

IDA A. STEELE, Willard and Alice Steele's sixth child, was born in April 1899, according to the 1900 US Census. Despite my grandmother's many prevarications as to her birth year, she had never wavered in maintaining that April 25 was her birthday and Agnes her middle name.

Not only did Ida A. Steele have five older siblings, but the census also revealed numerous Steele aunts, uncles, and cousins living nearby on Farmington Avenue. This would explain why the cast of Ida's photo collection contained the multitude of women, babies, children, and men resembling her. When I spoke with my father that evening, bursting with my discoveries, the fluctuating pitch of his voice told me that he, too, was excited, although as usual he maintained a calm facade.

"Really great work, Annie. It looks like you may have something here," he said. "But we need more proofs." After a career of directing scientific studies, his standards of proof were rigorous.

Years of seeing promising leads go nowhere had increased his innate skepticism. Once, in the early 1990s, Uncle Al had been convinced that he hit the jackpot when his research on international ship passenger records turned up an Elof Hanson, potentially Frank's father, who had arrived in New York in 1903 after a circuitous voyage from Sweden via South Africa. That angle had proven a dud, like all the others. Now, my dad the scientist wasn't going to accept my discoveries until I could make an airtight case, with multiple pieces of corroborating evidence. As for his emotions, they stayed under wraps.

I, too, was wary after so many years of fruitless research, but this discovery seemed different. Each new finding, such as the names of the erstwhile Willard Howe's siblings, correlated precisely with some detail of my grandmother's stories.

For the next two weeks, every waking hour not spent working, commuting, eating, going to the gym, or seeing Marc, I researched the Steeles. New names took root in my brain and dominated my thoughts. New Britain. Steele. David, Eugene, Daniel. My grandmother's six brothers and sisters. The Steeles appeared to have New Britain roots stretching back generations.

Seemingly mundane family trivia from the Hanson past assumed new significance. Uncle Harvey's middle name had been Myron. One of Ida's brothers was Myron too. Now I knew where the name came from, if this magical connection was real—"if" being the operative word. I was my father's daughter, after all.

When I arrived home from work on Wednesday, July 16, an envelope with the vital records I had ordered from the New Britain City Clerk was in my mailbox. Yanking my mail from the box, I unlocked my apartment building's lobby door and sprinted the flight of steps up to my apartment.

Stepping inside and closing the door, I dropped my purse and backpack in my small foyer and tore open the envelope.

"Alice Howe Steele," said the cursive script on the death certificate of my grandmother's mother, Alice.

Howe. Yet another match. Ida had always claimed that Howe was her maiden name. It appeared instead to have been her mother's maiden name. Alice was born in Naugatuck, Connecticut, while Alice's parents, Frederick Howe and Ellen Fox, were born in Sheffield, England.

Sheffield. Naugatuck. I had heard these place names before. Sheffield, of course, was the legendary English city of yore from which Ida always claimed her parents, the noble Howes, had emigrated. The town of Naugatuck, Connecticut, had entered the picture during the 1953 genealogical interview, when Ida told Aunt Virginia that after arriving in the US, her father initially stayed there before buying the farm in Brooklyn.

Documents in hand, I relocated to my usual place on my green living room couch under the lamp. Alice Howe Steele died at home on September 24, 1914. The certificate stated her cause of death with dreadful simplicity: carcinoma of the breast. The same cancer that claimed her daughter, my grandmother Ida, in 1960. Alice was only forty-three. Almost eighty years after the fact, looking at her death certificate, I felt a wave of sadness for this poor woman and her family. I hoped the doctors had given Alice plenty of laudanum, a painkiller containing morphine and codeine that was widely available without a prescription until passage of federal restrictions in December 1914.

The date of Alice Howe Steele's death also had a familiar, dismal ring. September 24, 1914, perfectly fit the claim Ida made during Harley's childhood of having lost her mother when she was in her early to midteens. Oddly, in 1953, Ida distinctly stated to faithful scribe Virginia that her mother Alice died on September 24, 1922. Why did she change the year from 1914 to 1922?

Next was Willard Steele's death certificate. He died of pneumonia at age forty-nine on February 29, 1916, a year and a half after his wife's death. This, too, matched my grandmother's stories. Ida always told my father that her parents died within a few years of each other, although she never discussed the exact dates or circumstances.

My eyes widened when I came to the death certificate of Eliza Andrews Barnes Steele, the Eliza A. Steele of the wobbly grave photo. Eliza, Willard's mother and Ida's grandmother, died at age eighty-seven on February 27, 1916, just two days before Willard.

During Harley's childhood, Ida once mentioned that after her parents' deaths, her grammy had looked after her until she, too, died.

"Wonderful woman. She took care of me." That was the sum total of Ida's comments on Grammy.

Less than a year and a half after Ida lost her mother to breast cancer, her father and grandmother died at virtually the same time. Although painful for anyone, this would have been especially devastating for a sixteen-year-old girl. As for me, the child with no memory of her grandmother, for whom Ida had crocheted the delicate blue-and-white-cotton teacup as a token of her love, I reflexively pushed sadness to the back of my mind. Propelled by curiosity, that most energizing of emotions, all I wanted was to learn more.

Each new fact in these New Britain documents echoed, often with eerie precision, some detail of my grandmother's stories, even as the big picture they presented flatly contradicted her account of the past. Always frugal, Ida had created a fantastical patchwork quilt when she invented the Howe family tree for Aunt Virginia in 1953. Steeles became Howes, Howes turned into Andrews, Andrews morphed into Foxes. Connecticut natives firmly rooted in New Britain soil fluttered across the Atlantic Ocean to take up residence in Sheffield, England. Surnames traded places here, generations switched there, dates easily hopped barriers immutable in life. How had my grandmother kept track of all this?

However, Ida's claim that she grew up on a farm did seem to be absolutely true. Her pet pig Tug-Tug, whose misfortune it was to wind up on the family dinner table, appeared to have passed his days on a farm belonging not to the Englishman Willard Howe of Brooklyn but to the thoroughly American Willard Steele, son of a family with deep Connecticut roots.

Ever since my futile college-era search for the Prospect Park farm of my grandmother's tales, this mythical homestead had been hovering in my mind, uprooted and placeless. Now, the farm finally was returning to its true incarnation, in New Britain, Connecticut. After that first July 3 voyage into the past with HeritageQuest, the Hanson family research project was never the same.

The Saturday after I received the New Britain vital records, a hot and sunny day, Marc and I headed west on the Massachusetts Turnpike, bound for Fairview Cemetery in New Britain. It was midafternoon and I was anxious about our late start.

"It's going to be late by the time we get there," I said. "What if the cemetery is closed?"

"We'll get there in time," Marc replied, ignoring my peevish tone.

During the past two weeks, I had collected reams of information on the Steeles, but I still didn't understand how it all fit together. Who was in the special grave that my grandparents had visited over and over? Who was in the other graves they visited? Most of the Steeles I had found so far were interred in Fairview, New Britain's large nondenominational burying ground. I needed to go to the actual scene, walk where my grandparents had walked, and see what they had seen.

Leaving Massachusetts behind, we continued southwest along Interstate 84 in Connecticut. About ten miles later, we saw an exit for Ruby Road.

"One of my grandmother's older sisters was named Ruby," I said. "Seems like a good omen."

Half an hour later, zipping through West Hartford on I-84, we were almost there. Just a few miles from New Britain, we saw an exit for Flatbush Avenue.

"Wouldn't it be funny if the Flatbush Avenue your grandfather lived near wasn't in Brooklyn and was really this Flatbush Avenue?" Marc asked.

We laughed. Anything seemed possible.

At last, we reached the exit for New Britain. We headed south down Farmington Avenue, into the outskirts of the city. Before going to Fairview Cemetery, I wanted to see if any of the houses on Farmington Avenue, where the Steeles had lived so long ago, were still standing. The numbering system had changed during the last 130 years, so it was hard to be sure where the houses would be. But according to MapQuest, and one of the New Britain maps I had printed out, some of the addresses still existed. We rolled slowly along Farmington Avenue, passing winding lanes with humble ranch and saltbox houses dating from the 1940s and 1950s. I had always thought of New Britain as a crumbling former industrial town, but here, at the outskirts, it felt like a modest suburb.

"Pull over! Oh my god, look!" I cried. "There. That house. That's one of the houses from their pictures."

To our left stood a two-story nineteenth-century wood house with pale yellow siding and a small third-story attic window peeking out from under the front eaves. My grandparents had taken photos of this house in 1955 and 1956. It was the one with the "Beware of Dog" sign in front.

We got out of the car and stood on the sidewalk across the street, looking at the house. I had brought the 1950s photos and we compared them with the dwelling in front of us. It was definitely the same place. Although the house had new siding and an addition, the essential original structure remained.

"My grandmother has got to be from New Britain," I said. "She has to be Ida Steele. Why else would they come here, why else would she take a picture of this house?"

Some might wonder how I could still be doubting, in the face of mounting evidence. The answer, in part, is that while I was intimately acquainted with research failure, I wasn't used to success and to my findings being real. This hot July day, under the beating sun, I just might be stepping into the past I had been seeking for so long. As certainty came ever closer, I felt it all the more necessary to be absolutely sure.

To the right of the house was a sign for the Pulaski Middle School, by a long, narrow driveway of several hundred yards that ended in a cluster of tan and light red brick school buildings of 1960s vintage. We walked down the school driveway to get a look at the side and back of the yellow house. The small side porch resembled one I had seen in photos that I had printed from the bag of old negatives. Behind the house stood a battered grayish-brown wood barn that might once have been red. Again, it matched the barn in the old farm photos featuring people who looked like my grandmother.

"Hey, look, there are animals in back," Marc said.

Two tan sheep with black heads and legs ambled about within a fenced-off yard at the back of the property. Outside the fence, the land sloped gently downhill to the school. This could be the same hill where Ida had photographed three laughing children playing with their sled, on a long-ago snowy day.

Encountering this house literally minutes after arriving in New Britain, I saw the first pieces of the jigsaw puzzle of my grandparents' photo collection snapping into place. We took some photos of our own, got back in the car, and continued south toward the center of New Britain, en route to the cemetery.

When New Britain was established as a town in 1850, the former farming community had already experienced two decades of industrialization as its small blacksmithing and toolmaking shops began their rapid growth into hardware manufacturing empires. Although farming remained important in the outskirts, where we had just stopped, New Britain's center became a bustling industrial powerhouse that earned it the nicknames "Hardware Capital of the World" and "the Hardware City." The city's population soared in the late 1800s and early 1900s, with migrants streaming in, not only from New England communities but also from impoverished regions throughout Europe, drawn by plentiful jobs in the thriving city's many factories and businesses. Then, in the second half of the twentieth century, manufacturing closed down or moved away, precipitating a decline similar to that in countless former industrial cities in the northeastern US.

As Marc and I skirted the edge of downtown, evidence of the city's decline surrounded us. We passed boarded-up buildings and empty storefronts, we encountered little traffic, and we saw few pedestrians on the sidewalks. Highways bisected the city from multiple angles, making it hard to get our bearings in those pre-smartphone days. When we stopped at a dilapidated shopping center on East Main Street in search of a cold drink, we could not locate a single open store selling water. Winding our way along eerily quiet streets, we finally found a CVS drugstore. A blast of chilly air slapped our faces as we entered, a reminder that we were in a national chain.

While we were standing in line at the register, a headline in the *Herald*, New Britain's daily newspaper, caught my eye. "Graves vandalized." Five monuments at Fairview Cemetery had been knocked over or smashed into pieces, including a five-foot angel that had been decapitated. Shivering in the air-conditioning, I bought the paper along with our water.

At Fairview Cemetery, we found a peaceful green oasis with gentle hills and lanes snaking through the one-hundred-plus acre property. As a child, I had run gaily with my friends through the graveyard on the grounds of our Quaker school. In adulthood, I avoided cemeteries as a rule, viewing them as a gloomy reminder of the fate we all share. Today, however, Fairview Cemetery was my friend and ally. I was ready to plunge in and skip along its paths, where the tombstones shone white and silver in their green beds.

Our first destination was the grave of David and Eliza Steele, Ida's grandparents. The cemetery office is closed on Saturdays, so Christine Raia, the helpful secretary, had left a map for us inside the screen door, marking the locations of the graves we sought with a big red X.

We parked the car and began walking up the winding road toward Section 9, at the edge of the older part of the cemetery, where large, ornate monuments attested to New Britain's prosperous industrial heyday, which had continued until the 1950s.

"Look, that stone has a piano on it," Marc said.

"My goodness, that's Teddy Wilson," I replied.

We walked over for a closer look at the elegant tombstone, which featured a grand piano and the phrase "Mozart of Jazz," along with Wilson's name and dates. A renowned jazz pianist who enjoyed his greatest success during the swing jazz era of the 1930s and 1940s, Wilson had played with the likes of Louis Armstrong, Benny Goodman, and Billie Holiday, I explained to Marc.

I first learned of Wilson during a course on the history of African American music at Wesleyan. Later, during my years in the Boston swing dance scene, I had loved dancing to recordings that featured his sophisticated piano performances. Still a fan of jazz and swing music, even though I had dropped out of the dance scene, I felt oddly at home when we encountered my old friend Teddy Wilson.

"I wonder how he ended up here," Marc said.

When I looked it up later, I learned that Wilson, who grew up in Alabama and later lived outside New York City, had spent his last years in New Britain before his death in 1986.

With the map as our guide, Marc and I continued toward our destination in the cemetery's southwestern corner.

The light gray headstone, just over four feet high, was planted firmly in the same sloping hillside on which my grandparents had stood fifty years earlier.

"DAVID STEELE DIED DEC 31, 1877, AGED 51," the first line of the inscription said. Underneath, it continued: "ELIZA A. HIS WIFE."

After my long search for this grave, I was finally here. Right where my grandparents had been. I felt like Dorothy when she first beheld the wondrous

Emerald City, except that my set was a grassy hillside, and the backdrop verdant groves beneath blue sky.

The thick rectangular slab of the gravestone rose to a gentle arc across the top. It rested on a base with STEELE inscribed in large letters, which in turn was mounted on a broad slab anchoring the stone to earth. The monument was larger, and more substantial, than I had expected. So intently had I examined my grandparents' small snapshot that, in my mind, the stone had shrunk and become tiny indeed. Below David and Eliza's names, I saw more Steeles, including Grove F. Steele, one of their sons. In 1956, the oversized potted plant placed in front of the stone had obscured these names—perhaps intentionally?

Beyond David and Eliza's headstone, outside the cemetery boundary, the trees and wood house of my grandparents' photo had been replaced by the roaring asphalt of Route 9. After manufacturing began exiting New Britain in the 1950s, urban renewal schemes of the 1960s and 1970s included construction of state highways 9 and 72 right through the city's core, with a portion of Route 9 running along Fairview Cemetery's border. The idea had been that altering the city's infrastructure to accommodate speeding automobiles would promote economic resurgence. Ironically, the highways only accelerated New Britain's decline, while their construction sliced through the city's heart, rendering portions of the historic center almost unrecognizable and splitting the core into disconnected sections.

Yet despite the desolation just below, in 2003, Fairview Cemetery remained a bucolic refuge above the once-grand city my great-great-grand-parents, David and Eliza Steele, had known. The span of their combined lifetimes, from 1827 to 1916, included the commencement and heyday of New Britain's manufacturing prosperity.

Marc took photos of me standing behind their headstone. Attired in my usual summer outfit of a short denim skirt with a swirly-patterned top and sunglasses, I rest my hand atop their stone, just as I might place it on the shoulder of a seated relative in a family reunion picture. My wide smile exudes happiness, although within I felt a trace of uncertainty. This was my first photo with these long-sought ancestors. Was a jolly demeanor appropriate when posing with deceased relatives I had just discovered? I didn't want to be disrespectful. I bet etiquette expert Emily Post never covered this scenario in her advice columns.

Next, Marc and I headed to Section 25 to find Willard and Alice, my grandmother's parents. Had my grandparents done their visiting in the same order, guiding the Studebaker along Fairview's winding, narrow lanes? I could see the car parked in the background in some of their photos.

As we entered the section, I stopped short.

"Look," I said. "There's the Williams headstone." The naturalistic Art Nouveau cut of the monument, so familiar from my grandparents' photos, was unmistakable. The special grave with no stone that my grandparents had visited and photographed repeatedly in the 1950s had to be nearby.

There it was. The site had changed markedly since Ida and Frank's last photo in 1959. Then a simple grave without any visible marker, now it contained two headstones and a flat plaque, all of which were shrouded by two giant cone-shaped coniferous bushes almost as tall as I was. At ground level, needle-covered low branches and undergrowth spread like tentacles over the stones.

The flat plaque was in exactly the same spot where Ida had knelt in prayer in the 1950s photos. After tugging at the branches that clung to it like claws, Marc brushed away the undergrowth that obscured the inscription.

"Willard Steele. His wife Alice," I read aloud. "Those are my grand-mother's parents."

"That's sacred ground," my father had said when I showed him the photos depicting the unmarked grave to which Frank and Ida had returned time after time. Now, I knew that this hallowed ground was the burial place of the parents my grandmother had lost in her midteens.

Also obscured by the grasping talons of the giant shrubs was the head-stone of Elsie Bigge, one of my grandmother's sisters, who died in 1984. A third grave nestling within the prickly embrace of the overgrown bushes was that of James Roden. Below James's name and dates was the name Alice, born in 1913, with no date of death.

Roden. Could the mysterious "Poden" I had sought so unsuccessfully actually have been Roden? Moreover, with no date of death for Alice, she must, at age ninety, still be alive.

On our way back to Boston, Marc and I stopped for dinner at an old inn near Sturbridge Village, a recreation of a colonial-era Massachusetts town. As we strolled hand-in-hand about the inn's leafy grounds and the sun bowed to a mellow summer evening, the historic location seemed appropriate. Over seafood entrées in the softly lit dining room, Marc and I rehashed what by any measure had been a hugely interesting and successful day. I still hadn't found the name or grave of the mystery boy Grampa had cut out of the photos, but with all the information I had collected, I now felt certain that this discovery was only a matter of time.

"Weren't those little trees weird?" I asked Marc. In my grandparents' last photo, in 1959, two seedlings in pots had been placed on either side of the site. "I bet they planted them, and now they've grown into these huge, crazy bushes that have taken over the whole gravesite."

Mostly, however, I spent dinner repeating the same phrases.

"I can't believe it. Finally. After all this time. The death certificates, the graves, that house—my grandmother definitely was Ida Steele."

"You've got to wonder, what could have happened to make her change her whole identity," Marc said.

"I don't know, but it had to be something big."

Because of Grampa's loaded pistol by the bed and his work in construction, I had assumed that he was the one with troubles to hide. Although that could still be true, I now knew, beyond any doubt, that my grandmother was not who she claimed to have been. Why did Ida smash and reassemble her family tree? Why did she say she was from Brooklyn, assume her mother's maiden name, and claim she was an only child? Why, in short, did she fabricate that crazy quilt, consisting of scraps of truth mixed with invention, which obliterated her past?

CHAPTER 12:
SWAMP YANKEES

"COULD I SPEAK to Martin Roden, please?"

The day after Marc's and my New Britain excursion found me at my usual post on the living room couch, handset of my 1980s teal landline phone propped between my ear and shoulder, pad of paper on my lap, with pen ready.

"That's me." The voice on the other end of the line sounded raw at the edges, uncertain. "Uh, you want me or my dad?"

I made my best guess. "Your father, please."

"Dad!" the voice hollered, and I heard muffled conversation in the background. Gripping my pen tightly, I sat and waited.

I was following up on our discovery in Fairview Cemetery of a tombstone with the name Roden, located right next to the headstones of my great-grandparents, Willard and Alice Howe, as well as those of my great-aunt Elsie Bigge and her husband. Using an online phone directory, I had looked up Roden in New Britain and found Martin Roden. He lived on Farmington Avenue, apparently next door to the simple Victorian house from my grandparents' photos, where Marc and I had stopped and seen the sheep grazing in back.

This was my first attempt to contact a member of my grandmother's family. Her real family. The one she said she didn't have.

A gruff older man's voice came on the line.

"Hello." Martin senior sounded suspicious. No doubt he thought I was a telemarketer.

Being a veteran of both reporting and sales, I was good at cold calling—the art of convincing someone, within twenty seconds, that I was on the level and worth a minute of their time. I plunged in.

"Hi, my name is Anne Hanson. I live in Cambridge, Massachusetts, and my grandmother was Ida Steele," I began. "I've been doing genealogical research on my family, and I think that Elsie Bigge was my grandmother's sister. Do you have a few minutes to talk?"

After a pause, he answered, "Yeah, OK."

"As I said, I'm Anne Hanson, and my great-grandparents were Willard Steele and Alice Howe Steele, and they lived on Farmington Avenue in New Britain." I took a breath. "My grandmother, Ida Steele, left New Britain some-time in the early 1920s and never came back. She had six brothers and sisters, and one of them was Elsie Steele."

"Yeah, Elsie was my grandmother," he said. "And I'm Marty. Not Martin." To my relief, the suspicion in his voice was fading.

My grandmother had left New Britain and erased her past, I explained. She married my grandfather, Frank, and raised four sons, including my father, but the Hanson boys never knew that their mother had changed not only her name but her entire history. They never suspected she was from New Britain.

"I found you because I saw the gravestone of Martin Roden next to my great-grandparents' grave at Fairview Cemetery, and I looked you up in the phone directory," I told him.

"That Martin Roden grave, that's my dad," Marty said.

"Did you ever hear anything about my grandmother, or why she left New Britain?" I asked.

"We always knew there was someone that went away, but we didn't know nothing about it," Marty replied.

Marty's mother, Alice, my dad's first cousin, was a young girl of ten or so when my grandmother left New Britain. Marc and I had seen Alice's name on the Martin Roden gravestone, with a 1913 birth date but no date of death. Now ninety, she was one of the few people still living who might know the circumstances that had caused her Aunt Ida to so thoroughly renounce home and family.

"Would you mind if I spoke with your mother?" I asked Marty.

"She don't talk no more," he replied. She had severe dementia and lived in a nursing home, he explained.

Throughout our conversation, Marty listened politely and, with a genial tone, answered my questions as best he could. But he didn't ask questions in return or make any comment to indicate he was excited or even pleased to hear from his long-lost second cousin. As our chat continued, a sense of disappointment began welling up inside me. Although Marty was cordial, he appeared to know and care little about the secrets of our family's past that I was working so hard to uncover.

Nonetheless, Marty was willing to help.

"You want to talk to my cousin's wife," he said. "She's into all the genealogy." He looked up the number of Joy Medvec, the Steele family historian, and gave it to me.

"Well, good to meet you, cousin," Marty added as we said our goodbyes.

After hanging up, I sat on the couch, deflated by my first contact with the Steeles. While Marty had provided a potentially valuable contact, I perceived no enthusiasm or interest on his part. "Wow, this is amazing! I can't believe it. It's great you found me," Marty would have exclaimed in my preferred alternate version of our conversation. Then he would have continued, "My grandmother used to talk about Ida a lot. We always wondered what happened to her."

So absorbed had I been in my quest to unravel the twisted strands of my grandparents' fabrications, that, up to now, I had given little thought to what might happen if I found living, breathing descendants. The exception, of course, was Grampa's baby sister Florence, with whom I envisioned having a pleasant chat on unknown topics in an imaginary nursing home. As for the rest, they had been a lumpy, amorphous mass. Only when my expectations were not met did I realize they existed.

After a few minutes of disappointment, I rallied and again picked up the phone. My next call was to the contact Marty had given me, Joy Medvec, the Steele family genealogist, whose husband, Paul Medvec, was my father's second cousin.

Given that her husband occupied a different branch of the Steele tree than I, Joy had never heard of my grandmother or her disappearance from New Britain. Nonetheless, she was friendly, curious about my research, and happy to share her extensive knowledge of Steele family history. To my astonishment, Joy said that my Steele lineage stretched all the way back to the original English settlers of New England in the 1630s, who were part of a colonization movement genealogists call "The Great Migration." John Steele, my great-grandfather many times over, in 1634 owned land in the heart of today's Harvard Square in Cambridge, Massachusetts. John Steele's former property apparently was right by today's famed Harvard Yard and just a few short blocks from my apartment building.

Joy told me that John Steele subsequently led a party that migrated south to form English settlements in today's central Connecticut. Establishing himself on properties first in Hartford and then in Farmington, which later became New Britain, Steele was town clerk for both of these entities. These details are recounted in a genealogical history of the Steeles, published in 1856, Joy explained.

Totally bizarre. By this time, I knew the Steeles had been in New Britain for generations. But now, she was saying they were one of the founding families of Connecticut, dating all the way back to the 1630s. In my quest to discover my grandparents' missing past, I had never imagined finding deep North American roots that extended to the earliest English settlements in today's Massachusetts and Connecticut.

Joy would become a dear friend over time, as well as my staunchest research ally. In our first conversation, she provided information on the Steele family that appeared to destine my grandmother's Catholic upbringing for the same fate as the mythical Prospect Park farm.

"What was the Steeles' religion?" I asked.

"When your grandmother was growing up, they belonged to the First Baptist Church," she responded.

The Steeles had drifted among various Protestant denominations during their centuries in New Britain, Joy explained. But contrary to what Ida repeatedly told my father about her Catholic girlhood, the Steeles were not, and had never been, adherents to that faith.

A few days later, stationed on my usual time travel launching pad—my green couch—I called another newly discovered Steele relative. This time it was my father's first cousin, Dorothy Varano, born Dorothy Roden. Daughter of my grandmother's oldest sister, Ruby, seventy-two-year-old Dorothy, born the same year as my dad, grew up next door to Marty on Farmington Avenue. Like Marty, she had spent her entire life in New Britain, moving with her husband in the 1950s to a modest two-family home in a quiet neighborhood west of downtown.

Our conversation was eye-opening, if disillusioning.

"Nope. Nothing. I never asked," she told me. "I always say, leave well enough alone."

That was Dorothy's curt reply when I asked what she knew about her aunt Ida.

Her mother and Aunt Elsie had often discussed their vanished sister and wondered what happened to her, Dorothy said several times. Nonetheless, she claimed no knowledge of, and zero interest in, the circumstances of Aunt Ida's departure from New Britain.

"I never wondered about it," she said. "I haven't the faintest idea what happened."

I might have believed Dorothy's assertion of ignorance if, like her cousin Marty Roden, she had spoken to me in a natural, straightforward tone. When Marty took my out-of-the-blue call, his voice had relaxed into affability after the first minute. In that conversation, I heard a man who, while knowing little of his vanished aunt, had nothing to hide.

By contrast, Dorothy's voice was tight, and her responses seemed a little too pat, as if prepared in advance. Unlike when I called Marty, Dorothy knew of me in advance. Joy Medvec, the Steele genealogist, had told her about me in an attempt to lay a friendly foundation.

"No one ever asked. No one was interested," Dorothy kept saying.

When I told her that my grandmother came back to New Britain in the 1950s and took photos of the Steele family farmhouse, right next door to her own childhood home, she refused to be drawn in.

"If Ida was standing in front of the house taking a picture, I'd have no idea who she was," she responded tartly. "If she wanted to get in touch, obviously she could have."

In the latter part of our conversation, Dorothy relented ever so slightly when I asked about her childhood and the lives of other family members.

"My parents didn't have much. They were always busy working and tending the farm," she said. "I had a brother Willard that died. I knew nothing about him either."

Dorothy did recall the funeral of Aunt Elsie's second husband, George Bigge, who was waked at home when he died in 1943.

"I remember this clearly," Dorothy said. "It was the first funeral I ever went to."

Widowed in her late forties, Elsie got a job in the fabric department at the Fair store in downtown New Britain, while also taking care of her daughter Alice, who was often ill.

"She was very hardworking," Dorothy said of Elsie.

Yet when it came to Aunt Ida's departure from New Britain, whatever Dorothy might know, she wasn't saying. She wouldn't budge from the rebuff she had issued at the start of our conversation.

"Leave well enough alone," she repeated. "Let the dead be dead."

My new friend, Joy Medvec, tried to help me understand Marty's and Dorothy's seeming indifference to our shared past.

"Deep down they care a lot and feel a lot, but they find it hard to show it," she explained.

As for Dorothy's unfriendly tone?

"She thinks you want to dig up dirt," Joy said.

Dorothy was half right. I did want to dig up stuff, but I wouldn't call it dirt. I'd call it the truth.

Later, I learned that Dorothy's sons, upon hearing of the appearance of a long-lost cousin asking questions about Aunt Ida, had told their mother not to speak with me. Given the awkward position she found herself in, Dorothy deserves credit for being polite and bearing with me until I ended the conversation. She easily could have refused to talk and simply hung up. Maybe she had mixed feelings about her sons' directive.

Before I discovered the Steeles of New Britain, my ideas of the quintessential Yankee WASP featured professors in bow ties carrying battered leather briefcases. The women wore understated, well-tailored garments accessorized with real pearl necklaces. These Yankee Brahmins, or aspirants to such status, summered in cool coastal towns, where they passed afternoons sailing. The males of the species might be identified by their lime-green shorts girded at the waist by duck-printed belts, while the women's trademark polo shirts, with collars upturned, were an inspiration for 1980s preppy fashion. Members of this tribe went to college, traveled in Europe, and resided in older upscale neighborhoods of northeastern cities.

My first conscious encounter with the Yankee Brahmin occurred the summer I was sixteen, when I joined a Quaker boarding school friend on her family's vacation in Cape Cod, Massachusetts. To my astonishment, the summer home of my friend's grandparents turned out to be a mansion with a grand central staircase, down which her grandfather slowly descended in a purring motorized seat. That week, appropriately enough, I went sailing for the first time.

My Connecticut Steele family seemed to have little in common with such Brahmin tribes. In the late nineteenth and early twentieth centuries, although the Steeles retained some land, most of the children left school and began working as soon as they hit their teens, according to US Census records. In 1870, when Ida's father Willard was three, his thirteen-year-old sister Eliza was already laboring in a New Britain knitting mill, even though their father, David Steele, was still living and only forty-three.

As for the twenty-first century, Marty had struck me as a straightforward, plain-spoken working man, while Dorothy, although less candid and far warier, seemed an offshoot of the same steadfast tree.

"There are lots of people descended from early New England settlers who are like that—they're Swamp Yankees," an acquaintance told me when I related the tale of my first conversation with Marty.

When I looked up "Swamp Yankee," I learned that this term, which no doubt had existed in everyday speech for generations, entered the scholarly lexicon via a 1963 article by sociologist Ruth Schell.

The Swamp Yankee is "a rural dweller—one of stubborn, old-fashioned, frugal, English-speaking Yankee stock, of good standing in the rural community, but usually possessing minimal formal education and little desire to augment it," Schell wrote.[1]

The Steele family, while apparently enjoying some elevated status during the founding of New Britain, seemed to have experienced a diminishment of its fortunes during subsequent centuries. When I visited the city library's Local History Room, I could not find a single Steele in the files on prominent people and families in New Britain's history. The name Steele also is absent in the books that faithfully record the movers and shakers who, from the mid-1800s onward, built New Britain into the prosperous manufacturing city dubbed the "Hardware Capital of the World."

The obituaries of Willard Steele and his five male siblings, as well as those of their cousins, all cite the family's place among New Britain's founders or their birth at the old Steele homestead on Beaver Street, just north of downtown. However, none of these eulogies hint that the latter-day Steeles occupied prominent positions in the business, cultural, or political life of their community.

One of the centerpieces of Ida's tales, her wealthy English gentleman papa, might have come from a wishful grafting of her English maternal grandfather, Frederick Howe, onto her robustly respectable, yet more modestly circumstanced, father, Willard Steele. My research later revealed that Frederick regularly bought and sold land in New Britain before he and wife Ellen returned to Sheffield, England, in the mid-1890s. When he died in 1902, his will's multiple bequests included real estate in both New Britain and Sheffield, as well as a gold Albert watch chain and a diamond ring. I wonder if Frederick's bequests, no doubt much discussed within the Steele family when Ida was a child, inspired her later tales of the "English Fortune."

When I first began thinking about my family history in junior high, I sometimes wished for a spicier mix than my father's pale, blue-eyed northwestern European porridge and my mother's multiple flavors of hearty German stock. At least, being Swedish was cool. Even though I had just one Swedish grandparent, Grampa, I knew and loved him, and I bore his surname. Sweden's reputation as an enlightened, progressive society attracted me further.

As for class, during my formative years, I didn't believe it applied to me. Although I always knew that both my parents came from working-class backgrounds, to my immature brain that seemed a faraway island in my forty-year-old parents' ancient past.

"Being educated is a way of thinking," I recall my dad saying when I was twelve or so and we were hanging out in the kitchen one evening. "It's a class in itself. It's not about money."

I always identified, instinctively, with this view of the world. The Hansons were, without doubt, a tribe defined by education.

Now, in 2003, my unexpected New England ancestry was throwing a new ingredient, Swamp Yankee blue blood, into my ancestral stew. Spicy it was not. What it meant, I couldn't yet say.

CHAPTER 13:
WHEREABOUTS UNKNOWN

MOTHER'S FUNERAL AS SON IS DYING

Willard Steele Succumbs to Pneumonia—Funeral Tomorrow

As the funeral services for his mother, Mrs. Eliza Ann Steele, were being held in the chapel of the First Baptist church yesterday afternoon, Willard Steele was breathing his last at his home on Farmington Avenue. When his children returned home from their grandmother's funeral they found that their father had died during their absence.

Mr. Steele was a victim of pneumonia. He had been suffering from a hard cold for some time and a week ago yesterday gave up and went to bed. His giant physique was unable to stand the ravage of the dreaded disease and he passed away at 3:45 o'clock yesterday. He was 49 years and one month old and had always lived in this city, having been born on the old Steele homestead on Beaver Street. For two score years he was employed at Humason & Beckeley's, but about eight years ago he retired. Mr. Steele's wife died a year and five months ago.

Mr. Steele was well known in this city and almost every day of his life he drove his team into the center where he greeted his friends and did his business. Because of his great strength and health, his many friends are shocked today at his sudden death…

~ New Britain Herald, March 1, 1916

WEDNESDAY MORNING, July 23, found me and my Subaru zipping along Route 9 south of Hartford, Connecticut. I was en route to New Britain once again. I had taken a vacation day from work and had planned a full agenda of research. As a newly minted Connecticut Society of Genealogists member, I had the ability, in 2003, to personally search the original birth, death, and marriage records stored in each Connecticut city or town hall. Today, I was headed for New Britain's city hall, where I would look for my grandmother's birth certificate.

I took the New Britain exit off Route 9 and followed the signs toward downtown. Around me yawned a desolate chasm of concrete highways, a parking lot, a deserted lot, and on one corner, a complex of modern office buildings. Turning left on Chestnut Street, I followed the signs toward the center of town, where two grand old stone church spires reached for the sky behind a Firestone tire store.

After parking in a municipal garage, I walked the few blocks to city hall. Discount stores, a check-cashing joint, fast-food outlets, and a few cheap corner marts were the only commercial activity evident, interspersed with empty storefronts. Human life was almost entirely absent, with only a handful of pedestrians on the sidewalks and little traffic. Along Main Street, amid worn two- and three-story buildings from the 1960s and 1970s, stood several taller mercantile buildings from the late nineteenth century that topped mostly deserted storefronts at street level.

This desolate scene bore little resemblance to the vibrant, industrial New Britain of the past. Indeed, so creative had been the Yankee inventors behind the city's manufacturing ascendancy that, between 1890 and 1900, the city had one patent, on average, issued for every 367 persons.[2] Downtown had been full of factories, railroad and trolley hubs, and a large army of workers, not to mention a bustling commercial, civic, and cultural life that had included grand office buildings, department stores, banks, churches, theaters, restaurants, clothing and shoe stores, doctors and dentists, pharmacies, beauty salons, and barbershops, along with myriad related organizations and services.

In 2003, during my first walk downtown along the drab empty streets, I was saddened to see such stark evidence of the city's decline.

Then, my first surprise.

In front of me arose an apparition from my grandparents' photo collection, come to vivid life in the sunshine. An imposing Beaux-Arts style limestone monument, standing more than forty feet high, reigned over Central Park, at the north end of Main Street. Flanked by four massive columns, this memorial, the Soldiers' Monument, honored Civil War veterans and was erected in 1899. Perched on top was a gold Winged Victory statue offering an olive branch. In my grandparents' photo, the monument had been underexposed, depicted in flat shades of dark gray, but there was no mistaking those columns and the Winged Victory statue.

Before my July 3 breakthrough, I had trawled the internet for photos of public monuments in the northeastern United States, hoping I would be lucky enough to find the subject of my grandparents' photo among the countless online images. Now, it seemed that I couldn't spend more than five minutes in New Britain without encountering one of their photographic subjects.

As I gazed at the monument, the sun glinted off Winged Victory, seeming to wink at me from the sky. Another piece of my grandparents' photographic puzzle snapping into place. I took a photo of my own and walked the last block to city hall.

Located in the back of a majestic five-story late-nineteenth-century brownstone-and-red-brick building on West Main Street, the interior of the New Britain City Clerk's office reminded me of the municipal offices I used to frequent as a reporter covering local government in Minnesota. People idled in line at the front counter, waiting for attention from staffers, who were mostly forty- and fiftysomething women in casual clothes and comfortable shoes. Low-walled rust-colored cubicles stretched across the back of the large room. Scores of photographs of dogs festooned the entire wall of a pet lover's cubicle. Today, however, instead of interviewing an official about a zoning controversy or the latest school-funding fight, I was hoping that records tucked away somewhere in this ordinary city office would shed further light on Ida Agnes Steele.

"I'm here to do genealogical research," I said after catching the attention of a fortysomething woman with blond hair. I held out my CSG card and driver's license.

Looking them over, she nodded. "OK, come in," she said. "Have you been here before?" She ushered me to the side of the main room, where she photocopied my credentials, and I signed in. "The records are this way."

I followed her into a long L-shaped room full of cabinets and tall shelves stacked with record books and binders.

"All the early indexes are here," she said, pointing to a metal shelf holding thick twenty-four-by-ten-inch books. "Once you find your record in the indexes, you look for the certificate in the books over there." Following her gesture, I saw rows of tall metal shelves filled top to bottom with fat dark red or black record books. "Let me know if you want copies made," she said and disappeared back into the main office.

After stashing my purse on a table where I could keep an eye on it, I got to work. First, I reached up to the index shelf and pulled down a massive book that covered people with last names beginning with letters from P through Z, for the dates 1850 through 1905. It must have weighed twenty pounds. I wouldn't have time for the gym today, but at least hefting books on and off shelves could serve as a light weightlifting routine. I laid the giant tome flat on the table and began turning its large pages. If my grandmother was Ida Steele of New Britain, and at this point I was banking on it, her birth certificate would be in this index.

Each page was filled with neatly typed entries for each birth, marriage, or death that had occurred, with an X under B, M, or D to indicate which it was. The rest of the line contained the person's name and information, including the date, parents', groom's, or bride's name, and where to locate the original certificate. Arriving at the S section, I saw lots of Steeles, but no Ida. I continued scanning row by row.

April 25, 1899. When I saw that date, I knew I had found my record. A girl Steele, no first name given, had been born to Willard Steele and Alice Howe. This had to be Ida. Ambiguous about her birth year, my grandmother never wavered from April 25. I walked over to the shelves containing books with the original certificates, pulled out the plump red volume, and began carefully turning the pages, each of which had a fragile yellowed original certificate attached.

Cradling the book in my arms, I came to April 25 and the birth certificate of baby girl Steele. She was the sixth child of Willard Steele and the former Alice Howe. Thirty-two-year-old Willard was born in New Britain, while twenty-eight-year-old Alice had been born in Naugatuck, Connecticut. They lived on Farmington Avenue. Everything matched.

I continued researching the rest of Ida's family and purchased copies of the certificates. I needed proof, after all, and this was as official as I could get. The birth certificate of Ida's younger sister, Edith, born in 1901, also lacked a first name. Had Willard and Alice run out of names? Gotten tired? Alice would have been exhausted. Marrying Willard at sixteen and giving birth to Willard Jr. ten months later, she had just turned thirty when she bore Edith, her seventh and last child. The number of miscarriages and stillbirths Alice might have endured is unknown.

Before leaving the city clerk's office, I checked the huge index book for Elida and Elof Hanson, Grampa's parents, as well as for Frank himself. They weren't there, of course, but I had to look. Just in case.

Back outside in the warm afternoon sun, I began walking to my next destination, the Berlin Probate Court. Despite the court complex's location just across Elm Street east of downtown, a feeder highway surrounded by yawning moats of parking lots created a gauntlet of high-speed traffic that threatened the unwary pedestrian.

After carefully navigating the intersection and a parking lot, I entered the probate court building. Probate documents are excellent resources in gene-alogical research. If a will exists, it is a veritable snapshot of a person's life at its end, listing property, possessions, and family members. If a will does not exist and the deceased person has assets, the documents generated during the years it can take to settle the estate still provide a wealth of information about the decedent and heirs.

The probate record room was floor-to-ceiling cabinets and shelves, arranged by date, the old section containing huge, heavy books in which clerks had created handwritten copies of all the probate documents handled by the court. The quiet, spacious room reminded me of the orderly offices of the county land use planners I used to report on back in Minnesota.

The Steeles of the nineteenth and early twentieth centuries didn't seem to believe in wills. Not only Ida's grandparents, David and Eliza Steele, but also her parents, Willard and Alice, had died intestate.

One by one, I began hauling enormous volumes off the shelves. I was looking up Letters of Administration, which the court issues when a person has an estate but no will, and Return of Distributions, which say who gets what once the estate is finally settled. The Steele estates remained unresolved, and hence in probate, for decades in some cases. According to the probate documents, the main Steele assets were land, buildings on the land, and property related to farming. They cite few possessions or cash. Although I gleaned a multitude of additional Steele names and details useful for further research, the documents yielded no clues related to Ida Steele's departure from New Britain.

I turned to the Return of Distribution document for the estate of my grandmother's father, Willard Steele, who had died on February 29, 1916. His estate, unlike those of his parents and wife, was settled relatively quickly. According to the loopy cursive script of the court clerk, on June 18, 1918, each of Willard's seven children was to receive $390.35 from his estate. In twenty-first century money, this comes to more than $7,000 each. A tidy sum, but hardly the estate of a wealthy country gentleman.

Wait a minute. As I skimmed the court clerk's list of the Steele siblings, I stopped short. The court had distributed Ida's $390.35 inheritance not to her but to her guardian, a man named Thomas Keevers. The clerk had entered my grandmother's name as Ida Steele Keevers. Maybe her story about the guardian really had been true. However, she always said her guardian, formerly her father's lawyer, had been Jewish, and Keevers didn't sound like a Jewish name. It also seemed odd that she would take on her guardian's last name.

Although the faded ink was stating the obvious, I couldn't see it yet. So central a character had the Jewish lawyer guardian been in Ida's stories, he had embedded himself in my mind too, blocking the new scenario that was right before my eyes.

Lugging more weighty books on and off the shelves, I found a Letter of Administration for the estate of Ida's mother, Alice Howe Steele, dated May 2, 1929. This time, the clerk copied the names of the Steele siblings in a plump, upright hand, with fat loops and ample Os, adorning each capital with a flourish. I skimmed down the list, looking for my grandmother.

"Ida Keevers, Whereabouts Unknown."

It took a minute to sink in as I stared at the page. My grandmother, in 1929, was listed as Ida Keevers. Finally, I processed the obvious. The Thomas Keevers listed in the 1917 document as her guardian had been her husband. I also knew that when this Letter of Administration document was issued in 1929, my grandmother, by then known as Ida Hanson, was living in Akron, Ohio, with her husband Frank and their two young children.

Whereabouts unknown. The court clerk's chubby script offered no further explanation.

Hastily gathering up my papers, I made photocopies of the document and hoisted the book back up on the shelf. I had to get back to the New Britain City Clerk's office and check for a marriage certificate. The clerk's office closed at 3:45 p.m., in fifteen minutes.

Bolting out of the building and across stretches of baking asphalt, I retraced my path along Chestnut and Main streets at a gallop, sweating in the heat, scurrying back past the Winged Victory monument to New Britain City Hall and the city clerk's office, now almost empty.

"I'm back," I said to the woman behind the counter, who looked less than pleased to see me. "I know you're closing soon, but I'll be really quick."

In the records room, I grabbed the heavy book of indexes for 1906 through 1940, which covered last names beginning with K, and plopped it on the table. *Keevers, Keevers,* I whispered as I skimmed the index page. It didn't take long: Ida Agnes Steele married Thomas Francis Keevers on April 26, 1917.

After scanning the next few lines, I gasped. On April 12, 1918, Ida Steele Keevers gave birth to a baby boy, Thomas Francis Keevers Jr.

CHAPTER 14:

BACK IN THE PICTURE

CIRCA 1916 *(Imagining the past)*

IDA HEAVED A SIGH OF RELIEF as she climbed aboard the trolley in her winter coat and boots, although the chilly interior provided scant respite from the bitter cold that had numbed her feet and fingers as she stood waiting in the weak early-morning light. She sank down in an empty seat. The half-mile walk down Farmington to the start of the trolley line was wretched on frigid mornings, but at least she always got to sit.

"Mornin', miss." The conductor nodded as she handed him the five-cent fare. "Cold one today, eh?"

This new conductor had been on her morning trolley ride for a few weeks now. Ida liked how he wore his cap pushed back on his head, revealing a widow's peak and lots of dark, almost black, wavy hair. Even though his lanky frame barely filled out his uniform, he stood tall and confident as he sauntered up and down the moving car. He reminded her of her brother Myron, a big, tough guy who always made sure nobody messed with his little sisters.

"Yes, indeed," she murmured.

"Another day, another dollar, eh? 'Tis a shame, a pretty girl like you workin' your fingers to the bone every day." For a long moment, his brown eyes held hers. Flushing, she looked down at her gloved hands.

Seventeen-year-old Ida was indeed headed to her shift as a timekeeper at the Stanley Rule Company. After the deaths of Grammy and Papa, she had quit school, abandoning her dream of attending normal school to become a teacher. It was the only thing she could do. Already scarred by watching Mama's slow, painful death, Ida was haunted by that awful moment when she came home from Grammy's funeral to find Papa lifeless in his bed. The memory of his open, frozen eyes, staring at nothing above the luxuriant silver mustache he had so carefully tended, gripped her with the hard, suffocating vise of a nightmare that would not end. "No! no! no!" she screamed every night as she wailed herself into a troubled sleep that yielded scant respite.

It had almost been a relief when she and Elsie realized that, with Papa gone, they didn't have enough money to make ends meet, let alone pay normal school tuition. Elsie's estranged husband, the no good Henry Woeche, had moved out a few months after their daughter, Alice, was born in 1913. Since then, the bum had drifted from one floozy to another, refusing to pay a dime to support his wife and child.

Now that Ida was working at Stanley Rule, the busy hubbub of the floor forced her to concentrate, leaving no time for her mind to slide into the mire of grief. The knowledge that her earnings helped Elsie and young Alice, the sweet blond cherub named for their mother, eased Ida's pain, at least temporarily.

She looked up, startled. The trolley had screeched to a halt at New Britain's Central Park, and its occupants were clomping out in a dark mass of heavy coats and boots. She had missed her stop. She stood up and hurried to the door, hoping to beat the bundled wave of humanity pushing to board.

"Looks like you was lost in a daydream, miss." The conductor was standing right in front of her. He tipped his cap. "Tom Keevers, at your service," he said, grinning. His brown eyes crinkled at the corners, creating a web of spidery rivulets. Still half-dazed, Ida looked into Tom Keevers's eyes and found herself wondering what it would be like to trace her finger along those fine lines.

JULY 2003

AFTER DISCOVERING THE BIRTH of Thomas F. Keevers Jr., I headed out of city hall onto West Main Street and strode along the baking sidewalk toward the New Britain Public Library. Since breakfast, I hadn't eaten anything but a Clif Bar and an apple, washed down with the water I always carried, but I wasn't going to waste time on food.

Images shuttled through my mind in rhythm with my rapid footsteps. Over and over, they returned to the photo my father had named "The Madonna by the Lake." Ida stands on a rise in front of a body of water, holding little Thomas, who is enveloped in a long white gown. Clutching a stuffed animal, he perches upright and faces Mama. Ida's hair, pulled softly away from her face in a bun, frames a serene visage. The sun reflects off Thomas's white gown and illuminates him, while mother and child seem to tilt toward each other in the sun's glow. Transcending time, this black-and-white image radiates love.

But this beautiful child had died. I couldn't wrap my mind around Ida's intense grief, any more than I could conceive of any alternative scenario. I pressed on in my quest to learn more about my grandmother's first husband, Thomas F. Keevers Sr.

As I approached the library, I stopped, startled. I had to laugh. The grand arched windows and tall Ionic columns flanking the building's original main entrance were old friends. I had gotten to know them last winter via the portal of my magnifying glass, when I scrutinized the small photo depicting that edifice, hoping for a clue as to its location. Where my magnifying glass had yielded only a meaningless blur, now, as I neared the columns, I could see, carved in the stone, "LIBRARY OF THE NEW BRITAIN INSTITUTE." Yet again, I had only to spend a minute in New Britain before an object of my grandparents' photos materialized in front of me.

Inside the stately old library building, the central gallery was a veritable shrine to the public good of knowledge available to all. Honey-colored wood columns stretched from floor to lofty ceiling. The walls were paneled in the same warm hue, and the late-afternoon light streamed in through massive arched windows.

I sat down at a table in the gallery to study my bounty from city hall. Ida Agnes Steele wed twenty-seven-year-old Thomas Francis Keevers on April 26, 1917, one day after her eighteenth birthday. The marriage license stated Ida's occupation as timekeeper and Thomas's as conductor. They were married by a pastor in the rectory of the Church of Saint Mary, New Britain's oldest Catholic church. The name Keevers sounded Irish and Catholic. According to Steele genealogist Joy Medvec, my grandmother's family was firmly Protestant. Was that why the couple married in the rectory?

Thomas Keevers's signature on the marriage certificate was shaky, the shapes of the letters jagged, as if he had labored to write his name. It was the handwriting of someone who did not often pick up a pen. Ida's older sister Elsie, as Ida's guardian, also had affixed her neat cursive signature to the document, giving Ida permission to marry. With both parents gone, it appeared that twenty-one-year-old Elsie, legally an adult, had served as the family guardian to approve her eighteen-year-old sister's marriage. Thomas Keevers then became Ida's legal guardian for three years, until she turned twenty-one. That is why, in the 1918 Return of Distribution document for Willard Steele's estate, Thomas received Ida's $390 inheritance. The Jewish lawyer guardian of Ida's stories, who had supposedly approved her marriage to Frank after she turned twenty-one, was, as of yet, nowhere to be found.

Thomas Jr. arrived on April 12, 1918, a year after the marriage. The multiple cropped photos of a youthful Ida, from which Grampa had excised a young child, portrayed my grandmother, then Ida Keevers, with her son, Thomas Keevers Jr. A half brother my dad never knew he had.

Marc and I had not seen Thomas Jr.'s grave during our visit to Fairview Cemetery earlier in the month. I wondered if young Thomas could be in one of the many unidentified graves my grandparents had visited and photographed in the 1950s. Child mortality was all too common in the early decades of the twentieth century. If little Thomas had died, the trauma could have broken his parents' marriage and precipitated Ida's departure from New Britain. Or maybe Ida had divorced her husband and left New Britain with her son, who subsequently died. Explanations such as these were the only ones possible, given the intensely devoted, self-sacrificing mother my dad had known, a woman who dedicated her life to nurturing her sons and ensuring their education.

I remembered a story Marc had told me about his family. Six years before his birth, his parents' eldest child, a boy named Jackie, had died of leukemia at age eight. Marc and his sister, who was born a year after Jackie's death, had no idea of Jackie's existence until they were seven and eleven years old, respectively. His parents never talked about it. No photos of Jackie were displayed around the house or appeared in the family photo album. Maybe my grandmother, like Marc's parents, had tried to escape the pain by removing any evidence of the deceased child's life. The difference, of course, is that unlike my grandparents, Marc's parents did eventually tell Marc and his sister about their lost sibling.

When Thomas Jr. was born, Thomas Sr. and Ida were living in the Hotel Washington, located at the northern edge of downtown New Britain. Very strange. Why on earth would Ida and her husband be living in a hotel? Ida was surrounded by family. If money was short, any number of relatives could have provided at least a temporary home. Ida's sister Elsie, who had approved Ida's marriage, was living with young Alice and their widowed uncle Daniel in the Steele sisters' large childhood home. Numerous Steele aunts, uncles, and cousins resided nearby on longtime family properties. Obvious explanations springing to mind were that Ida's family didn't like Thomas, or Thomas didn't like Ida's family. Thus far, I had zero evidence to support any interpretation.

I entered the row of library stacks that housed New Britain city directories from the early twentieth century onward. Maybe some detail in these worn brown books would give a hint as to what had happened.

In the 1914 directory, several Keevers were listed, including Thomas, whose occupation was driver. Putting 1914 back on the shelf, I opened 1917, the year Ida and Thomas married. There he was again, still working as a driver. My grandmother was not listed, though this meant nothing because married women were routinely excluded from city directories until the mid-1920s. Although these directories can be an excellent research resource, they are frequently incomplete or out of date and often miss new immigrants and the very poor.

I pulled the directory for 1918, the year Thomas Jr. was born. Thomas Sr. was living in rooms at the Hotel Washington, which corresponded with the information on Thomas Jr.'s birth certificate. Thomas Sr. worked for the Connecticut Company trolley line, explaining the cryptic occupation "conductor" listed in the marriage license. He must have been a trolley conductor.

The late-afternoon sun pierced the window at the end of the row of stacks, adding heat and light to the dusty smell of old books. Year by year, I pulled the directories that listed Thomas Keevers through the 1920s and into the 1930s. He moved frequently, sometimes residing at the same address as others named Keevers, while some years, he had his own lodgings. He could have been unemployed during the first half of the 1930s, the worst years of the Great Depression, because for many years, the directory listed no occupation.

I was all by myself in the stacks, suspended in a time warp, with the still, musty air pressing against the bare skin of my arms and legs. As I held each brown book and tracked the path of the peripatetic Thomas Keevers, I didn't know what I was looking for. I was simply following one of the foundational principles of investigation: Follow the data, wherever it may lead. One never knows how or where a key clue will pop up.

By 1936, Keevers was working as an assembler at Corbin Screw Corp., one of New Britain's major manufacturers. Good for him to have a steady job, at a time when the Great Depression had not relinquished its grip on the US economy. In 1937, Keevers also had a new wife, named Stasia. I made a mental note to copy the page. My eye drifted down to the next line.

Thomas F Jr, curtain worker.

I stood, frozen. I stared at the faded typescript in the old brown book.

Thomas F. Keevers Jr. My grandmother's son. He had not died. The brown-eyed boy who had snuggled close to his mama in those cropped photos had lived, and he had remained in New Britain.

CHAPTER 15:
FINALLY, HE BELIEVED

DRIVING THE ONE HUNDRED MILES home to Cambridge, I sat bolt upright in the driver's seat, eyes straight ahead on the road, both hands on the steering wheel. Reflexively I watched the traffic, checked my mirrors, and signaled before changing lanes. The car was quiet except for the steady low hum of the engine and the whoosh of other vehicles on the highway. The radio, usually my constant companion on long drives, was off. I didn't need anything to occupy my mind.

I didn't really see the road, the cars, or the long shadows cast by the late-afternoon sun. I saw fresh-faced young Ida Keevers in a striped summer frock, leaning against a wood fence, cuddling the toddler Thomas as she poses for the photographer. The little boy clutches a toy truck, his big brown eyes, smile, and dimples conveying simple happiness.

Before I saw Thomas Jr.'s name listed in the 1937 directory, it simply hadn't occurred to me that my grandmother might have left her son behind.

Everything I knew about her said this could not be true. After my initial discovery, a few quick checks of subsequent years had confirmed that first finding: Thomas Jr. lived with his father and stepmother until he enlisted in the US Army in the early 1940s. After returning safely home from his military service by 1946, he moved to Hartford. Simple words printed year after year in the city directories—*Thomas F Jr, curtain worker, Thomas F Jr, US Army*—proved that the impossible was, indeed, fact.

Arriving home with just fifteen minutes until Marc picked me up for dinner, I turned on my computer to investigate Thomas Keevers Sr. in US Census records.

On Saturday, January 3, 1920, census taker Edward C. Connelly stopped by the household of Thomas and Ida Keevers as he walked up and down New Britain's Allen Street, north of downtown. Connelly's strong, clear cursive script gave me a bare outline of the couple's lives. Thomas, thirty, worked as an installer for an elevator company, while Ida, twenty, was an inspector at a rule factory. They were renters. Their son, Thomas Jr., was a year and eight months old.

It seemed unusual for a woman with a young child to be working outside the home in 1920. Money must have been tight. Did Ida's family take care of Thomas Jr. when she was working?

Switching to the 1930 census, I looked up Thomas Keevers again. My grandmother's former husband was now living with his widowed father, John, along with his son, Thomas Jr., in an apartment just east of downtown.

My landline rang.

"I'm here," Marc said.

He was waiting, double-parked, in front of my building, the rushing Massachusetts Avenue traffic threatening to sideswipe him.

As soon as I hung up, the phone rang again.

"Hi, Annieeeee!"

It was my father. We had spoken briefly during my drive home, and he was calling back, eager for all the details.

Walking down to Marc's car, phone at my ear, I told my dad of the day's discoveries. Knowing him, I led with facts: the marriage and birth certificates, the probate records, the 1920 census information, and especially the 1930 census and 1930s city directory entries. Together, these constituted overwhelming evidence that Ida's son had lived and remained in New Britain.

"This is really something, Annie," he said, his voice rising with excitement. "That explains a whole lot of things."

Finally, my father believed. Ida Agnes Steele, of New Britain, Connecticut, was his mother. Prior to this day's revelations, he had not been able to fully accept my findings, even though he had eagerly awaited my almost daily phone updates.

His skepticism stemmed in part from the fact that he was, to his core, a scientist who demanded multiple, corroborating proofs. Yet beyond science and proofs, my dad also was Ida Hanson's son. Although he never doubted the quality of my investigations, at a fundamental level, he was finding it difficult to comprehend the extent to which his strict, proper, and intensely devoted mother had lied about her past. He had suspected it for years, at some level even known it, when my college-era research had proven that the Prospect Park farm of Ida's girlhood could not have existed. However, it was one thing to know, in the abstract, that his mother had lied about her past, and an entirely different matter to face detailed evidence.

The disturbing revelation that Ida had given birth to a heretofore unknown older brother, and left him behind in New Britain, seemed inconceivable in light of the mother my dad had known. Nonetheless, these fantastical new truths, combined with my father's lifelong questions about his mother, were creating a new framework that made complete sense to him—especially when considering the lengths to which my grandparents went to hide the truth.

My father and I continued talking as Marc expertly wound his car through the crowded, narrow streets of Cambridge's Central Square neighborhood, en route to a Korean restaurant.

"You know how your mother said that after her parents died, she had a Jewish guardian who had been her father's lawyer, and he gave her permission to marry Grampa when she turned twenty-one? Well, she did have a guardian, but it was her sister. Her sister's the one who gave her permission to marry Thomas Keevers when she turned eighteen," I said.

"Hmm! I wonder where she got the Jewish lawyer from."

"Well, her father might have had a lawyer, and your mother probably knew some Jewish people in New Britain, but I'm willing to bet they weren't the same person," I said.

Ida's claim of attending normal school also failed to withstand scrutiny. Although New Britain was the site of Connecticut's first normal school, founded in 1849, she could not have attended.

"Your mother got married the day after she turned eighteen, and she was already working at a factory," I explained.

"Maybe she worked at the normal school," my dad said. "She did know how to teach kids to read and write."

"Could be," I replied. "I think she said she attended normal school and taught because that's what she wished she had been able to do."

I didn't yet understand how deeply this information disturbed my father. I just knew that my discovery of his mother's lost son caused my dad to accept these revelations.

As Marc and I sat down in the restaurant, the last rays of the July evening sun streamed in through the broad sidewalk windows and then yielded to the soft darkness of a summer evening, punctuated within by dim incandescent lights. My half of our scallion pancake appetizer grew cold as I continued pouring out my discoveries to Marc. Across from me, his blue eyes were calm yet attentive, and his smile met mine between bites. Two years ago, Marc had been inducted into the Hanson family mystery, and now, as the quest entered its new phase, he continued to support and accompany me.

I had eaten little all day, but I couldn't stop talking. My bibimbap, a steaming, spicy stew that I normally gobbled down immediately, sat untouched for twenty minutes.

"It's amazing," I kept saying. "I never expected this. I was always much more focused on Grampa, trying to figure out what kind of trouble he was in. And all the time it was my grandmother."

That's what I said, in the excitement of the moment. However, Frank's history, including how and when he entered Ida's life, remained a mystery. Prior to those happy days with Ida in the summer of 1924, which were captured in their photo collection, Frank Hanson's early path and whereabouts remained entirely unknown to us.

Back in my apartment late that evening, I investigated what happened to my grandmother's first son, Thomas F. Keevers Jr. Hoping against hope that he might still be living, I turned to the online Social Security Death Index, an indispensable tool for twentieth-century family research. If someone dies and a survivor claims the Social Security death benefit, basic information about the deceased person goes into the public record and is available free of charge on numerous genealogy websites.

Within three minutes, I had my answer. Thomas F. Keevers Jr. died at age eighty-one on August 14, 1999. His birth date of April 12, 1918, exactly matched that on the birth certificate of my grandmother's son Thomas F. Keevers Jr. Ida's former husband, Thomas F. Keevers Sr., had died in 1963, three years after my grandmother.

I logged onto the *Hartford Courant* website in search of an obituary for Thomas Jr., hoping to find names of surviving children who might be able to tell me more about what had happened between Ida and Thomas Sr.

KEEVERS, Thomas F.

Thomas F. Keevers, 81, of Newington, husband of Mary (Madenski)

Keevers, died Saturday (August 14, 1999) after a long life. He was born in New Britain and resided in Newington for the past 48 years. Thomas was a decorated US Army Veteran of World War II and retired from the State of CT Highway Dept. after many years of service. Besides his wife, he leaves his daughter, Cyndi Loomis of Rockaway, NJ...[3]

When I read his obituary, the man Thomas Keevers Jr. became real to me. No longer was he just the brown-eyed mystery child in so many photos or a name in the New Britain city directory—a hidden, unknown part of my grandmother's past. Thomas had lived a long life with a wife and daughter who loved him. I felt the sadness behind these simple words.

With a few quick taps on the computer, I found a phone number for Thomas's daughter, Cyndi Loomis. As I always did before one of these "cold calls," I jotted a brief outline of topics I wanted to cover on a white notepad. That night, I was nervous, not so much because I was calling a relative who had never heard of me but because I had the feeling this wasn't going to be a happy story.

CHAPTER 16:
A MEAN SOB

CIRCA 1923 *(Imagining the past)*

"THERE'S NO POINT IN TALKING TO HIM," Ida said. "He can't help me—no one can help me."

"At least give him a chance. Mr. Saxe was real good when Alice's father was so mean. He's a very smart man. It don't hurt to talk."

Elsie gave her sister's arm a quick squeeze. Ida shook her head with a deep sigh.

The two young women, clad in calf-length frocks whose origin in the previous decade had been concealed by strategic alterations to mimic the streamlined low-waist fashion of 1923, were walking along Main Street in downtown New Britain. Ida's tricorn hat, adorned with a jaunty feather, was no longer the height of style, but she and her sister Elsie, both tall with erect posture and a commanding step, still cut a striking figure amongst the never-ending tide of factory workers, shoppers, office clerks, and passersby who streamed up and down the busy sidewalk. The Hardware City was booming in the 1920s.

As the sisters passed the train station, a multicar freight line thundered down the tracks. With the din of the train and clanging of trolleys, the clatter of horse hooves, and the added roar of automobiles, Ida and Elsie had to lean in close to hear each other.

Despite their hometown's remarkable nineteenth-century transformation from a farming community into a prosperous industrial city, the sisters' family, the Steeles, had fallen into obscurity from the elevated status it had enjoyed three centuries earlier, when brothers John and George Steele had figured amongst the community's founders. Nonetheless, Ida and Elsie, aged twenty-four and twenty-seven, respectively, remained intensely proud of their Steele heritage. They were members of the Daughters of Liberty, an ancestral membership organization for descendants of women who had actively supported the patriots' cause prior to and during the War of Independence. Indeed, some of the sisters' happiest girlhood memories involved the days they dressed up all in white for Daughters of Liberty events.

"Here's his office," Elsie said. They stopped in front of 338 Main Street, a three-story red-brick building with multiple businesses listed on the placard by the door. The most prominent name was that of Morris D. Saxe, Esq., an attorney with large offices on the first floor. Ida grimaced.

"Come on now." Elsie touched Ida's shoulder, looking into her lowered eyes. "Let's listen to what he says." She opened the door and followed her younger sister into the building.

JULY 2003

THE PHONE RANG a few minutes before eleven on Friday morning. I was working at my home office, which meant I was sitting at my usual place on my green living room couch. Laptop computer positioned atop phone book on my lap, glass of water on the side table to my left, teal landline phone on the couch to my right, I tapped rapidly on the keyboard, preparing for a conference call.

"Is this Anne Hanson?" A woman's voice delivered the words in a quick rush, her voice quivering ever so slightly.

"Yes, this is Anne."

"This is Cyndi Loomis. You left a message for me the other night about your grandmother. I just got it. I was away."

"Hi, I'm really glad to hear from you." I glanced at the clock. Almost eleven. "I really want to talk with you, but I'm working, and I need to go to a meeting right now," I said, sounding as reassuring as I could. "Will you be there for a while? Can I call you back right after I'm done?"

"OK, that's fine," she said. "I'll be here, at the number you called before." I could hear relief in her voice. Was it relief that I sounded nice and normal, or relief at a temporary reprieve before heading into uncharted territory?

For the next hour, I was all business as my colleagues and I calmly discussed plans to implement controls that financial auditors required in the software system for which I was responsible. I had flipped the off switch to my personal world, putting my excitement and anticipation of talking to Cyndi on hold.

Just before noon, the meeting was over, and I was free. After sipping some water, I sat for a minute, taking long, slow breaths in and out. Then I dialed Cyndi's number.

"I couldn't believe it when I got your message," she said, her words tumbling out in a rush. "Tell me everything."

I gave her the short version of my story, beginning with how my father grew up in Akron, Ohio, believing that his mother was Ida Howe of Brooklyn, New York. My dad had never heard of the Steeles or Keevers, I explained, and he never knew that his mother had any connection to New Britain. I told her about my genealogical research, and how I had gone to New Britain and discovered my grandmother's marriage to Thomas Sr. and the birth of Thomas Jr.

"My father had absolutely no idea that his mother had been married before, or that he had another brother," I said.

"Oh my god, this is unbelievable." Cyndi's tone was both agitated and excited. She knew almost nothing about the marriage of her paternal grandparents, Tom Keevers Sr. and Ida, beyond that Ida had left and the marriage had ended. Tom Sr.'s mother and brothers subsequently stepped in to help raise Cyndi's father, Tom Jr.

Cyndi was blunt in her assessment of Tom Sr.

"My grandfather was a mean SOB," she said.

As I continued to jot notes of our conversation on my usual white pad, Cyndi related an unpleasant childhood memory related to her grandfather. The details were jumbled and I couldn't quite follow the story, which involved the gift of an engraved watch to her grandfather. Nonetheless, Cyndi's point was clear: Tom Sr. had been hardhearted and thoughtless. As for Stasia, Tom Sr.'s second wife, whom he married after his divorce from Ida?

"I didn't like her," Cyndi said. "I haven't seen her since my grandfather's funeral in 1963."

Cyndi was clear and unequivocal that, unlike her grandfather, Tom Sr., her father, Tom Jr., had been kind and loving.

"He was a wonderful man," Cyndi said. "He was a great and fair dad."

Decorated for the valor of his World War II service, Tom Jr. married Cyndi's mother in 1944, with Cyndi, their only child, arriving in 1949. In the early 1950s, the family moved to Newington, just east of New Britain, where Tom Jr. remained for the rest of his life.

When Cyndi was growing up, her father rarely discussed his childhood and never spoke about his mother to her. Except once.

"When I was little, I saw a photo of a blond lady," Cyndi said. "I asked my father, 'Who is that?'"

"'That was my mother, and she left me.'"

Fifty years later, her father's harsh, terse response echoed in Cyndi's voice. "My father was very angry all his life," she said.

During her own childhood, Cyndi never met any of her Steele relatives. When, at twelve or thirteen, she suggested to her dad that they try to contact the Steeles, he wanted nothing to do with it.

"They'd come after us with a gun," he told her.

Another time, Tom Jr. referred to Ida's family as the "Clan of Steeles," Cyndi recalled. However, given that her father had no contact with the Steeles, it is likely that Tom Sr., who was hardly an impartial party, was the source of these invectives.

It was clear that Cyndi's father, Tom Jr., whom she had adored, had been deeply scarred by his mother's departure. Cyndi's tone always hardened when she referred to our grandmother.

In this initial conversation and others to come, Cyndi never referred to "my grandmother" or "our grandmother." It was always "Ieeh-dah," the I chewed with a grimace. When describing her father's pain and bitterness at being abandoned, her flat tone throbbed with accusation, as if she were about to cry.

I got it. Thinking of the intense pain young Tom Jr. must have endured filled me with sadness. It also was obvious that Cyndi herself was suffering deep grief over the loss of the dad she had adored. Nonetheless, eighty years later, my mission was to uncover and understand the truth, and not to condemn or blame. In light of the intensely loving, protective, and self-sacrificing mother I knew through my dad's stories, I was sure the truth would be neither simple nor straightforward.

Moreover, given that Tom Sr. was a mean SOB, as Cyndi herself had immediately volunteered, surely the kindness and strength Tom Jr. displayed his entire life must have derived, in good measure, from the love and nurturing he received from his mom, Ida, during his early years. I refrained from making that comment.

As Cyndi and I talked, I found myself questioning whether the connection between my grandmother and her father was one hundred percent real.

"Why aren't you sure?" Cyndi asked, incredulous, when I voiced my uncertainties. "I'm totally positive. There can't be any doubt."

I was pulling back because I sensed the deep, hot rage that simmered just beneath Cyndi's excitement. Although I appreciated her directness and especially her love for her dad, her anger made me uneasy. With Cyndi in the picture, the stakes of my investigation were escalating by the minute. People who had already been hurt were now involved, making it all the more imperative to avoid mistakes.

After her father died in 1999, Cyndi learned that, in the mid-1930s, Tom Keevers Sr. had hired detectives to find Ida. He wanted to remarry in the Catholic Church and needed an annulment from her to do so.

"They never found her," Cyndi said.

Tom Sr. ultimately had to settle for a civil union. The source of this intelligence was Marilyn Keevers Bozzuto, a cousin with whom Cyndi had previously had little contact.

"Thank you for finding me," Cyndi said as we wrapped up our first conversation.

We agreed that our next step would be to swap old photos via email. Late that night, I emailed Cyndi four pictures of my grandmother with Tom Jr., from the batch of cut-up photos whose negatives I had found and reprinted. In one, Ida sits with toddler Tom Jr. on a wall in front of a lake. She wears a dark dress with a long, pointed white collar and a large dark hat. Tom nestles in her arms, his dark eyes and mobile baby face framed by a white hat tied under his chin and topped with a trio of white pom-pom tufts. He is wearing a white gown, with his little knees and calves bare above dark shoes and white socks. Mother and child squint into the bright sun as Ida tugs at the brim of her hat, trying to shield her eyes.

My phone rang Saturday morning. It was Cyndi.

"I have that exact same picture of my father at the lake!" she exclaimed. "But it's with my grandfather. It's dated August twenty-eighth, 1919."

She emailed it to me. Sure enough, her photo portrayed the same wall, the same lake, and little Tom in exactly the same white pom-pom hat and garment. The only difference was that posing with him was his father, Tom Sr., wearing a hat and suit, as people did for outings in those days.

"My grandparents' photo collection has lots of photos of people I don't know," I said to Cyndi. "Why don't I email a few to you, and maybe you'll know some of them."

"OK, send them. Do you have pictures of anything else?" she asked.

"Yeah, I've got lots of pictures of houses."

"What do they look like?" Cyndi asked.

"Well, there are a bunch of different ones. A few ranch houses, a lot of older houses."

"Send the ranch house photos."

I scanned a few photos and emailed them to her. Minutes later, the phone rang again.

"I'm falling on the floor," she said. "That's my house!"

Among the photos I had sent Cyndi was a hazy September 1955 snapshot of a small ranch house taken from the interior of my grandparents' Studebaker with the windows rolled up. A spindly newly planted tree in the front lawn was stretching frail limbs up, as if in supplication. Finally, after a half century of silence, the plaintive cry of that fuzzy photo was delivering its message.

"That's the house I grew up in." Cyndi's voice trembled. "My mother still lives there."

On that September day, my grandmother returned to the son she had left behind some thirty years earlier. Driving up and down Indian Hill Road in Newington, Frank and Ida had stopped in front of Tom Jr.'s house, number 117, taking one photo at each pass. Thirty-seven-year-old Tom, living in that small house with his wife and young daughter, was totally unaware of this visitation by the mother who had vanished so long ago. He never knew that his mom, who had protected and cosseted him during his earliest years, had been sitting in her car just yards from his home, looking at it, thinking of her firstborn.

As for the emotions coursing through Ida's brain during those moments she and Frank sat in the car, looking at Tom Jr.'s home, I can only speculate. Perhaps she was remembering the last time she ever saw Tom Jr. Had she kissed his forehead as he slept, gently stroking his soft brown hair, and whispering her love? Or maybe she had waved bye-bye as he stood in the door with an aunt or cousin, after repeated assurances of a speedy return.

I wondered how Ida found out, in 1955, where her grown son lived. With no smartphones, internet, or social media, you couldn't find someone with a few quick taps on your device. Maybe my grandparents went to libraries in and around New Britain, looking in phone books until they found Tom Jr., who had moved into the newly built ranch house in 1952. Or back in Akron, my grandmother could have dialed the operator and asked to be connected long-distance to the New Britain operator, repeating her request in nearby towns, until she found the listing. Either way, it would have taken a lot of effort.

After getting off the phone with Cyndi, I called my dad.

"Hi, Annieeee!" he greeted me. "I bet you have some more updates!"

Just two days after a most eventful excursion to New Britain, I did, indeed, have even more news. I told my dad about finding Cyndi, about her stories of her father and grandfather, and about the matching photos of Ida and Tom Sr. with toddler Tom Jr.

"Really good work, Annie!" he said, his voice buoyant with enthusiasm. "So this woman you made contact with, she's the daughter of my mother's son."

I was tossing so many new names at him that he wanted to make sure he was keeping the relationships straight.

I also told him that two of the photos from my grandparents' collection, from their 1955 road trip, were of Tom Jr.'s home in Newington, Connecticut. They had driven up and down Indian Hill Road, taking photos of number 117 with the car windows closed.

"Good Lord," said my dad, the most unreligious of men.

For the past three weeks, ever since I first connected the Steele grave of the wobbly vacation snapshot with the Steele family on Farmington Avenue in New Britain, the edifice of my grandmother's past had been crumbling. Some patently false bricks and stones came tumbling down with a thud from the walls of fabrications, which had been the foundation of my father's life for seventy-one years. Other details, pebbles of fact, clung tenaciously like old vines to a brick wall, clutching at air even as the supporting structure collapsed.

Engrossed in the history detective adventure of my life, I didn't yet grasp the pain and shock that were percolating beneath my dad's unruffled demeanor. Ever the scientist in search of truth, he embraced each fact as I proved it. Yet accompanying the genuine delight he felt in finally learning about his parents' past, was his deep shock upon learning about Tom Jr. So deeply embedded were my dad's memories of his mother's relentless, suffocating drive to nurture, protect, and of course control her sons that for her to have left a child seemed impossible. It was incompatible with her nature.

Nonetheless, my father remained the same outwardly calm man who had listened patiently when I called him via pay phone during my adolescent escapades. By 2003, however, the former wild child had grown into an energetic and determined investigator who was rocking the foundation of his own past.

"I find it very hard to understand," he commented. "It seems inconceivable." And then, as always, he encouraged me to continue digging.

"Keep it up," he said. "Truth is best."

When I met Cyndi a few days later at a Friendly's restaurant outside New Britain, a tall woman with short, stylishly cut dark hair, almond-shaped brown eyes, and my grandmother's chin stood up to greet me. I was en route to Philadelphia, while Cyndi was in Connecticut helping her mother, who was becoming increasingly debilitated by dementia.

Between bites of fried egg and toast, we talked, and Cyndi showed me photos of her father as an adult. Little Tom had grown into a handsome man with a long face and brown hair and eyes. In his coloring and facial features, Tom Jr. took after his father. Cyndi also brought the handful of photos she had of her dad as a child. I recognized them immediately.

"I have those same pictures," I told her.

Until Cyndi showed me her photos of Tom Jr. as a child, I hadn't realized how many of the mystery babies, toddlers, and youngsters pictured in my grandparents' collection actually were Tom Jr. He was one of those children whose appearance changed markedly from when he was a round-faced, dimpled baby up through when he had grown into a thin-faced child of five or six with dark, straight, glossy hair. In these later pictures, when his face had lengthened and taken on a different cast, he appeared to change from photo to photo, depending on the angle.

"I didn't realize that these other pictures, when your dad was older, were Tom," I said.

As it would many times, our conversation turned to speculation over what happened when Ida left New Britain.

"I can see why she would leave my grandfather, but I don't understand how she could leave my father," Cyndi said. "Why didn't she take him with her?"

"I don't know" was the only reply I could muster. I, too, didn't understand it. Based on all my father had told me of my grandmother, this behavior was completely out of character. "I think we're missing a lot of information. We don't know what happened."

Cyndi showed me a photo of herself as a little girl in front of her house, the same small ranch house that Ida and Frank photographed from inside their Studebaker in September 1955. When they took those photos, the driveway was empty, as if no one were home. I wonder how many other times my grandparents might have driven by that little house, only for a car in the driveway to indicate someone was inside. As the green Studebaker rolled by slowly on a Saturday afternoon, Tom Jr. might have been out mowing the front lawn. Seeing her grown son, in his thirties the spitting image of his father at the same age, Ida would have felt not only a gut-wrenching pain but also a shock of recognition and intense anxiety, as if the husband she had left so long ago had stepped from her troubled past onto the lawn in front of her. Little Cyndi, her dark hair and eyes echoing Tom's appearance as a child, might have been outside too, playing with the two blond children from next door.

"Keep going, oh, keep going," Ida would have cried to Frank, her voice thick with suppressed sobs. That man was her beloved little Tommy. How often had she dreamt that she was approaching him, scooping his warm, delicious little body into her arms, only for him to slip away, just beyond her entreating embrace. Those dreams then became nightmares and sweet little Tom morphed into Tom Sr., the angry husband from whom she had come to shrink in terror.

As they passed Tom's house, Ida craned her head around, straining to keep her son in sight as long as possible.

A few days later, I pulled over on the Garden State Parkway in New Jersey to take a call from Cyndi. Her voice trembled with raw hostility. "She left him lying in his crib!"

Earlier that day, we had met up again in central Connecticut to visit Stasia Keevers, Tom Sr.'s ninety-two-year-old widow, whom I had tracked down at a nursing home near New Britain. Although Stasia had severe dementia, I had spoken to a nurse who said that she had occasional lucid moments. Cyndi and

I were hoping she might know how her husband's first marriage had ended.

We were out of luck. Stasia was not having a good spell. Throughout our visit, she maintained the same uncomprehending grin and was unable to utter a word.

Afterward, as I continued my drive to Philadelphia, Cyndi had located one of Stasia's family members, with whom she hadn't communicated for more than four decades. After speaking with this relative, Cyndi was reporting back to me, with complete conviction, the story of Ida abandoning Tom as a baby in his crib.

"I don't think that can be right," I replied, keeping my tone calm and even. "My grandmother's photos show that she was in New Britain with your dad at least until Tom was five or six."

Although one may debate whether it is worse to leave a child in infancy or at six, it didn't matter. Cyndi was primed to judge harshly and believe the worst of our grandmother, no matter what.

"Shame on her, that she didn't love him enough to take him with her," she said.

Although I still appreciated Cyndi's warmth and directness, I was becoming increasingly wary, because her barely suppressed rage seemed to be escalating. While I, too, was disturbed by my discoveries, I would not rush to judgment.

"Give me a child until he is seven, and I will show you the man." This saying, attributed to Ignatius of Loyola, founder of the Jesuit order, as well as to Aristotle, always ran through the back of my mind whenever Cyndi spoke about how wonderful her dad had been. The countless photographs of young Tom Jr. in my grandmother's collection, beginning in infancy and continuing in a steady stream until he was about six, testify that Ida had been a loving, nurturing, constant presence in her first son's early life. She played a huge role in making him the wonderful dad Cyndi had adored.

Moreover, I was pretty sure that Tom Sr., in explaining his first marriage to the woman who became his second wife, would portray himself favorably and Ida as the villain, regardless of what really happened. A truism of relationships is that if you get dumped during a bad breakup, the stories you tell your next partner about your ex will not be pretty. On the other side of the equation, my grandmother, Ida Agnes Hanson, had failed to provide any version whatsoever of what happened, leaving the door open to opinion and speculation.

"I bet he beat her up," my father said of Tom Keevers Sr. He repeated that comment often. In his view, only extreme fear could have caused his intensively protective, loving mother to leave her first son.

Trolley conductor Thomas Keevers, twenty-seven, was arrested for punching a garbage man whose sleigh was blocking his trolley at eight a.m. on Thursday, March 23, 1916, the *New Britain Herald* reported. Police court Judge James T. Meskill dismissed the charges two days later, saying the man's threats justified Keevers's hard punch, which resulted in "closing the garbage man's eye."[4] A Connecticut Trolley Company attorney represented Tom Keevers in court.

Throughout my dad's childhood, his mother always said, "You don't hit people. Period." Did Ida hold this view so strongly because her first husband had hit her? Neither Frank nor Ida ever physically disciplined my father and his brothers, just as my father never struck me. So fundamental was the Hanson moral opposition to personal violence that my dad never knew Frank to raise a hand against anyone, and he, in turn, never did either.

Tom Keevers Sr. clearly knew how to fight, which suggests that his punching of the garbage man was unusual for him only in that the incident was reported to the police and made the news. If he assaulted my grandmother in the early 1920s, she would have been extremely unlikely to report it, due to shame and fear, as well as the unfortunate reality that domestic violence was not then considered a crime.

"Then why would she leave her son with an abuser?" Cyndi countered, when I suggested that Tom Sr. might have physically abused Ida. A reasonable question, to which I could respond only with conjecture. Tom Sr. might have hit his wife but not his son. Or, given that multiple members of the Keevers family helped raised Tom Jr. after Ida left, perhaps she knew they would step in to care for him. She might even have discussed arrangements with one or more of them.

Distrusting Cyndi's eagerness to condemn, yet striving to maintain a cordial relationship, I found myself channeling my dad, and maintained a neutral, calm tone as I speculated about possible scenarios. Tom Sr. might have pointed a gun at Ida and ordered her to pack up and leave. On the other hand, it also is possible that Ida Steele Keevers was so unhappy in her marriage, and so despondent about the future, that she thought her son would be better off without her. There had to be an explanation somewhere in the murky tunnel of the past, if only we could uncover it.

Despite the tension that simmered between Cyndi and me over our differing views of our grandmother, the stories about her father that she generously shared opened a singular window into the life of my father's lost brother. Attending Catholic school until he quit after eighth grade, Tom held a series of jobs in the early 1930s before joining the Civilian Conservation Corps, one of President Franklin D. Roosevelt's New Deal employment programs, where he worked on environmental projects in Washington and Oregon. Tom subsequently served in the US Army Signal Corps in North Africa and Italy during World War II, receiving the Soldier's Medal for risking his life to save fellow soldiers.

Upon returning home after the war, Tom married and created a stable, happy family with wife Mary and daughter Cyndi. He worked for the State of Connecticut Highway Department as a bridge foreman, and as a snowplow operator in the winter.

At home, he was a hands-on dad and partner with Mary. He hugged, cuddled, and pitched in with kitchen tasks, Cyndi told me.

"He didn't think cooking was just for women. He made fantastic home-made bread."

Cyndi's mother worked nights, so Tom oversaw Cyndi's homework, particularly enjoying helping her with geography.

"The nuns were tough," Cyndi recalled.

He even was in charge of curling her straight dark hair, a task he took on gamely, fumbling through as best he could.

"He was secure in himself," Cyndi told me. "He was a stay-at-home guy. He loved the house, Ma, me, the neighborhood, our yard. He and Ma had a wonderful group of friends—friends he had till the day he died."

Tom became a man of whom Ida would have been proud. She must have thought about him, the child she left behind, every day for the rest of her life. Whenever she said she had four boys, or mentioned that Frank Jr. was her oldest, a small, persistent voice, emanating from a back corner of her extraordinarily retentive mind, would have silently contradicted her. The self-righteousness with which she judged others may have been fueled by an internal duel in which she was always the party whose behavior deserved censure.

In the days and weeks after I learned my grandmother's secret, I thought of it constantly. I still went to work, spent time with Marc, and got together with friends. But when no action was required, I just stopped and thought. The groove in my brain that in past months had been etched deeper and deeper by each contradiction, discovery, and irreconcilable fact had finally gotten a piece of the truth it craved. This only whetted my appetite. I wanted more. I wanted to understand what happened.

At my small, noisy gym in Cambridge's Central Square neighborhood, instead of grabbing a magazine or watching TV during cardio workouts, I'd stare into space. On the treadmill, my mind would begin reverberating in concert with the din of fifty other T-shirt-clad exercisers pumping and thudding away in the windowless, low-ceilinged room. *It's true*, I'd repeat over and over to myself. *The pain she must have felt.* Thoughts whirled round and round my head, drowning out the pounding motorized symphony around me. *What the hell happened?*

CHAPTER 17:
LAST NAME BEGINS WITH H

I SAT AT THE END OF MY GREEN SOFA a few minutes before 11 p.m., a glass of red wine and a cup of water on the tiled side table to my left. It was July 27, three and a half weeks since the July 3 breakthrough when I learned that my grandmother was Ida Steele.

In the living room of my tiny apartment, my gaze drifted from one object to the next, resting on the prints, photography, and ceramics collected during my travels. The last gift Grampa ever gave me, the baby duck he carved from butternut wood at the nursing home, perched in its appointed place on my bookshelf. Next to it, the white crocheted teacup and saucer with blue trim that Ida made for her granddaughters occupied its position of honor. Usually the memory of how I acquired these items, as well as their patterns and colors, filled me with pleasure. Tonight, however, they could not quell my restless discontentment.

During the last few weeks, the Hanson family research had morphed into an investigation of my grandmother. I had pried away the seemingly impregnable barrier hiding Ida's past, unearthing the eighty-year-old drama of a young woman's secrets that astonished and confused me. But Grampa was the one I had known and loved, and he was nowhere to be found. How did Ida and Frank meet? How did Ida Agnes Steele, daughter of a family with deep New Britain roots, transition from being the wife of Thomas Keevers to her life as Ida Hanson, wife of Frank Hanson of Brooklyn, New York? So far, I had uncovered nothing in my grandmother's past connecting her to Frank.

Fueling my unsettled mood was the lackluster reception I had received from my newly found Steele relatives. Joy Medvec, a Steele by marriage and the family genealogist, was the only contact who seemed unreservedly happy to hear from me. Cyndi's emotions were always a fraught mixture of enthusiasm and fury, while the discomfort of my dad's first cousin, Dorothy Varano, had been palpable. Although I would later become fond of Marty Roden, my very first Steele contact, his genial disinterest had been discouraging.

Where might Ida have gone after leaving New Britain? I wondered. How, and where, did she meet Frank? She had told my father that, as a young woman, she was employed at a sanitarium near Bear Mountain, up the Hudson River north of New York City. She had worked with kids and taken them on outings, she said. Once, she showed Harley a photo of a steamer ship she called the *Clermont*, on which she and Frank had enjoyed an excursion on the Hudson River.

By now, I knew that Ida's tales usually contained morsels of fact, albeit deftly scrambled up in a collage that obscured the truth. The trick was to figure out which parts were real, as well as their original arrangement.

The photographic evidence, combined with Ida's stories, did seem to indicate that she had spent time near Bear Mountain and the Hudson River north of New York City. Maybe Ida had left New Britain for New York state and found a job at a sanitarium north of the city. In a set of 1922 photos from my grandparents' collection, Ida shepherds a group of children on what appears to be a nature outing. Surrounded by ten youngsters, of similar age and bearing no familial resemblance to one other, Ida smiles at the photographer as the group stands together in a shallow pond or stream, immersed halfway up to their calves. Attired in a loose blouse and baggy pantaloons hanging to her knees, with strands of wavy hair that had escaped her bun dangling across her face, Ida smiles broadly, exuding a relaxed joy. On the back of the photo, she had penciled in the date 7-8-22.

When I examined the photo more closely, however, I realized that one of the children was four-year-old Tom Jr., ever the chameleon in photos from his early years. So much for the Bear Mountain sanitarium. Perhaps Ida was a helper at the New Britain Fresh Air Camp, which in 1920 began providing outdoor activities for children during summer months. Or maybe she worked as an aide at the normal school and was taking her charges on an outing.

By the summer of 1924, Frank was in the picture, literally, with the first dated photos from their life in and around New York City beginning in June. In the set of photos overlooking the Hudson River north of New York City, I could see a large ship on the river. One of the photos had "CLERMONT" scratched into it, corroborating the story Ida had told young Harley.

Where did Ida and Frank meet? If Frank had grown up in New York state, maybe he had met Ida outside the city, and they subsequently moved to Brooklyn. Ida had just one story about Frank's family, which she repeated multiple times during my dad's childhood.

"Right after we got married, we went to his house to see his parents," she said. "When we got to the house, his mother was sitting on the porch, reading the newspaper. But she was holding it upside down!" Ida always paused, grinning, before she continued. "Later, we were in the kitchen, and his mother was cutting a big round loaf of bread by holding it against her belly with a knife and cutting toward herself. I was very alarmed—that's not how you cut bread!"

"It didn't happen like that," Frank protested in annoyance, although he never offered an alternate version of events.

So specific was the detail about Frank's mother cutting the bread toward herself that, to my ears, this anecdote had the ring of truth. The question was, where did it occur? I hadn't a shred of evidence that Frank was from New York, or from anywhere at all for that matter. And what of my grandparents' claim that they had known each other in grade school? So clever had Ida been in concocting the tales of her fictional past that distinguishing fabrication from truth was nearly impossible.

As I sat sipping wine and water that Sunday night, I got an idea. Turning on my laptop and placing it on the phone book on my lap, I logged into the HeritageQuest site. I had already spent more time than I cared to recall trawling New York and New Jersey genealogy records for Grampa's father, Elof. However, I had never searched for Grampa's family in Connecticut. Now that I knew my grandmother was from New Britain, checking Connecticut records for an Elof with any last name that sounded Swedish seemed worth a shot.

With a few quick taps, I searched for all men with the first name "Elof" living in Connecticut as of the 1920 US Census. About fifteen Elofs came up on my screen. Elof Johnson, Elof Swenson, Elof Gustafson. Of course, no Elof Hanson.

The one thing I knew for sure about Grampa was that he had a little sister named Florence. Ida had labeled the back of the photo of a smiling blond child with her neat script: "Florence H., 6-21-21, aged 3½." Ida had been precise in noting the date and Florence's age, as she was in all record keeping that didn't involve covering her trail. I was willing to bet her accuracy extended to the first letter of Florence's last name, H.

On the computer screen in front of me, only one of the Elofs living in Connecticut in 1920 had a last name beginning with H: Elof Harriander. Unusual name, I thought. It sounded Swedish. I clicked the link to view the original document filled out by the census enumerator.

Up popped the image. Elof Harriander's name was third from the top, captured by the enumerator's stubby, dark cursive script. On the line below Elof was his wife, Elida.

Elof and Elida. The names of Grampa's parents.

During the instant it took for my eyes to move to the next line and register the meaning of the dark squiggles, I shrieked out loud.

"I found them!"

Frank, age twenty, was Elof and Elida's oldest child. That fact, captured by the strokes of the enumerator's pen, was right in front of me, and it matched Frank's story. *My grampa. Frank Harriander.*

Elof and Elida's other children, listed by age, were Albert, Ethel, Helen, Carl, Vincent, Henry, and Florence. From Albert through two-year-old Baby Florence, the details exactly matched those that Grampa provided to Aunt Virginia in 1953, right down to the birth order. Frank's little sister May would not have been listed in 1920 because she died around 1918.

I sprang off the couch with a shriek, jumping up and down.

"I did it, I did it!" Still standing, I dialed my father's number.

"I found Grampa," I shouted into the receiver.

"What?" my dad asked. He had been dozing on the couch in his basement TV room.

"I found Grampa, I found his family!" My words tumbled out in quick blasts. "His last name was Harriander. They lived in Connecticut."

"Okay, that's very good," he said, his voice woolly and flat. "But we need confirmation." Even in his drowsy state, his natural skepticism prevailed.

I plopped back down on the couch after getting off the phone, rearranging the phone book and computer. The census image of the Harriander family was still on my computer screen. Looking at the small loops of the enumerator's careful script, some leaning left, others right, I knew that the symmetry between the names he had listed and the names of Grampa's family members was too perfect to be a coincidence.

I remembered how, when Marc and I were driving to New Britain for the first time two weeks earlier, we had passed an exit for Flatbush Avenue off Interstate 84 in West Hartford. He had said, "Wouldn't it be funny if this Flatbush Avenue were the Flatbush Avenue of your grandfather's childhood, rather than the Flatbush Avenue in Brooklyn?"

Now, sitting at my computer Sunday night, I scanned the top of the census sheet image that contained the Harriander family. *Connecticut, Hartford*, the enumerator had written in the top left corner, indicating state and county. My gaze traveled across the top of the image and then stopped abruptly. New Britain City, the enumerator had written in a tidy backhand.

New Britain.

Frank Harriander, my grampa, was from New Britain, Connecticut. Just like my grandmother. I sat on the sofa, my eyes boring into the computer screen. It took a minute to sink in. He wasn't from Brooklyn, or New York state, or even Flatbush Avenue in West Hartford. He was from New Britain.

On January 2, 1920, a frigid Friday, enumerator Raymond O'Neil had trudged up and down New Britain's East Main Street, northeast of downtown. At 315 East Main, he stopped at a two-family house. A widow and her grown daughter rented one unit. The other tenants were the Harrianders: Elof, Elida, and their eight children.

Elof, age fifty, and Elida, forty-three, were born in Sweden, just as Grampa said. Elof worked as an operator at a screw factory. Frank worked as a tool-maker in a machine shop. Like all the Harriander children, he was born in Connecticut. The second son, Al, was a sailor, which also matched Grampa's story. Seventeen-year-old Ethel was employed as a feeder in a printing office, while fifteen-year-old Helen was a sorter in a factory. Only the youngest four children, ranging from thirteen-year-old Henry down to two-year-old Florence, were not toiling for wages.

I gaped at the computer screen. I had broken through and penetrated the barriers of time and secrecy. The ghost ship of Grampa's past was evaporating in the mist. In its place was a raft of real people who had lived, breathed, and worked hard, as enumerator O'Neil, in his almost childlike script, had documented more than eighty years earlier.

"I don't think our parents ever existed," Uncle Al had said in 1992, when he gave up on the Hanson family hunt.

Al was right. We had been chasing phantoms invented by my grandparents.

Frank and Ida's photo collection had told the truth, as usual. The wood house in front of which young Florence had posed, and the country roads where Grampa's tough-guy motorcycle buddies had photographed each other, had seemed as odd for a man from Brooklyn as the barns and fields of my grandmother's early photos had been. They made perfect sense, on the other hand, for a couple hailing from New Britain, Connecticut. Although the busy core of the city hummed with commercial and industrial activity, on the outskirts, the farming community of an earlier era still existed in the first decades of the twentieth century. Outside of town, the rolling hillsides of central Connecticut, green oases from the bustling cities, were within easy striking distance for Frank and his biker gang.

It was 11:30 p.m. Time to prepare for the workweek ahead and get to bed. But I couldn't stop. I logged on to another genealogy website to do a quick search for Grampa's family.

"Harriander," I typed in the text box, punching the search button. Up came a few pages of records. What a pleasure to pursue real people. After all those years of coming up empty, now I got results. I found Social Security Death Index records for all of Grampa's siblings except Florence, leaving me with the faint hope that Frank's favorite little sister, Baby Florence, might still be alive. As for Frank Harriander, however, I found nothing beyond 1920. This left a big unanswered question: when and how had my grandfather ceased to be Frank Harriander and assumed his new identity as Frank Hanson?

CHAPTER 18:

NO STONE UNTURNED

JUDGE LOSES PATIENCE

Judge Meskill's patience was taxed to the limit this morning in the case of Frank Harriander, a 16-years-old boy, charged with assaulting Sam Falk, a milk dealer. Harriander was decidedly "fresh" and conducted himself in a manner highly insulting to the court, evidently believing himself to be a martyr to the cause of "gangdom." It appeared that Harriander is one of the leaders of a gang of young boys, ranging in age from a dozen to sixteen years, who take special delight in causing trouble on Hartford avenue. Monday they pelted Sam Falk with snow balls and when the milk man stopped Harriander punched him in the face and then, as he told the court, "took a sneak over the fence" so he wouldn't get arrested. Harriander and his young friends, Peter Tomshick and Clifford Renshaw, told an impossible story about trying to pick some burrs out of the mane of Falk's horse and said the milk man attacked them.

Harriander was fined $2 and placed on probation. No witness fees were allowed the other boys whose testimony was plainly fabrication.

~ *New Britain Herald*, March 29, 1916.

WHEN I PULLED OFF THE HIGHWAY into New Britain on July 30, three days after my Sunday night discovery of the Harrianders, the city seemed altered. On the outside, it remained a run-down former manufacturing town. Imposing church towers, reminders of a bygone era of prosperity, cast tall shadows over battered buildings that lined desolate streets. Now, however, the city's worn surfaces seemed to vibrate in the sun's hot rays. They resonated with the prospect of discoveries that could bring my father and me closer to Frank's real past.

After parking in a municipal garage, I headed up South Main toward city hall. When Frank and Ida had walked these same streets a lifetime ago, the air would have been humming with commerce and industry, punctuated by snippets of conversation from passersby and the clatter of trolleys. A block south of the Winged Victory monument, the sidewalks of Chestnut and Main would have been crowded with workers coming and going from factories, shoppers paused in front of store displays, clerks entering their offices, entertainment seekers streaming into theaters. I was willing to bet that Grampa's boyhood story of retrieving theater tickets from Brooklyn gutters and using them to get in for free had in fact occurred right here, in the flourishing and bustling New Britain of the early 1900s. This city had once boasted seven downtown theaters.[5]

When Harley was a boy, Frank had made a chance remark about seeing Ida's father get into his buggy. "He was a huge man, six six or something,"

Frank said. "He must have weighed three hundred pounds, and he was so big and heavy that when he stepped in the buggy, it went down like a rock on the side he got in."

Now, I knew that this scene had occurred right here, when these quiet streets had been full of life. Despite the downturn in New Britain's fortunes, the commercial buildings that remained from the city's heyday still stood proudly, their glory faded yet not vanquished. My love affair with downtown New Britain was underway. These grand old buildings, beautiful in their own right, were also, to me, symbols of my family's rediscovered history.

In the city clerk's office, I again showed my Connecticut Society of Genealogists card and driver's license to the clerk behind the counter.

"Yes, I've been here before," I told her. "I know where everything is."

I was an old hand at researching Connecticut vital records now, although I hadn't expected to return to this office so soon. Who knew what further surprises the day might have in store?

In the back room, I pulled down the huge index book that included last names beginning with H, for people born in 1899. Within seconds of heaving the heavy volume onto the white worktable, I found what I came for: Frank Elmer Harriander was born on May 8, 1899. Just like Frank Elmer Hanson. The index directed me to a fat book residing at the bottom of a tall metal bookshelf located smack in the middle of the stacks housing New Britain's original vital records.

Pulling out the red volume, I flipped through the pages as carefully and quickly as I could. On a fragile, yellowed sheet of paper, recorded in a clerk's spiky black script, I found the birth certificate I had sought for so long: Frank Harriander, born May 8, 1899, was the first child of Elof Harriander and the former Elida Johnson. The record showed that both his parents had been born in Sweden. Elof worked as a molder. All the information on Frank Harriander's birth certificate, other than his last name, corresponded to what Grampa had told Aunt Virginia fifty years earlier.

I stood among the tall shelves, cradling the plump, weathered book with both hands, drinking in the simple, yet to me hallowed, data that documented my grandfather's birth. I had been seeking and working toward this moment for more than two decades. During my first visit the previous week, I had checked for Elof, Elida, and Frank Hanson in the very same big index book with H surnames. Little had I known how close to the answer I was. If I had turned just a few more of those big pages, I would have seen the entry for the birth of Frank Harriander. Yet the neatly typed names had lain mutely, just within my grasp but completely beyond my comprehension. And when last week I had held the book containing my grandmother's birth certificate, within my hands had been Grampa's birth certificate too. Because my grandparents' birth dates are so close—April 25, 1899, and May 8, 1899—their certificates reside in the same volume, hers on page 242 and his on page 265. Just as Ida had always teased Frank, she was indeed two weeks older. Surely they also must have been in the same class in elementary school.

Today's plan was to look up everything I could on the Harrianders. Grampa's parents, Elof and Elida, were married in New Britain on October 28, 1898, by the pastor of the Swedish Bethany Church. Elida would have been almost three months pregnant with Frank. Some things don't change, I thought, chuckling to myself.

Elof and Elida's second child, Albert, arrived one year later, with more babies, nine in total, following every year or so. The family moved frequently within New Britain. When Grampa was born, they lived at 89 Fairview Street. A few years later, they resided at 128 Fairview, then at 232 Hartford Avenue, then 208 Hartford Avenue, and a few years later, at 315 East Main Street.

In May of 1913, Elida gave birth to her eighth child, a girl named May. Aside from Baby Florence, the only other fact about Grampa's family of which I had always been certain was that he had had a little sister named May, who died as a young child.

A quick search through the index books confirmed that May Harriander, just five years old, died on September 14, 1918. Examining her death certificate, struggling to decipher the jagged lines of the clerk's scratchy script, I could just make out the cause of death. "Probable pneumonia," the clerk had written. "Died suddenly after 4 days illness without medical attendance."

Poor little May. Her death had probably deepened Frank's attachment to his youngest sister, Florence, who was only nine months old when May died. Grampa never spoke of his family to me, but when my father was growing up, both his parents said that if they had had a girl, her name would have been Florence May.

When I had spent that long July afternoon a year earlier scouring New York City death records for a child named May who died between 1915 and 1920, my gut had been right, even if I had been laboring in the wrong archive, in the wrong city. The few snippets Grampa had revealed of his hidden past were essentially truthful and seemed always to be rooted in emotions deeply felt, if rarely expressed.

The sad end to May's short life provided yet another proof, in my dad's parlance, that Frank Elmer Hanson was Frank Elmer Harriander. Inside my head, a jubilant chorus chanted, "I found them! I found them!" Countering this joyous refrain, a wary, dour voice growled, "Are you *really* sure? How much would you stake on this?"

After so many years of searching and failing, at some level, I was struggling to believe I had finally discovered the truth. Despite the mounting evidence, I wanted more.

The last Harriander I planned to research that day, Baby Florence, did not let me down. Florence Harriander was born on January 1, 1918. On the back of my grandparents' one labeled photo of Florence, Ida had written "Florence H., 6-21-21, aged 3½." It added up: January 1, 1918, plus three and a half equals June 21, 1921.

Florence, born nineteen years after big brother Frank, was my best chance of locating someone who could tell me about my grandfather's family and early life, if I was lucky enough for her still to be living. To continue following the path of Florence and any children she might have had, I first needed to locate a marriage certificate, if it existed, to get her last name. A minute in the big index volume, and I had it. Florence married Roger Bergeron in New Britain on July 4, 1941, when she was twenty-three.

Her New Britain records trail stopped after her marriage. Combing through the indexes, I could not find evidence of the birth of any children. It was quite possible that she and Roger had moved out of New Britain. Each town in Connecticut maintains its own vital records, as birth, marriage, and death records are called. This meant that even if Florence and Roger had relocated just to the town next door, I still would find nothing for their children's births in New Britain vital records.

For all I knew, Florence and Roger had gone to Alaska. The prospect of requesting records from faraway states loomed unpleasantly in my mind. In the Hanson family, the four Hanson boys and members of the next generation had always been a rambling bunch. I expected the Harrianders would be the same.

Of course, Florence might not have had any children. I reflected, not for the first time, on how genealogical research can temporarily transform even the staunchest freethinker into a strict traditionalist.

"A woman without a man is like a fish without a bicycle," a student had spray-painted on a wall of the Wesleyan University "hippie dorm" where I lived one year. Although I hadn't really believed that mantra, regardless of what I professed at the time, I certainly had internalized feminist philosophies about choice. Marriage and children are an option but far from obligatory. Now, however, in my role as Hanson family genealogical sleuth, I wanted everyone to get married and have children, producing a boy if possible. Marriage and children mean descendants, always a plus in family research.

And because men almost never change their surname upon marriage, they are far easier to trace, while yielding the added bonus of carrying on the family name.

That is, unless the boy is born with the name Frank Elmer Harriander.

For reasons I did not yet understand, Frank Harriander had traded in his rare surname for the commonplace Hanson. About twenty Harrianders had trod Connecticut soil during Frank's youth, but as of 2003, I could find no living Harrianders in the United States. Absolutely none. So rare is the surname Harriander that any individual born in the United States in the twentieth century with this name in their family tree is guaranteed to be related to my grandfather—and to my father and me—by blood or marriage.

The name Hanson, on the other hand, is common among Americans of Swedish descent. It resides solidly on the second tier of the most prevalent Swedish American surnames, a notch below the ubiquitous Anderson, Johnson, Carlson, and Nelson. When I lived in Minneapolis, a town chockfull of the descendants of Scandinavian immigrants, the city phone book, today a relic of the predigital landline era, had contained five full pages of Hansons. In 1924, Frank slipped into the anonymous crowd of Hansons, with the first documented use of his new surname occurring on August 3, when he scratched "HANSON" at the top of a photo of himself at Brighton Beach in Brooklyn.

After ordering copies of all the certificates I could find for Grampa and his family, I retraced last week's walk along West Main Street to the New Britain library. Grampa had always said he quit school as soon as he was old enough to get a library card. Now, finally, I knew that New Britain's stately library building, which I had been startled to recognize from my grandparents' photo collection, was the repository in question.

"I may not know something, but I know where I can look it up!" Employing Grampa's practical motto, albeit in pursuit of information he had never intended for me to acquire, I entered through the main modern building entrance and turned left into the grand honey-beamed central hall of Grampa's childhood library. Completed in 1901, the construction of this edifice was funded by industrialist Cornelius Erwin, of New Britain's Russell & Erwin hardware manufacturing company.

Within this airy, elegant space dedicated to knowledge for all, I could imagine red-haired Frank Harriander, twelve or thirteen years old, his short, thin frame clad in the rough shirt and overalls of a working lad, perusing titles in the dimly lit stacks after a day's work in the factory. What would he have checked out? Books about his passion, motorcycles? Stories of adventures in faraway places? As a teenager, he might have read about the just-completed Panama Canal and dreamt of one day voyaging through it, as indeed he and Ida later did.

I headed toward the section of the stacks containing the old city directories, which a week earlier had begun revealing the secrets of my grandmother's past. Entries for the Harrianders began in the 1880s. The same few names appeared over and over in the early listings: Elof, August, and Peter. At first, they all lived at the same address, so they had to be members of the same family. The spelling of their unique surname seemed infinitely malleable: Harreander, Heriander, and Herriander were the most common early variants, with Herriander and finally Harriander winning out as time passed.

Young Frank made his debut in 1922. "Herriander, Frank E., carpenter," the faded typescript stated. He lived, along with several other Herrianders, at 315 East Main Street, the same address as in the 1920 census. Frank's information remained the same in 1923. No directory was published in 1924. By 1925, he had vanished from the directory. His parents, Elof and Elida, had moved to 28 Oak Street, just north of downtown.

In the years after Frank disappeared, the number of Harrianders and Herrianders in the directories expanded to a half dozen, still clustered at a handful of addresses. Grampa's brothers Henry, Vincent, and Carl continued to live with their parents, who, after still more moves, in the 1930s finally settled more or less permanently in a rental at 222 East Main Street. That building, along with a broad swathe of blocks on both sides of East Main, was later bulldozed to make way for unsuccessful urban renewal schemes and the highways that cut through the heart of New Britain beginning in the 1960s and continuing through the 1970s. The deserted shopping center where Marc and I had tried to find water during our first visit to New Britain stood right at the site of the bygone Harriander residence at 222 East Main Street.

My great-grandfather Elof, Frank's father, died in 1941, followed by Elida in 1948. Grampa's brothers Carl and Henry, by then in their forties, had still been living with her at 222 East Main Street. These two seemed to have been lifelong bachelors. I had found no records for marriage or the birth of children for Carl and Henry in New Britain City Hall. Another brother, Vincent, did marry, but I located no evidence of children.

When Carl died in 1967, he was living at the Hotel Sarsfield on East Main Street. I later learned that this establishment had once been one of the grandest hotels in New Britain, host to international entertainers, politicians, and sports figures. By the time it was demolished in 1972, it had become "a home for lonely men—bachelors, widowers, pensioners," according to the *Hartford Courant.*[6]

Via online research, I also learned that Grampa's brother Al married in 1929, only for his twenty-one-year-old wife to die in 1931, a week after giving birth to a baby girl, who herself had died shortly after birth. Although Al remarried, he did not again become a father. All this helped explain the lack of next-generation Harrianders, despite Grampa being one of five brothers.

Finding Grampa's little sister, Baby Florence, was the next goal of my foray among the New Britain city directories. I had located Social Security Death Index records for all of Grampa's immediate family except Florence, so she was my only hope of finding a living Harriander sibling. Florence Harriander Bergeron and her husband reappeared in the New Britain directories in 1952, when they moved back into the family apartment at 222 East

Main Street. They rejoined her brothers, Carl and Henry, who had never left. My earlier assumption that the Harrianders would be like the Hansons, apt to move in pursuit of education or opportunity, seemed misplaced.

Fortunately for my research, Florence and Roger stayed put. The directories showed that they remained at 222 East Main until the 1960s, shortly before the block was demolished for redevelopment. They subsequently moved to an apartment southeast of downtown, and Roger worked as a custodian at Central Connecticut State University, which had developed out of New Britain's Normal School.

After Roger's death in 1984, Florence remained in New Britain until the early 1990s, when she moved to the neighboring town of Berlin. The last phone and address listing for Florence in the Berlin telephone directory was from the year 2000, three years ago. I found nothing further in the New Britain directory.

At long last, I could be on the verge of connecting with Grampa's favorite little sister.

I'll have lunch and then I'll call her, I decided.

I needed time to compose myself. What would I say if Florence answered the phone? "Hello, my name is Anne Hanson, and I'm the granddaughter of Frank Harriander, the brother you haven't seen in eighty years." How often do you get a phone call like that? What if I caught her at a bad time? She might think the call was a scam. Or she could be too ill to speak with me, or she might be indifferent.

Gathering up my papers, I exited the library and headed back down the hot, quiet sidewalk, past the Winged Victory monument and the parking garage. After stopping to pick up a turkey sub, I carefully crossed the Elm Street highway and found a picnic table for lunch in front of the judicial complex. Dressed in my usual miniskirt, sandals, and pullover top, I felt my face, arms, and legs baking in the heat. I usually avoided the direct summer sun, but today I needed space to spread out.

Between bites of my sub, I jotted a few phrases in my notebook. "I am the granddaughter of your oldest brother, Frank Harriander," I wrote in blue ink on the lined white paper. "We have been looking for you for a long time." I took care to clearly print the surname Harriander. So unusual was this name that sometimes I couldn't remember it. I didn't want to draw a blank in the midst of introducing myself to Florence.

The sub consumed, I dawdled for a few minutes, my phone on the table beside me. Finally, after gulping down a mouthful of water, I picked it up and punched in Florence's number.

It rang a few times. My heart thumped. Any second, I might hear her voice.

The hollow three-part tone started on a low note, climbing an octave by its end. "The number you have reached is no longer in service," a robotic voice informed me. Crap. When the phone of an eighty-five-year-old woman is disconnected, the likely explanations are that she died or moved to a nursing home. My best hope was the latter.

I walked across the manicured lawn to the Berlin Probate Court offices, where a week earlier I had researched the Steeles among the heavy gray tomes. First, I searched for Florence Bergeron in the private index of the deceased. She wasn't there. That, at least, was good news. However, when I looked up Elof and Elida Harriander, I also didn't find anything. *That's odd*, I thought—*they definitely died in New Britain.*

"I can't find anything at all in the indexes for people who I know died in New Britain," I said to a staffer who had entered the back room. "Am I doing something wrong, or is there someplace else I should be looking?"

"If they didn't have any property that had to pass through probate, you won't find any case in their name," she replied. "You'd be surprised, in the past, at how often people didn't have anything at all."

Did the fact that the office had no probate documents for Florence mean she was still living or that she had died and had no property? I found an index card for one of Grampa's brothers, Henry, stating that he was insolvent when he died. For all I knew, it could be the same for Florence. Between the constant moves and lack of real property among the Harrianders who had remained in New Britain, I was getting the impression of a family living close to the financial edge.

My next stop was Fairview Cemetery. Out of the probate court and back behind the wheel of my Subaru, I got lost in a tangle of nondescript boulevards. The year 2003, of course, preceded the advent of ubiquitous smartphone navigation apps that prevent one from going totally astray.

Finally, I turned into the cemetery entrance off Smalley Street. In the office I met Christine Raia, the same helpful woman who had put cemetery maps inside the screen door for Marc and me two weeks earlier. Aged sixty or so, with thick reddish-brown hair, she exuded a matter-of-fact cheerfulness, which I found a comforting trait in an establishment devoted to the dead.

"What was the name?" she asked. "Florence Bergeron?" In a tall cabinet at the back of the office, she thumbed through a small drawer filled with index cards. "No, she's not here."

"How about Elof and Elida Harriander?"

Raia turned to the cabinet and flipped through a few more cards.

"They're in Section 33, Lot 111." She pulled out another cemetery map and circled a small section on the far side of the grounds.

Section 33 was newer than the final resting place of the Steeles but still bucolic, with tall trees lining the winding drive and providing shade. I got out of my car and began strolling among the graves, checking the names on the headstones.

HARRIANDER. I saw the inscription on a tall vertical stone topped with a cross. Underneath were the names Elof, Elida, and their sons, Carl and Henry. I stood gazing at the weathered white stone, bright in the rays of the summer sun. Here, right below me, were Grampa's parents.

Elof and Elida's tombstone was not among the grave photos in my grandparents' 1950s photos. It seemed odd that they would take so many photos of the graves of Ida's family and none at all of Grampa's parents' grave. Perhaps the visibility of the unique Harriander surname on the stone caused Frank to veto photos, or resulted in him destroying any that existed. On the other hand, perhaps Frank just hadn't felt the need for a photo. Uncle Al had hypothesized that familial conflicts were the reason Frank had left his past behind so completely. Maybe Al was right. Although Frank had seemed unable to discard any early images of Ida, he showed far less solicitude toward depictions of his own past life in New Britain. The prime exceptions, of course, were the multiple photos of Florence, several of his motorcycle gang, and one of his brother Al, the sailor.

While jotting down the names and dates from my great-grandparents' and great-uncles' headstone, I noted that both Carl and Henry had died at sixty-one. Being a Harriander bachelor did not seem conducive to long life.

The time was 3:30 p.m. In today's search for Florence, I had checked the city clerk's office, library, probate court, and cemetery. As I honed in ever closer, I couldn't stop. Where else could I go to search for her today? I reviewed my notes. The town clerk in Berlin, the location of Florence's last known address, was open until 4:30 p.m.

A half hour and several wrong turns later, I walked into the Berlin Town Clerk's office, which was located in a modern red-brick municipal building complex set back from the road.

"Could I look at recent death records?" I asked the woman behind the counter, showing her my CSG card and driver's license. "I just want to see the ones from the past two or three years."

"OK, come on back. All the most recent ones are here." She pointed me toward a Rolodex.

As I hastily thumbed through the cards, another staff member walked past and stopped short, alarm on her face.

"That's not available to the public!" she exclaimed.

I showed her my CSG card. "Hmph, OK," she said, her tone still a grumble.

Florence was not in the index. I went back out to the front desk.

"Do you know where this is?" I asked one of the staffers, pointing to my notebook, where I had printed Florence's Berlin address of 31 Colonial Drive.

"Yes, that's a senior housing complex on the other side of these buildings," the woman replied. "Just go back around, and you'll find it."

Driving a few hundred yards beyond the municipal buildings, I came upon a series of tidy one-story houses, clustered together townhouse style in groups of four.

"I'm looking for thirty-one Colonial Drive," I asked an elderly man. "Do you know where that is?"

After I followed his directions but failed to find the address, I encountered a woman of about seventy with curly dark gray hair.

"Thirty-one Colonial Drive? You need to go back out on the main road, get onto Robbins Road, then it's around there," she said. "That one, he doesn't have any idea where he is or what he's talking about," she added, gesturing dismissively at my first informant, who was still ambling about.

Colonial Drive was a quiet cul-de-sac ringed by tiny one-story wood dwellings. Three elderly women were clustered on a small but well-groomed lawn, chatting, as I pulled up. I got out of my car and walked over to them.

"Hi, I'm looking for Florence Bergeron," I said. "She's a relative of mine. Does she live here?"

"Oh yes, we know Florence," one of the women replied.

"She was very small and bent over," a second said. "And she had a daughter who visited her *every day*."

The women smiled their unanimous approval.

"Her daughter used to own a pharmacy around here, and she had Chihuahuas," the first woman said. "But Florence doesn't live here anymore."

My heart sank. "When did she leave?"

"It must have been about six months ago."

"Do you know where she went?"

"A nursing home," the woman replied.

"Do you know what nursing home she went to?"

Eager to help, the women speculated among themselves for a moment, trying to recall the details.

"I'm sorry, we don't remember which one she went to," one of them finally replied. "But if you check all the nursing homes in the area, you should find her."

Darn. I had come so close.

"OK, thanks anyway," I said with a sigh and a smile.

They had done their best. I walked back to my car, turned the key in the ignition, and began turning around. I was already planning how I'd call all the nursing homes in the vicinity of New Britain as soon as I got home.

Just as I was about to pull away, one of the women waved for me to stop. She walked over to my car, and I opened the window.

"We've been thinking about it some more," she said. "We think you'll find her at the Brittany Farms nursing home."

"Where is Brittany Farms?"

"Off Route 9 in New Britain," she said. "If you go up Stanley Street, that will take you near it."

Bless them. "This is wonderful, thank you so much."

Upon attempting to call Brittany Farms, I found my phone had no service. No matter, I could drive there. Today, it felt like my Subaru and I were careening around a bumper-car arena, ricocheting first in one direction and then off in another as I smacked up against each new piece of information.

Fifteen minutes and still more wrong turns later, I pulled into Brittany Farms, a large nursing home complex located in a green suburban corner of northeast New Britain. I entered the reception area.

"Do you have a Florence Bergeron living here?"

The young woman checked her computer. "Yes, she's here."

My heart pounded as I headed toward Florence's wing.

"Is Florence Bergeron here?" I asked at the nurse's station.

"Yes, she is," the nurse replied. "You can go see her if you want."

Now that I was finally here, visiting Florence straightaway didn't seem like such a good idea. She had no idea who I was, and I didn't know the state of her health. I couldn't predict how she would react to this latter-day Harriander apparition, suddenly descending upon her.

"Is there someone in the family I can talk to?" I asked the nurse. "She's my great-aunt, but she doesn't know who I am. She's never heard of me."

"You should talk to her daughter," the nurse replied with a quick raise of her eyebrows. She picked up the phone and dialed. "Hi, Linda," she began. "I have someone here to talk to you. I think I better let her explain."

CHAPTER 19:

REACHING THROUGH THE SKY

MY PULSE RACED AS THE NURSE AND I wound our way through wide white corridors toward Florence's room. I felt as if I were hovering above this scene, watching events unfold, as I hurried after my guide, clutching my handbag stuffed with notes. On a hot July afternoon in 2003, my years of searching for Grampa's family were coming to an end. In seconds, I would be face-to-face with his favorite little sister.

A few minutes earlier, at the nursing station, I had spoken with Florence's daughter, Linda Corazzo.

"Hi, my name is Anne Hanson," I began. "I'm the granddaughter of Frank…" I hesitated. What was Grampa's real last name again? As I had feared, for a split second, I couldn't remember my grandfather's unique surname.

"I'm the granddaughter of Frank Harriander, your mother's eldest brother." It came back to me just in time.

"Oh, my goodness! I can't believe it!" Linda said, her voice raised in astonishment.

I explained how Frank had left New Britain in the 1920s, become Frank Hanson of Akron, Ohio, and completely hidden his past from his children, except that he spoke often of his favorite little sister, Florence. "We've been looking for my grandfather's family for so long," I said.

After listening to me in puzzled surprise for a few moments, Linda responded with cordial friendliness. "We always knew her brother Frank went away," she said. "My mother always wondered what happened to him."

"Would it be all right with you if I visited your mom today?" I ventured. I was hoping Linda felt that this new relative, of whose existence she had been entirely unaware just minutes ago, was trustworthy.

"I… I think it would be OK," Linda had replied. "She's tired, so she might seem kind of out of it. I left there a little while ago. I must have just missed you." After a few more words, we exchanged phone numbers and agreed to speak again the next day. She later told me that because I had provided so many specific details, she instinctively felt my account was true.

As the nurse and I continued our trek to Florence's room, we passed clusters of elderly women slumped in wheelchairs lining the hallway walls. Although this facility was unmistakably clean and well maintained, I detected the scent of antiseptic cleansers mixed with the substances they had been applied to remove, but which always left a faint trace. The first time I had encountered this peculiar combination was when I visited Grampa in his nursing home twenty years earlier.

A wheelchair-bound woman with a pointed chin and thick iron-gray bangs raised her head as we approached, her eyes seeming to bore into mine. Startled, for a split second I wondered whether this was Florence.

The nurse and I continued a few more paces and finally turned into a room.

"Hello, Florence, you've got a visitor," the nurse announced in a loud, clear voice. After a murmur confirmed Florence was awake, the nurse left.

In the faded photographs my grandfather had kept his entire life, Florence was a slight child with a sharp chin, short blond hair, and spiky bangs crowning a generous forehead. She had smiled shyly at the camera with her head tilted, trust in her eyes. If she wasn't nestled in her brothers' arms, she was cradling a cat.

Now, lying in the bed before me was a tiny, frail woman with wisps of white hair and blue-gray eyes prominent in a bony, pale face. During her eighty-five years, Florence had never heard of me or any member of my immediate family. She had last seen her oldest brother Frank, my grampa, some eighty years ago.

"Hi, my name is Anne Hanson," I began. "I'm the granddaughter of your brother Frank."

Her head on the pillow, Florence gave me a long look, blinked, and continued to regard me steadily. My instincts as a former newspaper reporter kicked in. Speak slowly, be calm and friendly. But unlike when I was a journalist, this was intensely personal. I knew that the fragile old woman before me, whom instinctively I wanted to protect, could be the only living person from the past life Grampa had so carefully concealed.

I sat on a chair to the right of the bed and continued. "Do you remember your oldest brother, Frank? He never forgot you, and we've been looking for you for a long time."

"Yes, I remember Frank," Florence said, her voice faint. "It's a surprise to see you. He left a long time ago."

I strained to hear her. She would utter a few words and stop, fatigued by the effort.

I told her Frank had four children and nine grandchildren, and she said, "I'm glad."

Despite having looked so hard for Florence, I had barely considered what I would say if I actually found her. Now that I was here with her, Florence appeared beyond having an easy chat. Her gaze was clear but weary, and her gaunt frame, beneath a sheet pulled up to her shoulders, did not stir in the bed.

As we spoke, and I did my best to explain my improbable materialization at her bedside, I looked at Florence's wan face on the pillow, and Grampa looked back at me. Gone for twenty-one years, he had steadfastly kept the secret of his past to the end. What would he think if he could see me here?

"I should let you rest now," I said, and Florence nodded. "I'm really happy I found you. My father and our whole family are going to be so glad when I tell them I met you today."

"Come again," she said in a whisper as I got up to leave.

Back outside, as I walked across the steaming asphalt of the parking lot, the late-afternoon sun baked my knees and calves. I pulled out my phone to call the person who would most want to hear what just happened.

"I found Florence, Dad. She's alive, I just saw her!"

"Who did you find? Say that again, Annie!"

My dad, sitting in his old black wicker chair in the keeping room as I lobbed this fantastic news at him, was having trouble keeping up. During the past three weeks, I had been calling him almost daily to add yet another new name or person to the rapidly transforming landscape of his parents' past. His mother was Ida Steele, and she left a child? His father's last name was what—Harriander? Not only his mother but his father, too, was from New Britain? And now, I was telling him that, at this very moment, I was at a nursing home in his parents' real hometown, and I had just met the one sure character from Frank's past, Baby Florence. As always during moments of high emotion, my dad channeled his joy through the lens of a scientist.

"Every day you were bringing me something new. I was suffering from information overload," he told me later, when we looked back on the summer of 2003, that wondrous season of discoveries. "I kept saying, you need more proof, more proof. That's good spy craft. But when you found Baby Florence, that was real proof. Everyone knew about Baby Florence. My brother Frank did, my brother Al did. That clinched the whole family story. Florence is still with us!"

The fabrications of my grandparents' past were slowly dissolving, making way for real people and real lives.

"The truth will set you free," my dad began saying, and he meant it. But alongside his pure, genuine delight in my almost unfathomable findings, he also had to process the degree to which not only his mother but his father, too, had deceived him. At this point, however, he breathed not the slightest hint of his inner turmoil.

Two days later, I was back at Brittany Farms to see Florence again. This time, I first met her daughter Linda, a trim fifty-six-year-old with glasses and shoulder-length blond hair, attired in neat, comfortable jeans and a tropical-flowered blouse. Now, I could put a face to the daughter with the Chihuahuas, who had visited her mom in Berlin every day. After owning and operating an independent pharmacy in nearby Rocky Hill, Connecticut, for more than twenty years, Linda, an accountant, and her husband Tom, a pharmacist, had sold their business to CVS a few years earlier.

As we greeted each other in the lobby and sat down to chat before visiting Florence, panic suddenly gripped me. What if I somehow had made a terrible mistake, and zero family connection existed between this friendly, soft-spoken woman and me? Linda, however, seemed as relaxed as one could possibly be during a first meeting with a heretofore unknown, and entirely unanticipated, cousin.

My fears evaporated as soon as Linda opened Florence's family Bible, which she had brought in a large Ziplock bag, and began showing me old family photos. Beginning with the first image, featuring a little girl with a heart-shaped face and spiky blond bangs, the photos depicted a cast of characters I knew well.

When we went to Florence's room, she was reclining in a wheelchair next to her bed, a loose white blouse hanging on her thin shoulders. She wore large round glasses and had an oxygen line in her nose.

Florence did not recall my late-afternoon appearance two days earlier.

"Do you remember, Mom? Anne is Frank's granddaughter. She came and visited you," Linda reminded her gently. "She said that Frank always talked about you. She and her family have been looking for us for a long time."

"Yes," Florence said, nodding, her voice low and hoarse.

"Frank had four sons," Linda continued. "And they all went to college."

"Oh, good," Florence said faintly, inclining her head slightly.

"What do you remember about Frank?" I asked.

"Nothing much," she replied. Clutching a tissue, she slowly raised a shaking hand to dab her nose, then lowered her hand again.

Multiple bouts of pneumonia during the past year had completely debilitated Florence. Although she did not have dementia, my great-aunt was physically and mentally drained.

"Do you remember Frank's motorcycle?" I asked.

"Oh, he loved his motorcycle," she replied, curving one side of her mouth up in a small grin. "He gave me rides on it."

"What else did you do with him?"

"I don't remember," Florence replied, to this and most of my other questions.

She couldn't recall any girlfriends or the circumstances of Frank's departure from New Britain. She wanted to help, but her brain synapses just weren't firing anymore. Beyond Frank's love for his motorcycle and her gentle rides with him, she could tell me little of the brother who had left when she was six years old.

Yet the few scraps of childhood memories that Florence could pull up corresponded reassuringly with my dad's recollections of his father.

"We always ate whole wheat bread," she said.

Florence knew little to no Swedish. "They [Elof and Elida] always spoke Swedish when they didn't want us kids to understand," she said. "We never knew what they were talking about." Frank, the firstborn, probably understood at least some Swedish, although he claimed he didn't.

When taking leave of her after this second visit, with Linda's smiling permission I gave Florence a little hug, lightly touching her shoulder with my hand and brushing my cheek against hers.

"I wish you could have met my mom a year ago. She could have chatted away with you about anything," Linda commented as we walked down the hallway afterwards. She paused and added, in a lower, hesitant tone, "I'm not sure how much longer she's going to be here."

Meeting Florence was a gift, regardless of her weakened state. When I had called my dad from the steamy parking lot after finding her two days earlier, I felt as if I had soared up into the warm blue sky, plunging through billowy clouds to emerge in a new land on the other side. Finally, I had pierced the invisible barriers of time and silence.

In this brave new world, the phantom ancestral Hansons were breaking out of their two-dimensional cage, where they had perched, identities askew, on the twigs of false genealogical charts. They were morphing into the flesh-and-blood Harrianders, who had journeyed through the past eighty years in a universe parallel to, yet totally separate from, that of the Hansons.

CHAPTER 20:
YOU'RE MINE NOW!

THE MASSIVE BOUQUET stationed precariously on my Subaru's back seat bobbed up and down wildly, the open petals clamoring warnings of an immediate tumble whenever I hit a bump on the now-familiar route to New Britain. My father had insisted on paying for the nicest arrangement I could get, resulting in this extravagant symphony of white, yellow, and lavender. My windshield wipers thwapped back and forth steadily as they sluiced in sharp angles through the thick early September drizzle. Encumbered by unaccustomed high heels, plus a dark dress and purse, I had wobbled unsteadily behind my outsize cargo in Harvard Square that morning as I transferred it from the florist to my double-parked car. How on earth was I going to get these flowers inside when I arrived?

A little before noon, I turned into the parking lot of the Erickson-Hansen Funeral Home, a 1990s one-story red-brick building with white siding and columns, on the edge of downtown New Britain. A dark-haired man in a sober suit greeted me as I paused in the foyer.

"Uh, I've got this huge thing of flowers …" I began.

Before I could finish, he nodded and walked with me to my car. Once there, he swooped down and retrieved the flowers from the back seat in a quick, expert motion. Then he turned around and escorted me back inside.

And so it was that I made my entrance, trailing the funeral director as he bore my immense offering in his outstretched arms, the top petals swinging above his face. To the left, I saw a screen displaying a rotating series of photographs of Florence. Up came a comforting, sweet smile. In one of the photos, three-and-a-half-year-old Florence sat in the yard in front of the family's wood house, grinning at the photographer, her knees bare above dark boots and socks. I had gazed at the very same photo in my grandparents' collection so many times, trying to identify some little detail, a hidden clue, that would lead me to Baby Florence and Grampa's family. Now, I was about to enter their midst.

As my procession entered the room where the service would take place, a pair of startled, brown eyes locked on me. They belonged to a young man who was craning around in his seat to watch the unknown mourner with her floral honor guard. No doubt he was wondering who on earth was this red-haired stranger. Everyone else here had always been part of Florence's life. In a scene straight out of a soap opera, I was turning up out of nowhere at her funeral, a long-lost relative descended from a brother who disappeared eighty years ago. My giant flower arrangement nixed all hope of a low-key arrival, since my offering turned out to be the day's largest bouquet by far, due to local florists being closed for the Labor Day weekend.

I felt as if every eye in the room was on me. And they were. *Here I am, everyone!* What would they think of me, and I them? Nancy Drew never dealt with these kinds of questions.

During my years of sleuthing, I had rarely considered what, if any, relationship I might have with Grampa's family if ever I found them. Over the years, each research failure had fueled my resolve, strengthening the history detective's determination to discover the truth. When my big breakthrough came in early July, I had certainly hoped my new relatives would be happy to meet me and able to shed light on the secrets of the past. But as for today's solemn gathering? I was winging it.

If my father had been able to join me, at least there would have been a second Hanson to provide moral support, not to mention diverting attention. Unfortunately, my stepmother, Carol, who had risen high in the managerial ranks at Merck, was in the throes of a professional crisis that within six months would end her thirty-year career with the pharmaceutical company. My dad was committed to always being there when Carol needed him. As much as he wanted to honor the woman who from childhood he had known as Baby Florence, trips to Connecticut had to wait.

After the funeral director deposited my bouquet near Florence's casket, I sought momentary refuge in the restroom. At the sink, a stick-thin woman with short, sparse gray hair, wearing a baggy untucked blouse over loose trousers, was washing her hands. The deep lines etched in her somber face would have marked her as a smoker, even without the telltale odor of cigarettes.

Back in the visiting area, Linda stepped forward quickly as I hesitated.

"I'm so glad you could come," she said, instantly reducing my discomfort. "This is my husband, Tommy, and my daughters, Jennifer and Liz."

Behind his big mustache and bushy eyebrows, Tommy's eyes were kind, although I suspected he could be tough when needed. Linda later told me that when she first told Tommy about the startling call from me the day I found Florence, he was sure it was a scam.

Jennifer and Liz, their lively brown eyes and shiny dark hair echoing their father's southern Italian heritage, greeted me with warm smiles.

"Why don't you sit down and get settled, and then you can visit with Mom for a bit," Linda said.

At the front of the room, Florence lay in her casket, pale and fragile in a long-sleeved dress with a bluish-purple pattern.

"She just didn't look right without her glasses," Linda said. So, they had carefully placed the large round frames on her still white face.

Taking a deep breath, I squared my shoulders and stepped up to Florence's casket. She looked so tiny and frail.

Goodbye, I said silently to the motionless woman lying before me. *I'm glad I was able to meet you. I wish I'd had the chance to know you.*

Prayer might have brought comfort had I been a believer, but since I wasn't, I was stuck with my thoughts. Memories from Grampa's funeral twenty-one years ago pushed, unbidden, to the forefront of my mind. Aunt Virginia told me she had placed in his hands a folded blue bandanna similar to one he always had in his pocket. His casket had been closed.

With Florence's death, my elation over discovering my grandparents' past was joined by an unwelcome, yet familiar, companion. My grief over Grampa's death twenty-one years earlier crawled out from its subterranean lair and punched me in the gut. In the weeks to come, it would visit me periodically, raw and heavy. Again, I blamed myself, as I had many times before, because I hadn't visited Grampa one final time when he was so sick at the end.

"I don't know why I said that. I wish I hadn't," my father told me years later, when I asked why he had advised against my visiting Grampa again. I, in turn, have wished many times that I hadn't listened to him. I should have been there for Grampa at the end, the way he always was there for me.

When I visited Uncle Harvey in the hospice, I had arrived just in time to stand witness as he departed this world. Afterward, speaking with Virginia in the hallway in a state of shocked grief, I told her how I forever regretted not visiting Grampa again before he died.

"I think he would have understood," Virginia replied. "And you're here now, and you're representing your father. You'll always have a very special place with me because of this."

Those memories twisted in a painful knot as I stood among my newly found relatives, saying goodbye to Florence Bergeron, Grampa's Baby Florence.

Against all odds, here I was at her funeral service, surrounded by her family. Grampa's family. My family, too. Maybe being here to say goodbye to Florence could help make up for what I had failed to do twenty years earlier.

"Annie?" A small round woman with short, curly gray hair and smiling brown eyes hurried toward me as I returned to my seat. She threw her arms up and around me, enveloping me in a bear hug.

"Oh, I can't tell you how happy I am you're here!"

With that embrace, Jean Czako, the only child of Grampa's sister Ethel, entered my life. After a month of phone conversations, today was Jean's and my first in-person meeting. Just then, the service began.

"We'll talk later," Jean said, squeezing my hand.

The minister, the only speaker at the service, spoke of a conversation he had with Florence shortly before she died.

"I want to go home," she had told him.

"Now she has gone home," he said.

After the service, the family reconvened at Linda's home, a two-story Dutch colonial nestled at the end of a verdant, suburban cul-de-sac in Berlin. Although in the past two months, I had become a pro at making out-of-the-blue phone calls to relatives who had never heard of me, mingling with newly found Harriander descendants at a post-funeral gathering was entirely new territory. By blood alone, I was as closely connected as any of the twenty people gathered under Linda's roof, yet my branch of the family had traveled a completely separate path for the past eighty years. Until just over a month ago, I hadn't known their names, and they hadn't known mine. Could I really say I was a member of this family?

Part of my discomfort stemmed from the fact that many of the people in Linda's house lived in a world very different from that of the hypereducated Hansons. The bony woman from the funeral home restroom turned out to be Linda's sister, Diane, whom I came to know as a quiet, stoic person with a warm heart.

"I cried when I found out," Diane later told me, describing her reaction when Linda first called with the news that Frank's granddaughter had turned up.

By the time I met them, when they were in their fifties, Linda and Diane, my dad's first cousins, had traveled very different paths. Linda, like my dad, exuded the comfortable well-being of the financially secure, healthy early retiree. Fifty-nine-year-old Diane, on the other hand, with her worn skin, simple, gravelly speech, and teeth in need of dental attention, struck me as a woman who had lived hard and made choices with unfortunate outcomes. She also had endured the protracted illness of her husband, Richard Sr., which culminated in his death in 1998.

When I entered Linda's living room, whose cream tones and floral prints invited relaxation, I was introduced to Diane's daughter, twenty-seven-year-old Becky-Lyn. She stared at me blankly, telegraphing a message that felt like, *Who are you? What are you doing here?*

My spirits sank. I was doing my sincere best to be friendly and polite, with all possible respect to the family's grief and to their lifetime of memories with Florence.

Turning away from Becky-Lyn, I perched on a flower-patterned couch in front of the fireplace next to Geza (Jerry) Czako, Jean's husband. Jean had dropped out of high school at sixteen to marry Jerry, now seventy-two, who was still working in his longtime trade of auto body repair.

Right now, he was offering advice, I suspect unsolicited, to Diane's son, Richard, the young man who had craned around to look at me upon my arrival at the funeral home. Richard's pocked cheeks testified to the misery of adolescent acne.

"You've got to have a trade," Jerry exhorted his nephew, leaning in close. "If you have a trade, you can always make a living."

"Uh, OK." Richard nodded an uncomfortable assent with downcast eyes, shifting in his seat.

Near the kitchen entrance, I encountered Jean and Jerry's oldest son,

Jerry Jr., who was in the midst of a story about how he always brought dough-nuts to his buddies at the local police station.

"I can't help it." He laughed. "That's the kind of guy I am."

Short, with a sandy gray crewcut and blue eyes, Jerry greeted me with a direct, friendly gaze. I would never have guessed that he was legally blind, a consequence of the Type 1 diabetes that also had forced his early retirement from auto body work.

Next, I chatted with Jennifer, Linda's older daughter, who worked at the United Nations and lived in Manhattan. Like me, Jen was a college graduate with a multitude of interests. Also like me, she hadn't quite gotten around to finishing her master's degree. I took to her immediately, sensing that she lived in my liberal, free-thinking world.

"I like that!" She laughed, her merry eyes hinting at mischief, when I used the phrase "irrational exuberance" to describe the 1990s dot-com bubble, in a paraphrase of economist Alan Greenspan.

"So, you're the granddaughter of my grandmother's oldest brother, Frank?" Jen asked.

"Right," I replied. "Your mother and my father are first cousins. And that makes us second cousins."

Jean, who was standing nearby, smiled and nodded approvingly as she heard our exchange.

"See, now you're beginning to make the connections."

One of Jean's sons, David, died in an auto accident in 2000. He, like her three surviving sons, had been a skilled tradesman. Three of the boys followed their father's path into auto body repair, while Steve, the outlier, was an automobile mechanic. Kathy, the only daughter, married in her late teens and focused on raising her two sons. Although Jean's family could not have been kinder, I quickly realized that many of them held conservative views or were fundamentalist Christians, meaning their social, political, and cultural outlooks were very different than mine.

How was I going to fit in? It was easy enough with Linda and her family. She and her husband, Tommy, had trod a path similar to that of my father and his brothers during the middle decades of the twentieth century, whereby working-class kids achieved upward mobility and professional occupations through the determined pursuit of higher education. Like all the Hansons, both of Linda's daughters had gone to college. Liz became a pharmacist, like her father, while Jen, like me, tried out multiple careers before ultimately finding her calling as a pastry chef. I had spent my entire life around people like them.

Because of Jean's warmth and insightful nature, our relationship always felt natural to me. But I didn't, at first, know how I was going to get along with the rest of the family. Would I inadvertently come off as a snob? Would they look at me askance, thinking I was an egghead who had never gotten her hands dirty?

At Linda's house that afternoon, and in the months and years to come, I focused on what we all had in common and steered clear of politics and religion. I learned, soon enough, that Jean's husband and sons possessed the confidence and pride of skilled tradesmen, just as Grampa had. I came to see the link between Frank Harriander, the creative, resourceful carpenter who dropped out of elementary school to go to work, and Jean, who left school at sixteen to marry and start a family with hardworking Jerry Czako.

However, the big difference between Grampa and the family he left behind is that Frank actively discouraged his sons from following him into the building trades, or into any trade at all. Indeed, he had refused to teach carpentry to my dad and his brothers, which is ironic given that for several years Frank ran the apprentice-training program for his union.

"If they can't work with their head, they can work with their hands," he said to my dad, perhaps not giving full due to the intelligence and skills required to be a successful builder or construction supervisor, as he was.

Ida, and hence Frank, early on decided that higher education was the only path for their boys. Baffled as Frank had been by Harley's graduate studies in the then-esoteric field of behavioral psychology, he had supported him wholeheartedly.

"I was doing it, so he was for it," my dad said. When in the mid-1960s my dad landed his big promotion to director of neuropsychopharmacology at Merck, with the then-fabulous salary of $24,000, Frank's comment was, "I don't understand what you do, but it must be really important, because they pay you a lot of money." Of course, most of that big paycheck went straight to Quaker school tuition for me and my sisters.

Later that afternoon at Linda's house, I sat in her airy screened-in patio with Jean and Irene, the latter the stepdaughter of Grampa's brother Vincent. Bathed in a gentle gray light, we looked out at the flowers and shrubs of Linda's lovingly tended backyard, rendered soft and misty by the drizzly afternoon. Jean and Irene reminisced about "the boys"—Vinny, Cally, and Henny—as Grampa's brothers Vincent, Carl, and Henry were forever known.

Vinny, unlike the deeply introverted lifelong bachelors Cally and Henny, was outgoing and gregarious, with girlfriends aplenty during his youth.

"He was having too much fun to get married." Jean chuckled.

Returning home from his European World War II service with the initials of a German love tattooed on his arm, this carefree bachelor became a convert to matrimony when he met Annette, Irene's mother, who was estranged from her first husband.

Jean's expressive features and hands never stopped moving as she recalled the day Vinny proposed to Annette. Then a child of ten or so, Jean was living in the Harriander family apartment at 222 East Main Street with her mother, Ethel, her now-widowed grandmother, Elida, and the boys.

"Vinny was sitting in the easy chair in the corner of the kitchen, and he's got this big diamond on his little finger, and he was shining his shoes," Jean began. "And he said, 'Yup, got myself a ring!' And I said, 'You're not going to wear that?' And he said, 'No, I'm going to find a woman to wear that.' And I said 'What?' Then he says, 'Remember Annette? I'm going to marry her.'"

Creating a home with Annette in West Hartford, Vinny embraced his new roles as husband and parent to young Irene.

"He *was* my father," Irene stated firmly.

Outliving Annette by seventeen years, Vinny became a devoted grandfather as well. A photo from the 1980s shows him grinning broadly, with his hands around the shoulders of his grandchildren, Irene's sons.

Vinny, Cally, Henny. Florence, Ethel, Helen… As Jean and Irene reminisced on Linda's porch, these names swirled around like so many wisps in the soft, foggy air outside, enveloping me in a new world. Formerly abstractions on charts, these names were now living, breathing human beings, with all their attendant personality traits and quirks. The past that Jean and Irene recalled, the mundane accumulations of day-to-day existence over the decades, was, for me, a small miracle that inaugurated my arrival in a new world. Irene's calm voice, punctuated by Jean's enthusiastic exhortations, enveloped me in a cheerful time-traveling cocoon.

"Oh, I wish my mother was here today," Jean declared, a sentiment she would repeat many times. "She would have *loved* to meet you."

In our very first phone conversation, Jean had told me that Ethel and the rest of the Harrianders had known Frank was involved with an unhappily married woman and that he left New Britain with her. When Jean was very small, her mother first told her the story in simple terms: "They left because they loved each other so much."

Ethel, the third oldest of the Harriander siblings, worried until the end of her life about what happened to her beloved big brother Frank. The second child, Al the sailor, died in 1962, followed by Carl in 1967, Henry in 1972, Ethel in 1981, Vinny in 1990, and finally by Helen in 1993, at eighty-nine the longest-lived of the nine siblings. At the end of their lives, none of them knew how very hard Frank's children and grandchildren were trying to find them, struggling against the invisible walls erected by my grandparents that confined us within separate worlds.

Only Baby Florence lived long enough to see the broken strands of her family begin to mend. Just barely. I wished I had found her earlier, but I was grateful for the short time we had. If I had showed up a month later, it would have been too late.

"It was comforting to her to know that her brother had a good life," Linda told me. "It gave her a sense of satisfaction, of completion, to know, after all those years, that he was OK."

Although in the years that followed, my father and Carol came to Connecticut for multiple visits with our Steele and Harriander families, my dad never met Baby Florence, the last living family member who knew Frank Harriander before he became Frank Hanson. "I really wish I had made it up to see Florence," my dad said often afterwards. "I regret I didn't do that."

Eighty years and multiple lifetimes of experience separated me from the people assembled at Linda's house that drizzly Labor Day weekend, but the great majority of my new relatives, whatever their thoughts on my unexpected presence, treated me with kindness and warmth.

I didn't know it yet, but as Jean, Irene and I chatted in the sunroom, a new phase of my quest, and of my life, was beginning. Through Jean, I would come to know the family Grampa had left behind and the pain his departure caused. Like me, Jean grappled to understand the trajectory of events eighty years ago that had led to the annihilation of Frank Harriander and Ida Steele Keevers of New Britain, followed by their reincarnation as Frank and Ida Hanson of Akron, Ohio.

Most of all, I, the detective, focused always on solving the mystery of my grandparents' past, found in the here and now a warm and welcoming extended family I never anticipated.

"We always knew you had to be out there, but you didn't know about us," Jean said, her voice equal parts joy and wistfulness. Beginning the moment Jean first enveloped me in her arms that drizzly September day, I became part of her life, past and present.

"I adopt people, you know," she said. "You're mine now."

CHAPTER 21:
THROUGH A GLASS DARKLY

CIRCA MAY 1923 *(Imagining the past)*

FRANK'S EYES SCANNED BACK AND FORTH across the surface of North Street as he slowly walked along, squinting in the bright sunlight. His wavy red hair glinted gold atop his head, a bright contrast with his black leather jacket, scuffed boots, and weathered dungarees. He doggedly craned his head back and forth, peering nearsightedly at the street and into the gutters. On his ride home from an early-morning carpentry job, the kick-stand bracket bolt had fallen off his motorcycle right before he turned off North onto Oak.

Looking up, he saw a tall young woman walking down the sidewalk toward him. Even with his bad eyesight, he knew her silhouette immediately. It was Mrs. Ida Keevers, the former Miss Ida Steele. His pulse quickened. Mrs. Keevers wasn't beautiful in the usual soft way, but to Frank, the keen features and erect posture of his former Burritt School classmate outlined the most intriguing woman he had ever seen.

When Frank first encountered Ida a few weeks ago, after his family moved to Oak Street, he had recognized his elementary schoolmate immediately. Despite the passage of almost fifteen years, Ida's large hazel-gray eyes, strong jaw, and fresh complexion had been unmistakable beneath the hat that shaded her forehead.

Since that first meeting, Frank and Ida nodded a greeting whenever they passed each other. Usually, Ida was accompanied by her son, a thin-faced, dark-haired boy who was the spitting image of Ida's husband, Tom Keevers. After encountering Keevers a few times during a construction job at the Connecticut Company trolley garage, Frank had concluded that the man's belligerent attitude was trouble.

Today, Ida was alone. Frank lowered his eyes as she approached, although not before noting how the folds of her middy blouse and dropped-waist skirt hinted at the hourglass shape within. It was too bad this magnificent woman had married Keevers, Frank thought yet again. Ever since he first ran into her a few weeks ago, Mrs. Ida Keevers had been on his mind constantly.

As Frank looked up, preparing a polite nod of acknowledgment, he inhaled with a shock of dismay. Ida was breathing in and out in short gasps, her eyes red and swollen.

"Mrs. Keevers, are you all right?"

Ida was aware of blue-gray eyes looking intently into hers, full of compassion and something else, too.

"I'll… I'll be fine," she said. Just exchanging a few words with Frank Harriander, the skinny boy from the Burritt School now grown into a strong, handsome man, she felt relief enveloping her. His gaze bathed her in a calmness that banished the agony.

Frank noted, not for the first time, that Ida was several inches taller than he was. He dug into his pocket for a clean handkerchief.

"Here," he said. "I think you need this."

Taking Frank's blue bandanna, Ida wiped her eyes and blew her nose. "My goodness, what a mess." She smiled. "I'll wash it for you."

"Do you want to walk for a minute?" Frank was surprised to hear his voice asking this question.

Ida hesitated. Then, she nodded. The pair began slowly strolling down the sidewalk, a careful foot of space separating them.

TRYING TO PIECE TOGETHER the life of Ida Steele Keevers in the years after her parents and grandmother died was like peering into a foggy void, with images occasionally flickering across the blur for a brief moment before the curtain again dropped. The tales she spun of her formative years on the mythical Prospect Park farm featured Tug-Tug the pig, the "Burk" school, and smelly-footed Woofty Gordon. The years after her parents' deaths, on the other hand, were a shadowy mix of vague description and fuzzy outline, lacking texture, color, and detail.

"When I came to see you at Westtown, we'd go to Friendly's, and you always got a large Coke with no ice. Now, that's detail," my dad said, referring to his visits to the boarding school where I spent three years of high school. "That's what's missing from my mom's stories."

Photos from my grandparents' collection provided a moment's glimpse as the camera shutter opened, only for the door to slam shut an instant later, concealing the scenes that could bring the big picture into focus. It was the elusive sequence of events swirling within the misty chasm that I needed to grasp in order to understand my grandmother and the decisions she would later make.

A few items could be confirmed with reasonable certainty. In 1916, in addition to the shock and grief of losing her parents and Grammy, young Ida undoubtedly faced another problem: money, or the lack thereof.

When Ida came of age in the early twentieth century, modest parcels of land remained in Steele hands, but whatever family wealth may have once existed was gone. Far from attending the New Britain State Normal School to train as a teacher, Ida did not even graduate from New Britain High School. Her name is absent from both New Britain High School yearbooks and from normal school archives held at Central Connecticut State University, which list students who enrolled, regardless of whether they completed the training. A CCSU librarian was even kind enough to check normal school yearbooks to see if the name Ida Steele or Ida Keevers appeared as that of an employee. It did not.

Sometime in her midteens, Ida dropped out of New Britain High School and went to work. Taking the Farmington Avenue trolley to her job as a timekeeper at Stanley Rule might even be how she met trolley driver Thomas Francis Keevers. Irish American, Catholic, and ten years Ida's senior, Tom no doubt cut a handsome figure in his conductor's uniform, with his five-foot-eleven height and dark good looks. Just sixteen or seventeen, Ida would have been reeling from her multiple losses and yearning for security. In Tom, strong, unlettered, and tough, she might have seen a protector who could shield her from life's blows. Maybe he reminded Ida of her brothers, Norvin and Myron, both tough guys who drank too much and drove too fast but whom she could always count on. When she first met Tom Keevers, Ida could not have known what another member of the Keevers family later told me—that they always considered Tom a bully and a troublemaker with a mean streak who frequently caused pain to those closest to him.

When she met Tom, Ida might have found comfort in the certainties, rituals, and traditions of his Roman Catholic faith, even though she had grown up in New Britain's First Baptist Church. Something in Catholicism resonated within her, so much so that she later told my dad and his brothers that she was born and raised Catholic.

In October of 1917, six months after eighteen-year-old Ida married Tom Keevers in the rectory of St. Mary's Catholic Church, she was baptized a Catholic. She was three months pregnant. Her Saint Mary's baptismal certificate lists her name as Agnes Steele Keevers. Ida had substituted her middle name, Agnes, for her first name. The pattern of becoming someone else, of altering her identity as circumstances required, had begun.

Ida's young son, Tom Jr., is the star of my grandparents' New Britain–era photos. About sixty pictures and negatives portray him, more than of anyone else. Beginning with photos of her round-faced baby with big dark eyes as he lay in his bassinet, Ida lovingly recorded Tom Jr.'s development into toddlerhood, and then his growth into a tall five-year-old with straight, dark brown hair and a long, thin face. Tom Sr. is entirely absent from these images, except, perhaps, for two photos in which a disembodied man's hand, with shirtsleeve and jacket just visible, reaches into the photo to steady the toddler Tom Jr. while Ida snaps the picture.

During her marriage to Tom Keevers, Ida frequently visited Elsie, Uncle Dan, and nearby cousins at the Steele sisters' family homestead on Farmington Avenue. In fair weather, Tom Jr., Alice, and other cousins ran screaming around the farmyard with a dog, laughed at pigs in their pen, and clambered onto a wagon that Uncle Dan's two horses were pulling. The sisters and their cheerful flock also went swimming and rowboating at a nearby lake. During the winter, Ida's camera caught the cousins sledding on the long, snowy hillside that stretched way down behind the barns at 435 Farmington Avenue. If Tom Sr. joined any of these visits, Ida or Frank discarded pictures containing his image.

That Ida took and preserved so many family photos at or near the Steele homestead, and that she gave her brother Myron's name to Uncle Harvey for his middle name, suggests that Ida remained close to her family following her marriage. One wonders, then, why she and Tom were living at the Hotel Washington when their son was born in April 1918. If they were short of money, why didn't they stay, at least temporarily, at the Steele family home with Elsie, Alice, sister Edith, and Uncle Dan? Aside from the expense, a hotel, even if it was a residential facility with long-term guests, seems like a terribly inconvenient place to live with a newborn. Several Steele siblings had resided with their spouses at 435 Farmington or nearby Steele homes immediately following their marriages. Did Tom Sr.'s rough demeanor make him an unwelcome guest?

On the other hand, it's possible that the anti-Catholic, anti-immigration, nativist views held by Uncle Dan and Uncle Virgil were the real problem. Daniel Steele, who a few years after his wife's 1908 death had moved in with brother Willard's family at 435 Farmington, belonged to the Patriotic Order Sons of America, an avowedly nativist fraternal organization. If the proudly Irish and Catholic Tom Keevers had gotten wind of Uncle Dan's sentiments, he would have been understandably reluctant to live under the same roof.

Ida's family ties to Aunt Amelia and Uncle Virgil were particularly close because in the 1880s, two Howe sisters, Ida's mother, Alice, and her sister, Amelia, had married two Steele brothers, Ida's father, Willard, and his brother, Virgil. By the time Ida married Tom Keevers in 1917, Aunt Amelia and Uncle Virgil were rattling around a large, mostly empty house just one door down from 435 Farmington, because their adopted daughter had long since married and left home. Couldn't Ida and Tom have lived with them, at least temporarily? Maybe not. Virgil, like his brother Daniel, espoused anti-immigrant, anti-Catholic views, if his organizational affiliations are any indication. Virgil belonged to the United Order of Mechanics, yet another nativist organization, which meant he may have held views repugnant to Tom Keevers Sr., and possibly also to Ida, the Catholic convert.

Scraps of information gleaned from city directories and the US Census augment my patchy sketch of Ida's life during this period. By the early 1920s, Ida and Tom Sr. had moved their little family out of the Hotel Washington, renting apartments first on Allen Street, a few blocks east of Farmington, and then on North Street. The 1920 census confirms that Ida continued working as an inspector at Stanley Rule after her marriage and Tom Jr.'s birth. At the time, married women with young children rarely worked outside the home unless economic circumstances demanded, suggesting, perhaps, that Tom Sr. did not earn enough to support her and Tom Jr. Who looked after Tom Jr. when Ida was at work?

A set of photos among my grandparents' collection suggests an answer to that question. Several pictures depict an unknown woman on the porch of a wood house, usually posing with little Tom. The well-maintained, intricately carved wood brackets and balustrade trimming the porch suggest the home was inhabited by its owners. In a few of the photos, Tom Jr. is bundled up in winter coat and hat and appears to be waving goodbye to the photographer as he enters the house with the woman. Ida could have been dropping her son off at Aunt Amelia's or with one of her many nearby Steele cousins before heading off to work at Stanley Rule.

Yet I still had no idea how Frank and Ida had met and fallen in love. Regardless of the misery of her marriage, how would she and Frank have crossed paths and come to know each other again? Men and women did not freely mix and mingle in those days, especially when they came from such different backgrounds. Moreover, as a married mother of a young child, who worked outside the home, Ida would have been busy taking care of her family when she wasn't at work.

City directories indicate that by 1922, Frank was working as a carpenter. Perhaps he came to know Tom Sr. through a construction job for Keevers's employer, the Connecticut Trolley Company.

"That's it!"

From my usual seat on my green living room sofa, I stared at the screen of my laptop, which was placed, as always, atop a phone book on my lap. I had found the link that most likely brought Frank and Ida together.

On the sofa beside me were photocopies with the title *Permanent School Census Card* in bold letters at the top. Most of New Britain's old school records were lost, but during one of my visits to the New Britain library's Local History Room, librarian Pat Watson had managed to locate school records for several of Frank's siblings, including Henny, Vinny, and Florence.

When Watson first showed me the off-white five-by-eight cards with yellowed edges, covered with names and dates scrawled in pen and pencil, they hadn't seemed to offer much beyond confirmation of what I already knew. Henry, Vincent, and Florence attended the Burritt School until age fourteen or so, when they left to go to work. When my dad's parents told him they attended elementary school together at the "Burritt School" in Brooklyn, the name to his ears had sounded like the "Burt" or "Birke" school.

The real Burritt School was named for New Britain native Elihu Burritt, a self-educated nineteenth-century blacksmith who became an international activist and philanthropist. The grand 1871 Burritt School building, a local landmark of the French Second Empire style with a mansard roof, also had the sad distinction of becoming, in 1961, the first major edifice to fall victim to the wrecking ball in the ill-fated East Main Street redevelopment schemes.

At home on my sofa, as I scrutinized the school record photocopies, I noticed that the school years and addresses of the Harriander children didn't match the city directory entries that tracked the itinerant family's multiple moves from one rental to another northeast of downtown. For the 1923–1924 school year, the school cards definitively listed Henry and Florence Harriander's address as 28 Oak Street, which is just off North Street, a major thoroughfare north of downtown. Not until 1925 did the directory finally catch up with the family's ever-changing residence. I had seen this lag in city directory records numerous times, especially for families like the Harrianders, who occupied the lower rungs of the social ladder.

Something began clicking in my brain. What was Ida's last address before she left New Britain? Digging in my box of papers, I confirmed that it was

162 North Street. A minute of online research confirmed my hunch: the map on my computer screen indicated that as of 1923, Frank Harriander and Ida Keevers lived only one block apart.

It all made sense. In 1923, Frank and his family moved right around the corner from Ida. They were neighbors. Walking back and forth on North Street, Frank and Ida would have run into each other. When Ida told my dad that she and Frank had known each other at the Burritt School and met again years later when he was walking along the road looking for a part that had fallen off his motorcycle, she was probably telling the truth.

Whatever the other circumstances, the trajectory of Ida's and Frank's lives hinged on the geographical fluke that in 1923, the peripatetic Harriander household happened to land less than a block from unhappy couple Ida and Tom Keevers. Simple proximity was the tiny yet key factor that precipitated all that followed. If, in 1923, the Harrianders had found a cheaper rental in another part of town, the encounter that launched Frank and Ida's relationship might never have happened. But happen it did, setting off a train of events that would unhinge and radically alter the lives of Frank, Ida, and everyone who loved them.

CHAPTER 22:
ALL HER LIFE SHE WAS UPSET ABOUT IT

CIRCA JANUARY 1924 *(Imagining the past)*

"I CAN'T BEAR IT," Ida said, her voice quavering.

Frank and Ida huddled in the bitter cold behind a stand of trees in New Britain's Walnut Hill Park. After hovering low over the horizon, the hard edge of the late-afternoon sun had dissolved, leaving the snow-covered hillside cast in a dull slate gray, interspersed with the dark shapes of tree trunks. Frank and Ida were all alone in the park, which had become their regular meeting place on these January 1924 winter afternoons, when the early darkness provided a welcome, concealing blanket.

After finishing her shift at Stanley Rule, Ida had hurried through downtown to the park, where she carefully picked her way through the snow on one of the hilly side paths that were sure to be deserted this frigid afternoon. Frank, clad in a work shirt and overalls beneath his heavy coat, had carefully set his carpentry toolbox down on a slick shelf of packed snow.

"I can't go on, I don't know what to do," Ida continued. "He said …" She shuddered. "He said if I left him, if I took Tommy…" She panted, overwhelmed by anxiety. "He said he'd find me and kill both of us."

Her shoulders heaved and she began to weep with low, gasping moans.

Frank wrapped his arms around her, holding her silently until her body stopped shaking. Removing his gloves, he kissed her forehead and wiped the tears from her cheeks, stroking the strands of wavy hair that had worked their way free from her wool hat. He had been thinking about Ida's situation, this problem without a solution, for a while. The lawyer, Morris Saxe, had spelled out their options in no uncertain terms. Keevers knew about him and Ida. If Ida sued Keevers for divorce, the louse would use everything he had against her. He'd drag her name through the mud, and she would lose Tommy in the bargain. And that was a best-case scenario, because Keevers was a violent loose cannon.

On the other hand, if he and Ida ran off together and brought Tommy, the problems would be just as bad. Keevers might not care about Ida, but he would never stop looking for his son. Tommy, who was going on six, was old enough to remember his father. As he got older, he'd start asking questions. They would never be free of Keevers Sr.

Frank saw only one way out. It was time to say it.

"I know what to do." He looked directly into Ida's eyes, which had become dark pools in the blurry pale surface of her face, its edges indistinct in the fading twilight. "We'll leave here together. You and me." His words hovered in the cold air.

Ida's sharp intake of breath cut the silence. "And Tommy?"

WHENEVER I CALLED MY FATHER, he had come to expect that I was shortly to announce yet another startling discovery about his parents'

past. Still, when I called on August 12 with the latest I had dug up at the Connecticut State Archives, my news took him aback.

"I got your mother's divorce papers from the Connecticut State Library today," I said. "Thomas Keevers divorced her, but it wasn't until 1938."

"My mother didn't get divorced until 1938? Holy crowly!"

"He divorced her on grounds of desertion," I continued. "He started the divorce process in 1937, and the divorce was finalized on February eleventh, 1938. The papers say she left in March of 1924."

While absorbing this astonishing news, my father simultaneously performed some quick mental arithmetic. He was one month shy of seven years old when the Hartford County Superior Court of the State of Connecticut granted Thomas Francis Keevers Sr. a judgment of divorce from Ida A. Keevers.

"On the thirteenth day of March, 1924, the defendant willfully deserted the plaintiff, and has continued said desertion, with total neglect of all duties of the marriage covenant on her part," I read to my father from the final divorce document. "The court finds that at the date of this complaint the defendant was gone to parts unknown."

The 1938 divorce decree granted plaintiff Thomas F. Keevers Sr. custody of nineteen-year-old Tom Jr., who by this time was likely out west with the Civilian Conservation Corps, a New Deal program that put unemployed young men to work in environmental projects.

Running off with her lover and leaving her child behind was behavior entirely alien to the proper, straitlaced woman of my father's childhood, whom I had come to know through his stories. For my dad, it threw a sharp, bewildering light on the woman whose status as Mrs. Frank E. Hanson had formed the core of her identity.

During my dad's childhood, woe unto anyone, excepting Frank and the boys, who called Ida anything but "Mrs. Hanson." Even her one friend on Clifton Avenue, the English-born Mrs. Garforth, was subject to this rule.

"Mrs. Garforth calls me Mrs. Hanson, and I call her Mrs. Garforth," Ida said. "That's proper. That's the way it should be."

One day, however, Mrs. Garforth unwittingly crossed the line.

"She came into the house and called me Ida. Ida! I could scarcely believe it. Totally unacceptable. I told her that she should please call me Mrs. Hanson in the future. *Mrs.!*" Ida laughed during these retellings of her friend's misbehavior, poking just a little fun at herself.

Among the many birdhouses Frank built was a multicompartment wren house with the face of a cuckoo clock, which he attached to the side of the garage. Ida set the hands of the cuckoo clock to eleven o'clock because, she told young Harley, "We got married at eleven o'clock in the morning." However, the date of this happy event failed to make it into the story. Ida never took off her wedding ring and always signed her letters "Ida A. Hanson (Mrs. F.E)," the F.E. standing for Frank Elmer.

During their 1953 genealogical chat, Ida told Virginia that she and Frank got married on May 26, 1923—a Saturday. I wonder if this is actually the date of the encounter that heralded the start of their love affair. Perhaps they ran into each other at eleven a.m., with that time later resurfacing as the hour of their supposed marriage. If so, yet another scrap of real history recycled by the ever-frugal Ida, who topped it off, as usual, with a dollop of pure invention.

Both my father and I had instinctively assumed that his mother and Tom Keevers Sr. had divorced before or shortly after she left New Britain. No other scenario was possible, we thought, but we were wrong. The divorce document made it abundantly clear that fourteen years elapsed between Ida's 1924 departure from New Britain and her divorce date of February 1938. Somehow, the intensely devoted wife and mother my dad had known, Mrs. Frank E. Hanson, was the same person as Ida Steele Keevers, who had married at eighteen, given birth at nineteen, engaged in an extramarital affair with Frank Harriander, and run off with him in March of 1924.

In the months and years after I discovered the date of his mother's divorce, my dad and I never tired of his new joke: "My friends always said I'm a bastard—they were right!"

A week after receiving my grandmother's divorce papers from the Connecticut State Library, I called another newly discovered Steele relative. This time it was Irene Hannibal, my dad's first cousin, who had moved from Connecticut to Southern California in the 1940s. Born in 1921, Irene was the only child of Edith, the youngest of Ida's siblings.

Although Irene's gravelly tone revealed her eighty-two years, her speech was precise and steady. Quickly I launched into a concise explanation of who I was and why I was calling. By now, a month after my first contacts with my grandparents' families, calling relatives who were unaware of my existence while I perched on the edge of my living room couch had become practically routine.

"Oh, yes, of course I know about Ida. And you're her granddaughter?" Severe osteoporosis, lupus, and other maladies had not dimmed Irene's mental faculties. She knew exactly what I was talking about immediately.

"Mama used to talk about Aunt Ida all the time," she said. "She always worried about her, that something happened to her."

Finally, I had found a Steele who knew of my grandmother and cared about her fate. Just two and a half years old when Ida left New Britain, Irene did not remember her missing aunt. However, my grandparents' photo collection includes multiple pictures of Edith and toddler Irene. Photos of Edith, with her bobbed, sleek dark hair and square, elegant jaw, show her remarkable likeness to my sister Alex as a young woman.

Realizing that Irene was eager to share her mother's stories, I soon moved on to the question that most bedeviled me.

"Do you know what happened between Ida and Tom?" I asked. "Do you think she was physically abused? What did your mother say?"

"My mother never heard anything about abuse," Irene said. "The story I heard is that she ran away because of the religion problem. It was over the boy, how he was going to be raised. The priest convinced Ida the boy would be better off with his father."

Those familiar with Roman Catholic doctrine might consider Irene's account implausible. It's hard to imagine a priest advising Ida to run away and leave her child. Within the Catholic Church, marriage is sacrosanct and divorce prohibited, with a union ending only when one of the spouses dies. An unhappy couple's only options were to live separately and remain celibate or for the church to annul the marriage, based on it having been invalid.

When Tom Keevers Sr. hired detectives to track down Ida in the late 1930s, his goal was to annul his and Ida's marriage so he could remarry in the Catholic Church. If he had succeeded, an unfortunate result would have been that, in the eyes of the church, Tom Keevers Jr. was born outside of marriage and thus illegitimate.

In the early twentieth century, many Protestants in the United States harbored a deep distrust of Catholics, with conversion to Catholicism by a woman of Ida's background rare. Although by this time the younger generation of Steeles was only a rung or so higher on the economic ladder than New Britain's Irish and Italian Catholic working class, Ida's family took pride in its deep, thoroughly Protestant, Anglo-Saxon American roots. The Steele sisters had belonged to the hereditary Daughters of Liberty society, which espoused anti-immigration views, according to newspaper accounts.

Based on the stories Edith told Irene, the marriage between Ida and Tom had plenty of problems aside from religion.

"They fought constantly, Tom and Aunt Ida," Irene said. "They fought over his drinking and gambling. He was a gambler, a horseplayer. She thought he was not going to change."

Irene's mention of Tom's drinking as a source of conflict sheds new light on a story that Ida once told Harley, when he was a boy, about having to go fetch beer when she was young, before she met Frank.

"I'd go rushing the growler," she said. "I'd be sent down to the corner tap."

In early-twentieth-century slang, "rushing the growler" meant going to the corner bar with an empty bucket, getting it filled with beer at the tap, and bringing it home for rapid consumption. Ida never said who sent her out for beer. This story, which had always struck my dad as odd, made far more sense if Ida was rushing the growler for her husband, Tom Keevers. If Tom Sr. drank heavily during his marriage to Ida, this also raises the question of how he might have abused her, emotionally or physically, when drunk.

When Ida disappeared, Edith was shocked and hurt. Ida had concealed from her younger sister both her relationship with Frank Harriander and their plans to leave.

"My mother thought that maybe Ida didn't tell her what she was doing because she wouldn't approve," Irene said.

In 1920, Edith herself had married a man, Irene's father, who turned out to be an abusive alcoholic. By the late 1920s, her husband, William Skene, had racked up multiple arrests for drunkenness, disorderly conduct, and assault, including attacks on Edith. It took years for Edith to muster up the courage to leave him and file for divorce, which she finally did in 1929.

"Ida didn't think Edith had the guts to break away," Irene speculated.

Irene portrayed the Steeles as narrow-minded, controlling, and deathly afraid of scandal. Elsie, the second-oldest Steele sister, who turned out to be the sweet-faced woman in so many of my grandmother's photos, was the main target of Irene's resentments, many of which she had inherited from her mother.

"My mother's first husband beat her so badly he nearly killed her, but Elsie and the family still wanted her to stay married to him," Irene said. "Mama was ostracized because she got a divorce."

Given the life-threatening danger Skene's violence posed to Edith, as well as the public accounts of his wrongdoings in the *New Britain Herald*, it seems unlikely that the family shunned Edith for getting a divorce. After all, Elsie herself had gotten a divorce. It seems far more likely that both Elsie and Ida would have urged Edith to divorce as quickly and quietly as possible, rather than counseling her to remain with a dangerous abuser.

Elsie's own early marital history contained scenes that must have brought tremendous stress and pain. Her first marriage, in January of 1913, occurred when she had just turned seventeen and was six or seven months pregnant with her only child, Alice. This marriage, to Henry Wesche, took place not in New Britain but in the neighboring city of Hartford. Less than three months after Alice's birth, Wesche moved out.

This ill-fated union brings to mind the archaic term "shotgun wedding," which refers to a hasty marriage, driven by an unintended pregnancy, into which one or both parties are coerced by Papa's shotgun. I wonder whether Wesche sexually assaulted Elsie—date rape, in today's terms. Regardless of the exact circumstances, in contracting this manifestly doomed marriage, Elsie would have sacrificed her own happiness in order to protect her child from the stigma of illegitimacy. She filed for divorce four years later, citing the desertion and Wesche's adultery. She married her second husband, George Bigge, in 1919, in a union that lasted until George's death in 1943.

Even if, for unknown reasons, Elsie had opposed Edith's divorce, the details of her own marriage and divorce, which would have been well known within the family, meant she possessed zero moral high ground from which to lecture her sister on the sanctity of a broken marriage. Indeed, divorce and abandonment appeared to have been the rule, rather than the exception, for six of the seven Steele siblings. Only the oldest girl, Ruby, married once and remained married to the same man until her death. Among the other six siblings, I found eight divorces or desertions.

I immediately liked Irene's feisty spirit and I enjoyed her confident willingness to speak her mind. However, I wondered, at first, how reliable a source she was about her family's past and thus, by extension, about what might have led to my grandmother's departure from New Britain. Irene also related dramatic escapades in the lives of Ida's brothers Willard Jr., Norvin, and Myron that sounded straight out of a bad soap opera—outlandish and impossible.

But to my surprise, my subsequent research confirmed that her accounts of the Steele brothers' exploits were essentially true, albeit with a few details scrambled and embellishments added. Norvin and Myron appear to have been quintessential "bad boys" during their first decades of adulthood, struggling with relationships, alcohol, and reckless driving. Myron bore the additional burden of coming home from his World War I service shell-shocked, in the parlance of the day. Now, we would say he had PTSD. However, with the passage of time, both Norvin and Myron appeared to calm down, in middle age settling into marriages that lasted until their deaths.

Although Irene seemed to have most of the facts of her family's history right, her interpretations and explanations, based on her mother's memories and resentments, were imbued with her own forceful personality and emotions.

"It was Elsie's way or the highway," Irene said. "Everything she did, that was for the right and good."

That Elsie could be bossy, controlling, and self-righteous I had no doubt, as these adjectives exactly match my father's description of his mother's less desirable personality traits. Edith, too, had been endowed with a forceful personality, and she had resented the authority Elsie wielded over the family in New Britain.

"Elsie was the boss," Irene said. "Your life wasn't yours. You had to live it the way they wanted. Aunt Elsie had her thumb on the family, but she couldn't control Ida and my mother."

Conflicts over land and money seem to have been the underlying source of Edith's anger at Elsie. Edith had been furious, Irene told me, because she felt Elsie had unfairly gotten the lion's share of the family land and had failed to compensate her siblings. The oldest sister, Ruby, also felt shortchanged by Elsie, I later learned from Ruby's son, Ray Roden.

By the mid-twentieth century, Elsie did indeed own the vast majority
of the considerably diminished Steele holdings at the family homestead
on Farmington Avenue. How the land came into her possession I cannot
say, because the details are buried in family papers and unindexed records
in the real estate room in New Britain City Hall. I suspect that the forceful
personalities of the Steele women, combined with Elsie's insistence on being
boss, escalated these conflicts into enmity in a way that more moderate
individuals, with greater skills in defusing and resolving conflict, might
have avoided.

Edith, her second husband, Thomas Barron, and Irene moved to
Southern California in the 1940s, putting three thousand miles between
themselves and the New Britain Steeles.

"The family was so oppressive, I left Connecticut," Irene said. "I just
wanted to be me."

Contrary to Irene's views, Ida's photo collection creates an impression
of closeness between her sisters and her, and especially between Elsie and
her. Of all her family members from New Britain, more photos exist of Elsie
than of anyone else, save Tom Jr., of course. Indeed, Elsie's husbands may
have been the original source of Ida's curious fluency in German. Elsie's first
husband, Henry Wesche, was born into a German immigrant household
in New Britain, while her second husband, George Bigge, emigrated from
Germany with his family when he was a year old.

George settled in at the Steele family homestead after marrying Elsie.
When Ida told her sons that she learned her German from a neighbor, she
neglected to mention that this neighbor was one or more brothers-in-law,
who were living in the same house where she herself had grown up and visited
frequently after her marriage. As always, my frugal grandmother repurposed
scraps from her true past to create a new history.

Elsie's strong personality, in addition to her belief that she always knew
what was right, echoes the stories my dad told me about his own mom. In

both Elsie's and Ida's cases, painful memories of youthful misadventures that ended very badly likely fueled their unrelenting insistence on propriety, as defined by them, later in their lives.

Further muddying my ever-evolving portrait of the complicated Steele family is the fact that Ida wasn't the only one of Willard and Alice's seven children to vanish. Willard, the oldest, also disappeared.

"He ran away because he didn't like how Elsie ran the family," was Irene's opinion.

Although Willard's motives are unknown to me, he most certainly did leave the fold and cut all ties, just like Ida. The same 1929 probate court document that pronounces Ida Keevers as having gone to parts unknown also refers to Willard Jr.'s location as "Whereabouts unknown."

A studio photo commemorating a 1907 excursion to New York City by Willard Sr., Alice, Willard Jr., and his first bride, Grace, provides a few seconds' glimpse of Steele family dynamics. Alice and Grace, attired in long dark garments and hats topped with exuberant bows and feathers, sit in front of their husbands, staring fixedly at the camera with solemn faces, as people did for formal portraits in those days. Standing behind Alice, Willard Sr., sporting a jaunty bowler hat and bow tie, also looks straight at the camera, his immense girth barely contained within his suit and overcoat.

Only Willard Jr. doesn't fit in. Standing behind Grace in the back right of the photo, he shifts his body away from his parents and wife. He also averts his face and eyes from the camera, offering a visage at a three-quarters angle that highlights the high cheekbones of his handsome oval face. Perhaps even then he was contemplating, in the far reaches of his mind, a future removal to parts unknown.

By 1910, Grace and Willard had permanently separated, although the couple never divorced. Until her untimely death in 1912, Grace lived with her parents and worked as a clerk, while Willard left town to serve in the US Navy. He resurfaced in the neighboring state of Massachusetts in 1913, where he married nineteen-year-old Madeleine Williams. The last known domicile of Willard and Madeleine was Springfield, Massachusetts, in 1919, after which Willard's trail goes cold. Edith, and several of her Steele siblings, believed that Willard moved to Germany, probably in the early 1920s—a tale which, if true, might have contributed to Ida's interest in all things German.

In the 1920 US Census, Madeleine Steele, still legally married to Willard, was living on her own in a boarding house in an unfashionable neighborhood of Boston, earning her bread as a domestic. When she died in 1923 at twenty-nine, her residence was a rooming house in New York City. She was buried, alone, in Mt. Olivet Cemetery in Queens, a bucolic cemetery with a variety of horticultural specimens. Her death certificate indicated that Willard was still her husband. As of this writing, the post-1919 odysseys of Willard Steele Jr. remain unknown to me.

During my conversation with Irene, perhaps her most surprising comment was that after Ida left, her mother Edith remained on good terms with Ida's husband, Tom Keevers Sr.

"Oh yes, yes, they were in touch," Irene said. "My mother and Uncle Tom were real good friends." Edith considered him a good father, Irene said. "She said he was good to the boy, but not a stable person."

I wonder whether Elsie, too, remained in contact with Tom Keevers Sr. after Ida left, at least for a while. Along with many photos of little Tom, among Elsie's personal papers was a sheet of paper with a writing lesson that she or Ida had given Tom Jr. Underneath words neatly penciled by an adult hand—Thomas, sugar, cat, dog, rat, pig—the boy had practiced writing each word in the awkward stick letters of a beginner.

I can see Elsie seated with young Tom at the kitchen table, leaning over him and covering his small hand with hers, helping him laboriously form these mysterious letters. "There, that's it, very good, Tommy! D-O-G spells 'dog.'"

Elsie also kept a letter that Tom Jr. wrote to Santa Claus:

DEAR SANTA I WANT A TRAIN MOVING PICTURE MACHINE BYCICLE

THOMAS KEEVERS

When Joy Medvec, the Steele family genealogist, first showed me these two epistles from the hand of young Tom Keevers, the paper now brown with age, I was dumbfounded. My surprise turned into sadness, for the boy who lost his mother, for the mom who had loved her son, and for Tom's aunt Elsie, who had loved her sister's boy, and who saved these precious scraps of paper for the rest of her life.

If Edith and maybe Elsie had stayed in touch with Tom Keevers Sr. for at least a while after Ida left, this means that hostility between the Steele and Keevers families had not always existed. The bitter enmity that Tom Jr. had voiced to daughter Cyndi might have come later. Indeed, maybe it was entirely the creation of Tom Sr.

At some point, Tom Sr. may have decided that it was to his advantage to cut all ties with the Steeles. If Tom Jr. continued to spend time with Elsie and the rest of the Steeles, he would hear happy stories about his mom. As the boy grew up and was better able to incorporate complexities into his worldview, he would have heard a version of his parents' embattled relationship far different than his father's simple, angry retorts—"The Clan of Steeles," "They'd come after us with a gun."

After his buddy Edith remarried and moved first to Hartford and then California, it would have been easy enough for Tom Sr. to rebuff overtures from Elsie and simply end all contact. Then, he could revise the past to his liking, without interference from the bossy Steele women. Stories I later heard from another Keevers family member indicate that Tom Sr. was more than capable of such behavior.

"Tom [Sr.] wouldn't tell him what happened," Irene said. "All the way around, it wasn't fair, that he didn't tell Junior."

I wish I could ask Irene to clarify exactly what she had meant. She died before I could ask her to explain.

Irene's stories added another, sometimes discordant, element to the images bobbing across the stage as I peered into the dark tunnel of the past, trying to piece together what happened between Ida and Tom. Irene's opinion that Ida fled because of conflicts with Tom over religion—a "big, bad problem with religion," she called it—echoes the ambivalence toward Catholicism that Ida Steele Keevers carried into her life as Ida Hanson. She used to drum warnings against Catholicism into Harley and his brothers.

"Stay away from Catholics," she said. "They tell you what to do. They take your money."

I wonder how much Ida's adamant opposition to Al marrying his Catholic high school love, Lena Testa, stemmed from her desire to protect Al from the deep trauma she had experienced as a result of her own youthful decision to marry a Catholic and convert.

On the other hand, Ida consistently told Harley and his brothers that she was born and raised Catholic. If she disliked Catholicism so much, why would she say this? She had gone so far as to emphasize that after her parents died, her Jewish guardian, who had been her father's lawyer, ensured that she continue to receive a Catholic upbringing. Contradictory this is, but my grandmother was nothing if not complicated. These very complexities and anxieties were, to a great extent, the drivers of my dad's persistent desire to uncover the truth of his parents' past.

"I'd bet my eyeteeth it was religion," Irene said of the conflicts that drove Ida to flee. If the Steele family disapproved of Ida's 1917 conversion to Catholicism, Edith and her sisters, in trying to explain her departure, might have found it easier to attribute it to religion rather than to issues such as abuse, drinking, or simply the unending torment of her marriage. Due to shame or pride, Ida might have withheld the true nature of her misery.

Ida's disappearance further aggravated the friction between Edith and Elsie.

"Elsie probably didn't know where Ida was, but she wanted the rest of the family to think she did," Irene said. "Mama thought Aunt Elsie knew where she was and wouldn't tell her. They didn't speak for twenty years because of this."

Saddened by loss, riven by conflict between strong-willed personalities, the Steeles seemed to struggle with the ties of blood and affection.

"She sounds like a Steele," Joy Medvec had commented when I first described my grandmother's forceful nature to her. "They have strong personalities, strong will, strength. They feel a lot, but they don't show it," she said, trying to help me understand the family, past and present.

With countless possibilities and few verifiable facts, the route Ida Steele Keevers and Frank Harriander traveled as they fell in love, departed New Britain, and reinvented themselves was a messy tangle of clues, interpretation, and supposition. One of the few certainties, sadly, is the deep pain their disappearance caused so many family members.

Ida's mysterious departure from New Britain never ceased to haunt her younger sister, Edith.

"All her life she was upset about it," Irene told me. "Mama worshipped Ida. She thought they were buddies. She was always real hurt that Ida didn't get in touch."

It was too late to relieve the anguish of Edith, who died in 1989, yet at least I could assure Irene that Ida had lived a good life and had been deeply loved by Frank, the man with whom she fled.

"He was a kind and gentle man," I said. "He was devoted to her."

"I'm so glad," she said. "My mother would be so happy. She always talked about Ida. She thought the world of her."

As it turns out, Elsie probably knew at least a little more of Ida's fate than she let on to her youngest sister. In the fall of 2003, Joy Medvec arranged a small Steele family gathering at her home in southeast Connecticut, located on a wooded hill with dirt roads overlooking the Salmon River. The party consisted of me, Marty Roden, his wife, Hilda, Joy, and her husband, Paul. Marty Roden, of course, was the first Steele descendant I had ever contacted.

A white-haired bear of a man who must have been at least six foot three, Marty seemed to duck instinctively as he navigated Joy's home, which, although tastefully decorated with artwork, crafts, and family photos, did not possess ceilings designed to accommodate big, robust men like Marty.

"Hmm, that's my barn," he said, eyebrows raised, when I showed him photos of Tom Jr. and other children playing in a barnyard.

And the sweet-faced young woman in so many of my grandmother's photos? "That's Elsie, my grandma," he said, his blue eyes meeting mine in acknowledgment.

He nodded a few more times and smiled as I showed him my grandmother's photos. Although I think Marty had believed me during our first phone conversation, seeing my photos of his barn and his family made our connection feel real to him.

"I think that's my mom's uncle Dan," he said of a photo postcard from the early 1900s, which portrayed a clean-shaven man in his fifties with a prominent nose, full lips, and a generous head of white hair. Standing erect at a three-quarters angle from the photographer, Uncle Dan sported a bow tie and open suitcoat that revealed a vest buttoned up over a stocky torso. His fingers caressed flowers that the photographer had positioned in a vase by his right hand.

A small Cape Cod house my grandparents had photographed during their 1950s road trips turned out to be the home of Myron Steele, the brother just one year older than Ida. Yet another homeless dwelling returned to its rightful place on New Britain soil, thanks to Marty.

"He was a big, strong tough guy. He could do the work of two men," Marty said of Uncle Myron. "He had a bullet lodged in his body. He wouldn't ever say how it got there."

Just as when we spoke on the phone, Marty didn't recall anything about Aunt Ida beyond that she had vanished. Fortunately for me, the memory of his wife, Hilda, was better.

"Your grandmother came back," she said firmly, dark eyes intent beneath short salt-and-pepper hair that had once been thick black waves. Hilda's parents were Assyrian, a Christian group from the Middle East, and yet another nationality in New Britain's infinitely varied immigrant tapestry. "I didn't see her, but she was there."

After Marty and Hilda married in 1959, they lived for many years in one half of the Farmington Avenue farmhouse where my grandmother and Elsie had grown up. Marty's mother, Alice, and his grandmother, Elsie, lived in the other half. This was the same house Marc and I had spotted on our first visit to New Britain. Formerly 435 Farmington, the property became 771 after a change in numbering.

"She was a nurse," Hilda continued.

Wow. This I did not expect. I had just met Hilda, and I had mentioned nothing to her or Joy of my grandmother's 1950s nursing career.

Short and stocky, with deep facial lines that testified to her love of cigarettes, Hilda spoke in direct, matter-of-fact tones. She didn't strike me as the sort of woman who would gussy up incomplete memories with fictional frills. Although Hilda could not recall how she knew my grandmother had returned to New Britain so many years ago, her comment about Ida being a nurse convinced me that Elsie had heard from Ida.

It seemed like every time I spoke with someone new, another nugget of my grandmother's story surfaced, making the patchwork quilt of her history ever more complex and confusing.

CHAPTER 23:
THAT'S WHY HE
HAD THE GUN

CIRCA JANUARY 1924 *(Imagining the past)*

"YOU WHORE," Tom Keevers Sr. snarled, punching her chest with his fist. Ida hit the kitchen wall with a hard thud.

She shrieked, hot pain and fear coursing through her body. Tom pinned her to the wall, his face a gruesome, contorted mask.

"You filthy whore. I'll kill you and that pimp of yours too, before any wife o' mine be sluttin' herself." Seizing her jaw, he bashed her head against the wall.

Terror seized Ida, through the shock and pain.

He's going to kill me, she thought. *I'm going to die. He's going to kill me.*

"Tom, please, no, please, no, no!"

He threw her to the floor.

As she huddled in the fetal position, dreading pain and annihilation, his voice continued above her, hard and rough, like a blunt knife cutting her open.

"And don't go thinking you can leave 'n' take the boy. You try that, and I'll kill you and him too. See if I don't. I'll kill you and him, too."

He kicked her, hard.

IDA'S GHOST ROAMED for years among those she left behind in Connecticut. The Keevers family, as well as the Steeles, felt her shadow in their midst.

"My father used to say to me that the day Tom Jr. got married, there was a strange woman in the back of the church that no one could identify. No one seemed to know who she was. We always wondered, could it be Thomas's mother?"

Those are the words of Marilyn Keevers Bozzuto, with whom I spoke in 2005. Her father, James Keevers, one of the brothers of Tom Keevers Sr., helped raise Tom Jr. after Ida left, with support from their parents, John and Isabel. James Keevers even delayed his own marriage because of the financial responsibility he took for the little boy.

"My father was very involved in taking care of Tom," Marilyn said. "He was very attached to him."

A friendly, well-spoken retired banker, Marilyn had been close to her late father, who quietly confided in her numerous times about the ill-fated union between Tom Keevers Sr. and Ida Steele. Together, Marilyn and her father had often speculated about the events that might have led to Ida's disappearance. Although she and her dad had not known that Ida was having an affair, Marilyn, like Cyndi, was blunt in her assessment of Tom Sr.

"That your grandmother left—I don't blame her. I don't know that there's any other woman in the world who would put up with Tom Sr.," Marilyn said. "He never showed any signs of appreciation for anything."

Tom Sr. was a callous bully, unlike his gentle, soft-spoken siblings.

"He was a tough guy, controlling and bossing. He was just like his father, and his father didn't treat his mother well," Marilyn recalled.

Despite her emphasis on Tom Sr.'s mean streak, Marilyn did not believe he had been physically violent toward Ida.

"I think he could have been abusive mentally but not physically," she said. "My guess is he probably did drink. He probably was very nasty when he drank."

Ida might have left Tom Jr. behind when she departed New Britain because she thought her husband would never stop looking for her if she took him with her, Marilyn speculated.

"Maybe he would let her go, but he would never let the kid go. If you took his son away, maybe he would have haunted them," she said. "He would have hunted them, too."

Even though adults considered him a mean bully, Tom Sr. was great with kids, Marilyn recalled, echoing the comments of Edith, my grandmother's sister. If Tom Sr. did indeed have a way with children, it helps explain how Ida could leave her child with a man who abused her. She probably also knew that Tom's family would step in to care for her son.

"My grandmother was a sweet woman. Maybe Ida thought she would take care of him," Marilyn said.

Tom Sr. had a track record of instigating conflicts and causing pain to those closest to him, she continued. In the early 1950s, he gave his siblings and their families an ultimatum: they could have a relationship with him, or they could have one with Tom Jr., but they could not have relationships with both.

"Tom Sr. made the family choose between him and Jr.," Marilyn said. "He forced their hands."

Despite the deep affection Marilyn's father felt for Tom Jr., the sad result of Tom Sr.'s ultimatum was that the Keevers family withdrew from Tom Jr.'s life. Tom Sr.'s mean streak deprived not just Tom Jr. but also Cyndi of the love and support of an extended family.

Why did Tom Sr. instigate this rift? Marilyn did not know.

Not until her father's funeral, in 1999, did Cyndi again interact with Marilyn and other members of the Keevers family. Indeed, Marilyn was the source of Cyndi's story of how the devout Catholic Tom Sr. hired private detectives in the 1930s to find Ida so he could annul their marriage.

"The only reason he ever cared after she left was when he wanted to marry in the church," Marilyn commented. "My dad said he hired a PI to look for her. They tried to find her and never did."

It is no surprise that Tom Sr.'s detectives failed. They were, after all, searching for people who no longer existed. With Ida having escaped beyond reach, Tom Sr. had to settle for a 1938 divorce courtesy of the State of Connecticut Superior Court. Despite finally getting that divorce, Tom Sr. and his intended, Stasia Urban, still did not marry, although city directories indicate they were living together as husband and wife.

Tom Sr. and Stasia finally wed in 1941, traveling twenty-two miles west of New Britain to marry in Waterbury, Connecticut, a city where neither had any obvious ties. He was fifty-one and she was twenty-nine. Presumably, they chose that unfamiliar locale so no one in New Britain would learn that they weren't already married.

"Aunt Stasia, the only thing that saved her, she so totally adored him," Marilyn commented on the pair's relationship. "She totally subjugated herself to him. That's why they got along."

Did Tom Sr. beat my grandmother? I have no direct proof. However, I do know he was mean, he had been arrested for assault, and he probably drank. Moreover, in the 1920s, assaulting one's wife was not considered a crime, and battered women almost never reported these attacks to the police.

The fact that Frank shed his unique Harriander surname for the commonplace Hanson suggests that Tom Sr. knew about Ida and him. Although we probably will never know exactly what happened, a horrific, violent scene could have occurred between Tom Sr. and Ida after he learned of her affair with Frank. It might have been followed by another between Tom Sr. and Frank, both of whom were capable, in those days, of throwing a punch. My search of newspapers and Connecticut court records yielded no evidence of a fight between the two men, which might only mean that any such confrontation was not reported to authorities.

"In those days, cheating was so uncommon—I think it's all based on them hiding from Uncle Tom," Marilyn said. "I think she would have been afraid of him. It would have taken a lot of guts on her part to even think about cheating on him. To have the guts to leave my uncle, she must have been strong."

Deep fear for Ida's safety, and his own, explains why Frank Harriander became Frank Hanson. Knowledge of a lethal threat accounts for the loaded gun Frank kept by the bed for so many years. Regardless of how Ida and Tom Sr.'s toxic union shuddered to its conclusion, everyone who knew my grandmother told me that only intense fear and abject misery could make such a devoted mother leave her child.

"Who first came up with the idea of running away and changing their names?"

When my mom asked that question, I gave the same reply I always did: "I don't know."

"I bet it was Frank," she said.

"Why do you say that?" I listened intently. My mother knew both Frank and Ida and was quite capable of putting herself in another person's place. Despite her antipathy toward Ida, I knew that my mom, for many years an archivist and editor for a local history organization, would bring the historian's scrupulous lens to my grandparents' troubled history.

"She had a child. Leaving him would have been too big a mental leap for Ida to make on her own," my mom replied. "Your grandfather was in a motorcycle gang, which was a bit disreputable at the time. He was a problem solver. He did what he had to do. So, he came up with a solution: *let's disappear.*"

When Frank and Ida first began planning their flight, were they going to bring little Tom with them? If so, they might have changed their minds when they thought about how Tom Jr.'s life would play out over the years.

Seared into the boy's mind would be the day, just a month before his sixth birthday, that he, Mama, and the red-haired man, Frank, traveled far away. "Where is Papa? When can I see him? Why did we leave?" little Tom would have asked. As the years passed, my grandparents' standard dismissal of queries about his father—"He died. They all died"—would have become increasingly unsatisfactory.

The intense bitterness Tom Jr. felt about his mother abandoning him is understandable, especially because his only source of information about her was probably bloody drops of venom from his father. Yet Tom Jr.'s was a straightforward rage compared to the confusion and anger he would have felt as a member of the Hanson household, an older child who bore no physical resemblance to his much younger siblings, as he gradually became aware of the truth of his and his mother's past.

At some point, Tom Jr. would have wanted some real answers. He would want to find his father. Ida would never be free.

"Shame on her, that she didn't love him enough to take him with her." That stark indictment, uttered multiple times by Cyndi, sums up her opinion of our grandmother. Cyndi felt that regardless of the consequences, if Ida had really loved little Tom, she would have taken the chance and brought him with her.

I understand Cyndi's point of view, but I see things differently. Although Ida's state of mind can never be known with certainty, I believe she deeply loved her first child. Her New Britain photo collection contained more images of little Tom, taken throughout his first six years, than of anyone else. She took numerous photos of him in the days before she left. Thirty years later, she sat in a car outside his house, just looking at it. Every story I have ever heard about my grandmother emphasizes her intense love for my dad and his brothers and her overwhelming drive to protect and nurture them. Why would this fundamental quality have been any different with her first son?

If Ida had brought Tom Jr. with her, she would have lived in constant fear that Tom Sr. would find her and exact his grim revenge. Even if she and Frank had successfully evaded Tom Sr., what if Tom Jr., upon reaching adulthood, simply took the train to New Britain to reunite with his father? He would learn that Mama and the kind man he had come to call Papa weren't even married. In the mid-twentieth century, this was scandalous. Tom Jr. might reject Ida entirely, Ida and Frank's new family would be destroyed, and Ida would suffer unbearable shame and humiliation.

It is probably just coincidence that at around the same time as Tom Sr.'s detectives were trying to track down his runaway wife, Ida Keevers, the Akron, Ohio, woman known as Ida Agnes Hanson sank into a depression so severe she couldn't get out of bed. Maybe she was haunted by the memory of the child she left behind. Or, if she had ever harbored hopes of going back for Tom Jr., she might have realized that it was too late. A child when she left him, he had become a young man who, she must have realized, would feel deep anger toward her.

What would have happened if Keevers's detectives had found Ida? My father thinks he knows. If Tom Sr. had appeared at the Hansons' door in Akron, Frank would have pulled out the loaded gun he kept hidden away in the bedroom.

"That's why he had the gun—because of Keevers," my dad said.

In 2004, my dad and Cyndi met for the first time when he, my stepmom, Carol, and I got together with Cyndi and her husband, Roger, at a restaurant in New Jersey. "She reminded me of my mother" was my dad's first impression, he told me later.

Roger Loomis, a private pilot with a calm, friendly demeanor, had known his father-in-law well. In his view, even if Tom Jr. had lived long enough to learn what happened to his mother, it would not have helped him make peace with her.

"I don't think he would have been able to deal with it," he said, shaking his head. "He was pretty bitter."

Cyndi, who seemed to have adopted as her own the pain felt by her adored father, nursed an implacable fury toward our grandmother that she could not, or would not, let go. Nonetheless, for several years we maintained a friendly but cautious relationship, exchanging holiday cards, emailing, speaking occasionally, and getting together a few times.

Once, I arranged a family brunch for Cyndi and Roger at my dad and Carol's house. My sister Karen came, with her husband and son. Everyone but Cyndi was warm and friendly, happy to be there. Cyndi was polite, as always, yet she could not help telegraphing her barely suppressed fury.

"She's going to have to change her attitude if she wants to have a relationship with us," Karen commented afterward.

"Why do you say that?" I asked.

"I felt as if Cyndi was consumed by rage," Karen replied. "It was her body language, the way she held herself, the stiffness. I felt no warmth, no sense that she wanted to get to know me."

Ultimately, my relationship with Cyndi fell victim to her anger. When I shared a draft of this book with her, my speculation that Tom Sr. had physically abused Ida filled her with fury.

"It would be unfair to Pa and me to allude to abuse. IF IT WAS ABUSE," Cyndi wrote in an email. "Then it begs the question of why Ida would leave her child with an abusive father!"

When we spoke a few days later, Cyndi said that her grandfather hadn't been so bad after all, and that she stayed with him and Stasia once when she was a child.

"The first time we spoke, you said he was a mean SOB," I countered. "You said quite clearly he was not a nice man."

Packrat researcher and reporter that I was, I had, of course, saved my scrawled notes from our first conversation. In the middle of the page, in big letters, I had printed, "a mean SOB."

"I don't remember saying that," Cyndi replied. "That was a hard time for me."

July 2003 was certainly a hard time for Cyndi. Her mother's dementia had become so bad that she didn't always recognize her daughter. At the same time, Cyndi's grief over the loss of her beloved dad remained a palpable, open wound.

However, because they were so raw and unfiltered, the emotions and stories that had poured out of Cyndi during our first conversation struck me as the truest representation of her feelings. She had adored her dad, disliked Stasia, and felt ambivalent, at best, about her grandfather Thomas Keevers Sr.

"I know we see things differently, but we don't have to agree on everything," I said. "We can agree to disagree, can't we?"

After a pause, Cyndi replied. "Yes," she said, her voice small and unconvinced.

The truth is, she could not. Part of the reason, I think, is that her father's death in 1999 had left Cyndi with a wound that had not healed. Missing and grieving him so, she was determined to defend him because he was not here to speak for himself. For her, this meant refusing to forgive Ida and refusing to try to understand her actions. Maybe doing so would have felt like a betrayal of her father.

I think that Cyndi's attitude was far too rigid. For her, our grandmother could only be all good or all bad, her actions righteous or sinful. I did not perceive a willingness to accept ambiguity or to understand that good people can have major flaws and flawed people redeeming qualities. I feel that it should be possible to empathize with the deep pain my grandmother caused Tom Jr. while at the same time tempering judgment with understanding. An open mind is a prerequisite for comprehending the complex past of Tom Sr.,

Ida, and Frank. I wanted to keep talking to people and searching for more clues, in the hope that something, somewhere would turn up and shed further light on what happened.

Ida's wandering ghost paid a few more visits to New Britain in 2013. At Marty Roden's funeral, in November, I was introduced to my father's first cousin Dorothy Varano, daughter of my grandmother's sister Ruby. I will forever associate Dorothy with the pronouncement "Let the dead be dead," which she had issued during our first and only phone conversation in 2003. Ten years later, Dorothy was wheelchair-bound and struggled to speak clearly.

Nonetheless, Dorothy's immediate nod of recognition and direct eye contact indicated she understood who I was. She also knew exactly what she wanted to say and wasted no time in commencing her battle to get the words out.

"Grandmother left … messages … grave." Because the words came out in a spasmodic staccato, I had to ask Dorothy to repeat them several times.

"My grandmother Ida? She left messages at the grave?" I echoed the phrase back to Dorothy, to make sure I understood.

She nodded.

"Where was the grave?"

"Fairview," Dorothy stammered with difficulty. "Fairview… Cemetery."

Dorothy's sons, on the other hand, still seemed to be sticking with their refusal to acknowledge me. When I struck up a conversation with Dorothy's granddaughter, Erin, her dad, standing just a few feet away, pointedly refused to make eye contact with me.

Today, Dorothy had chosen to defy him, just a little.

At Marty's memorial service, I also introduced myself to Ray Roden, Dorothy's brother and another of my father's first cousins. After I explained that I was his missing Aunt Ida's granddaughter, to my astonishment, Ray's head snapped up in surprise and recognition.

"She's the one that left messages at the graves," he said, his eyes rolling up as memories flowed back. "She would leave notes in the cemetery, letting them know she was OK."

When I called Ray, a retired hospital administrator, at his home a few days later, I found him likable, articulate, and more than willing to speak his mind. After first stating his complete lack of interest in his family history, he commenced a description of what his mother, Ruby, and aunt Edith had considered to be Elsie's unfair land grab.

"You wouldn't believe what I found when I went through my mother's papers," he said. "There was a letter from the lawyer to my mother—they were all supposed to get part of the property. Elsie was supposed to pay them off for their share. Elsie owed them money."

After we said goodbye, Ray called me back ten minutes later, to further expound on what he considered to be the dysfunctional Steele family dynamics.

"I always felt there was something wrong with relationships among the family, because they all [Ida and Willard] disappeared," he said. "The family was very cold. There were no family reunions, no family dinners. We lived right next door to Aunt Elsie, but we never had an invitation to her house."

Dysfunction and coldness there may have been, but I also see love and loyalty. Buried among Elsie's papers, and given to me by Marty's sons David and Mark, was a postcard, postmarked in New Britain in 1956, from Ida to Elsie.

Dear Folks & Friends,

Just a few lines to let you know I am still alive and healthy, just passing through, expect to go where it is cooler. Don't worry about me as I am able to care for myself as I am still not too old. As I told you on phone, I took training for nursing. I am a Nurse + work 40 hours per wk. I am stopping @ cemetery to leave 2 flowers on parents' grave with love. The weather is rather warm here. The city certainly has changed since I was here last. Must be going. Give my love to all as ever.

Your sister Ida

This postcard seems to answer the question of how Hilda, as a young woman, learned that my grandmother was a nurse. As newlyweds, Hilda and Marty had lived in one half of the 771 Farmington Avenue farmhouse, while Elsie and Marty's mother, Alice, lived in the other half. (During Ida's childhood, before a numbering change, the farmhouse address was 435 Farmington Avenue.) Elsie or Alice must have told her about the postcard.

Ida sent Elsie another postcard, of the Duke University Chapel, after she and Frank visited my parents in Durham, North Carolina, during one of their 1950s road trips. Her short note contains similar bland platitudes, conceals where she lives, and omits all mention of Frank and the four sons of whom she was so proud.

Whatever the conflicts and complex relationships, my grandmother had loved her family, the Steeles. Even though Ida had created a new life in which her original family could play no part, she held on to countless pictures, she kept on returning to New Britain, and she communicated with family members at least a few times. She could never quite let go of the past.

Stories about Elsie depict a tough and complicated woman, who could be kind and friendly, yet also self-righteous and domineering—much like her sister, Ida. All the evidence points to her, the sweet-faced young woman who appears over and over in Ida's photo collection, as the sister to whom Ida was closest. Why didn't Elsie share her news of Ida with her youngest sister, Edith? No doubt the answer lies in the conflicted relationship between these two strong personalities.

In the years after Ida's departure, Elsie continued to look out for her sister. Among her papers was a clipping from the *New Britain Herald* newspaper on Tom Sr.'s February 11, 1938, divorce decree from Ida. Even after Ida's death in 1960, Elsie, who likely was not notified, continued to monitor Tom Sr. Her papers also included a newspaper clipping of his 1963 obituary.

When Ida was in dire straits in 1924, driven to flee her husband and her life as she knew it, Elsie might have been her only confidante, protecting her sister with her silence and continuing to do so for the rest of her long life.

CHAPTER 24:
WILL ANYBODY EVER LOOK FOR US?

CIRCA 1909 *(Imagining the past)*

"YOU'RE IT!" Seven-year-old Ethel shrieked with laughter as she pounced on her cousin Walter's back. Even though she was four years younger, short, and a girl to boot, she could always nab him.

"Ha-ha, bet you can't catch me!" Frank taunted Walter cheerfully, running in close and sprinting away when his cousin started after him. Switching directions abruptly, Walter turned on Helen, who was caught unawares. "You're it!"

From her seat at the kitchen table by the window, Ingar Herriander looked up from the lace she was tatting to watch her grandchildren darting this way and that around the back lot. Her hearing wasn't what it used to be, but their cheerful screeches pierced the closed window and filled her with contentment.

In the fading late-afternoon light, Ingar could no longer see her lace. She removed the glass chimney from her old kerosene lamp, lit the nub of protruding wick with a match, and replaced the chimney. Turning back to her work, now bathed in a warm glow, her fingers, although gnarled by arthritis, still knotted the white cotton thread and looped the shuttle with quick, practiced ease, creating perfect snowflakes that she would sew together into a larger piece.

"*Farmor!*" Frank and Walter, their fair faces flushed pink from exercise, stood in the doorway. "*Farmor,*" Frank repeated, "är *kakorna klara?*" ("Grammy, are the cookies done?")

The kitchen was filling with the warm aroma of the ginger cookies, pepparkaka, that Ingar had put in the oven a few minutes ago.

"Frank, talk English or you not have cookie," Ingar replied, trying, unsuccessfully, to compose her features into a stern expression. This English was hard work, but she wanted her grandchildren to be Americans.

"Sorry, Grammy," Frank said, giggling. "Are the cookies done yet?"

"Few minutes." Ingar smiled at her grandsons' eager faces. "I call they ready."

The boys pulled the door shut with a bang and ran back outside. "Cookies almost done!" they yelled.

IN THE EARLY 1940S, as the Hanson boys slumbered each night in black walnut beds squeezed into their tiny bedroom, five hundred miles away in New Britain, their cousin Jean Harriander curled up beneath the round headboard of her red-rock maple bed, in the room she shared with her mother in the fourth-floor tenement apartment at 222 East Main Street. Sounds of the radio wafted down the hall from the kitchen, where Grandma Elida, Ethel, and "the boys" sat in the evening.

Lying in the darkness, Jean often puzzled over the disappearance of her mother's eldest brother, Frank. "Where is Frank right now, what is he doing this very minute?" she would say to herself. "Wasn't he afraid to go far away? With no family? Nobody to take care of him?"

Far from being dead, as Frank Hanson always claimed, the family he left behind remained very much alive and well after the annihilation of Frank Harriander. Although Frank created a new life in which his original family could have no place, their everyday dramas continued, although perhaps never quite the same as before.

Ethel, just three years younger than Frank and the oldest girl, took his disappearance the hardest.

"She talked about him a lot," Jean told me. "My mother mourned him till the day she died. She suffered for him, grieved for him always. She wanted him to come back."

Frank and Ethel, along with Al and Helen, had been the "big kids" of the family, Jean explained. Close in age, they were a unit who grew up together, played together, and were expected to care for the "little kids," as the younger five were known. "That's why those four were close."

Ethel Harriander, an outspoken and honest free spirit, lived in a time and place where such traits were a liability for young women.

"She was born out of time," Jean said of her mother many times. Ethel wore slacks, swore, and smoked back when proper young ladies didn't do such things, Jean recalled. Photos of Ethel from the early 1920s depict a young woman clad in bloomers—pants—and a simple blouse, her straight dark hair chopped off in a severe, uncompromising bob, and never a trace of makeup or feminine frills.

"She was a real hellion when she was young," another family member said.

Marrying her first husband, Edward Allen, on a lark in 1923, after the pair served as witnesses for the city hall wedding of two pals, Ethel posed for the camera the day of her impromptu nuptials. Perched on a rock with hands clasped around her knees, she grins impishly for the camera.

A year later, she gave birth to a boy who died within days. When her husband subsequently began cheating, Ethel left.

"She was just not going to put up with it," Jean said. "She was not going to stand for that life, so she walked. She packed up and went home."

When Jean was born in 1936, Ethel, thirty-four and by then divorced for several years, was going to put her up for adoption. In those days, bearing a child out of wedlock was a terrible scandal, exceeded only, perhaps, by the disgrace that ensued if the sinning mother dared keep her child. Ethel's mother, Elida, ordered her to give the baby up. Elida had already endured the disgrace of Frank running off with another man's wife, followed by Ethel's divorce. With her renegade daughter now pregnant by a beau who refused to marry her, Elida desperately wanted to avoid further public humiliation.

"My mother had already cut off a piece of my hair to keep as a remembrance, and some of my fingernails even," Jean said. "But Elof, my grandfather, came to the hospital and told Ethel that she was not to let me go. She was not to go anywhere else. He said, 'We hardly have any grandchildren. We can't afford to lose this one. Bring that baby home.'"

Despite yielding to Elof on bringing Jean home to their East Main Street apartment, Elida never stopped resenting her dark-haired little granddaughter, whose expressive brown eyes, turned up slightly at the corners, lent her face a faintly exotic cast.

"She didn't talk to me, she never touched me. There are no pictures of us together," Jean said. "She was hard as nails. She was the hardest person I ever knew."

Unlike Elida, Ethel's sisters, as well as her bachelor brothers Vinny, Cally, and Henny, embraced Jean's presence.

"The boys, they were fabulous. They more than made up for Elida," Jean said. "They supported me and my mother, financially and emotionally."

At dinner, Vinny would let Jean eat off his plate.

"Vinny would make a dish of food, making extra for me, and I'd sit on his lap and eat it with him," Jean recalled.

In the winter, the boys took Jean ice-skating, and in the summer, fishing and swimming. Every Saturday, she went to Aunt Helen's for lunch, followed by a trip downtown to the movies, and then a family dinner.

"That's the beauty of children," she told me. "They take love where they find it."

For the first five years of Jean's life, Grampa Elof tried, usually without success, to teach his lively granddaughter his version of proper manners.

"He was strict," Jean said.

When the Harrianders sat down to dinner, the rule was that only Elof could speak. Jean, an irrepressible chatterbox, was unable to comply.

"I could not shut up," she said. "And he would take his fist and pound it on the table, and he would just grunt, 'Mmmn, mmmn, mmmn.'"

Straightforward Ethel didn't believe children should learn the truth by accident or gossip. Early on, she explained to Jean that her dad wasn't around because his family had opposed his marrying Ethel because she was divorced—although I suspect that Ethel's unrepentant nonconformity was also a factor. Within a year or two of Jean's birth, all contact ceased between Ethel and Jean's father because of what Ethel referred to simply as "problems." Jean never knew her father.

Ethel spoke often about Frank, her eldest and favorite brother, who fell in love with an unhappily married woman and left New Britain with her.

"She told me point-blank he ran away with a woman and it's OK, because they must have loved each other very much to run away from their families and not get in touch with anybody," Jean said.

The woman had a little boy, Ethel also revealed to her daughter.

"For the longest time, I thought the boy went with them," Jean added. "I don't know when I figured out that he didn't go."

Sometimes, when the adults were sitting in the kitchen, discussing Frank with voices lowered, Jean picked up hints about the strife in Ida's marriage. "I'm positive she was abused. She was very badly treated. He was not good to her," Jean said. "Those were all the nuances I got from the adults' conversation, when they thought I was not listening."

When Jean grew older, Ethel told her the Harriander siblings' first reaction when Frank became involved with Ida. "We knew it was going to be trouble."

For years after Frank's departure, his brothers searched for him, traveling to towns in Connecticut and to New York City. They visited city halls to request vital records, and they looked for Frank in all the local phone books. However, just like the Hanson family quest, existing in a parallel universe, the Harrianders' search, too, was doomed. They sought a man, Frank Harriander, who no longer existed.

"Will anybody tell us what happened to him?" Ethel said often. "Will anybody ever look for us?"

Mourning and worrying about her lost brother all her life, Ethel passed on her love for Frank to her daughter, who, as a child, struggled to understand her uncle's actions.

"Does he miss us?" Jean wondered. "Why doesn't he want to be here with me like my other aunts and uncles?"

Jean had only one cousin, Helen's son, Richie, until Florence's daughters, Diane and Linda, were born in the mid-1940s.

"There were so few of us. I used to wonder, 'Does Frank have children?'" Jean told me. "It used to drive me crazy."

When sixteen-year-old Jean married Jerry Czako, this dearth of children was one of the reasons she knew she wanted a large family. She also opened her home and heart to youngsters in need. Beyond her five biological children, Jean was mother to nearly twenty foster kids. In addition, the Czakos' door was always open if their children's friends needed a place to stay when things were tough at their own homes.

A thoughtful student of human nature, Jean was always trying to figure out my grandmother's emotional journey. In the early 1920s, how did Ida go from being a mother stuck in a miserable marriage to falling in love with Frank and trusting him enough to leave New Britain with him?

"You meet somebody, and you're going to run away with them? How can you know them well enough to trust them truly?" she said. "It's not like today, when men and women always work together, and you can get together easily." Ida couldn't just jump in the car, drop Tom Jr. at the sitter's, and drive off to meet Frank, Jean explained.

Frank also might have seen that Ida was in trouble and needed help, she added. "Remember, you told me he was a protector," she said. "It might be much deeper than what we know."

The two of us lamented, often, that we didn't have all the facts and there was no one we could ask. My dad, Carol, and I had once visited Marty Roden's mother, Alice, in her nursing home, in the hope that she might be able to answer some questions. Unfortunately, as predicted by Marty, her dementia rendered her unable to comprehend us or to speak.

Jean and I created a new family tradition we called "Swedish Lasagna." Every few months I drove down from Boston for Sunday lunch at her small apartment in Newington, a town adjoining New Britain. Jean always made lasagna, my childhood favorite. Full of ricotta cheese, spicy sausage, and tomato sauce, the only Swedish thing about it was the cook.

Cousin Linda, and sometimes Diane, Florence's daughters, came by on these afternoons. After we had stuffed ourselves with lasagna, Jerry would retire to the bedroom to watch TV, leaving us to hours of family stories, the cousins' reminiscences, and poring over boxes of photos both old and new.

I brought pictures of Grampa and the rest of the Hansons, which the cousins scrutinized, discussing who resembled whom.

"Your father reminds me most of Henny," Jean said as Linda and Diane nodded in agreement. Apparently, Henny and my dad shared what my dad always liked to call "my big Swedish blockhead."

Jean's stories breathed life into family members who for so many years had existed only as disembodied names perched on the branches of Aunt Virginia's genealogical charts. She led me into worlds I had thought forever beyond my reach.

Perhaps the account I least expected to hear was of the day in May of 1899 when twenty-two-year-old Elida gave birth to her first child, Frank.

"His head was large and she couldn't get him out," Ethel told Jean. Overcome by the agony, Elida didn't understand what was happening. "She went and she hid in the closet to get away from the pain," Ethel had continued. "They had to pull her out of there to make her go to the hospital so she could have the baby."

As the babies kept coming, giving birth in a hospital became a luxury beyond the means of Elida Harriander.

"The first three she had in the hospital, the second three with a midwife, and the last three she delivered herself, on the dining room table," Ethel's story went. With the birth of each new child, the family would move once again, in search of yet another inexpensive rental big enough for their ever-growing brood.

Elida was forty-one when Florence, her ninth and final baby, arrived on January 1, 1918. With the family gathered around, Elida went into labor on the dining room table. Then, chaos: Elof bumped into the heater stove, causing the flue vent connecting the stove to the chimney to come crashing down.

"All the tin came apart and the smoke's coming in the room, and she's trying to have this baby, and there was no heat," Jean said, retelling Ethel's story. "It was awful. That bothered Frank terribly. He was very upset, and he felt bad for Elida."

Her dramatic arrival in the world behind her, Florence became everyone's, and especially Frank's, favorite.

"She was Frank's little darling—he kind of gravitated to her," Ethel told Jean. One Sunday, Diane brought a blurry photo of Frank and Florence sitting together on his Indian motorcycle. Bundled up in a winter coat and hat, Florence, a toddler of two or three, perches in front of a grinning Frank. They might have been about to embark on one of those motorcycle rides, a gentle lap around the block that Florence recalled when I met her eighty years later.

Jean believed in labeling the people in her pictures, occasionally right on the image of the individual in question.

"That's May," she said, pointing to a little girl tilting her head at the camera in a 1917 group shot covered with scribbled names. "May had red hair too, you know. Elida was pregnant with Florence when this was taken."

"That's May?" A start of recognition went through me. I had seen that wavy hair, square face, and pointed chin before. "I have a picture of her. I didn't know who it was."

In a photo from my grandparents' collection, this same little girl, sitting on a patch of grass with two older boys, had been one in the vast universe of mystery children who had so confounded me.

"We mourned hard over the loss of her," Ethel said of May's death, echoing the deep grief that Frank had expressed to my dad. May died a few weeks before the 1918 flu pandemic hit the northeastern states. The Harrianders found comfort in Baby Florence, then just eight months old.

"I don't know what I'd do if I didn't have another baby to hold," Elida said often after May's death, according to Ethel. The woman Jean knew as cold and hardhearted could be loving after all, even if Jean never experienced it herself.

One Sunday, after we had finished our lasagna and cleared off the table, Linda pulled a locket out of her bag.

"I thought you might like to see this," she said. "It was Ethel's. She gave it to me."

I held the round, gold-colored locket case in my palm. It was about an inch wide.

"You open it up like this," Linda said, gently unsnapping the tiny clasp.

Tucked into one side of the locket case was a black-and-white photo of Grampa's brother Al as a young man, wearing a round sailor hat. The photo had been snipped into a circle to fit in the locket. Facing Al from the other side of the locket case was a photo of my grandfather, back when he was Frank Harriander.

"Oh my goodness," I said. "Grampa showed me that photo when I was a kid."

An intense young Frank stared straight at the camera, with his improbably full head of wavy hair. This was the same photo Grampa had pulled out for me during that summer visit to Akron when I was twelve. I had never seen that picture since, until this Sunday visit at Jean's.

"You can take his picture out," Linda said.

After carefully removing Frank's photo from the locket, I saw Baby Florence's face peeking out at me from its hiding place underneath, her tiny toddler head engulfed by a frilled sunbonnet. My grandparents' photo collection included the same picture.

Ethel wore the locket necklace frequently when Jean was a child. She had kept her absent brothers close to her heart—Frank, who had vanished completely, and Al, who sailed the world as a trombonist in the US Navy band—together with their favorite baby sister. Turning over the photo of Grampa, I saw the name "Frank" penciled lightly on the back.

When she was a teenager, Linda wore the locket on a long black velveteen ribbon, unaware of the heartache behind the photo of Frank.

"I was a little more interested in the picture of Al, because I knew him," she said. "Every once in a long while, he would come to visit."

"If the old country was any good, we'd a stayed there."

This quote from Elida, the only direct reference Frank ever made to his mother during Harley's childhood, appears to have summed up Elida's feelings about the land of her birth. She wanted her children to be Americans. "We were forbidden to speak Swedish," Frank told young Harley. Nevertheless, based on snippets Frank dropped here and there, and his penchant for reciting the occasional Swedish nursery rhyme, Harley got the impression that Frank understood and spoke Swedish, although he was embarrassed to admit it.

When I researched Elida's family in the Skåne region of southern Sweden, I learned just how bad it had been. Her father died when she was ten and soon thereafter Elida, her mother, Carolina, and brother moved to another village. In 1891, four years after her father's death, Elida left for "Amerika" by herself. Claiming to be seventeen, she had in fact just turned fifteen. Two years later, Elida's mother, who had not remarried, gave birth to a baby boy. He, too, later immigrated to New Britain, leaving mother Carolina on her own back in Sweden. Elida commemorated her mother by giving Ethel the middle name of Carolina.

From 1870 until 1920, about a million Swedes, or a fifth of the population, left Sweden for North America—one of the highest rates of emigration from a European country.[7] Poverty, a rising population, and lack of jobs and land, along with forced military service and religious intolerance, pushed this mass tide of Swedes onto ships bound for "Amerika," as the promised land was called in emigration records. It was unusual, however, for a fifteen-year-old girl like Elida to make this voyage alone. She had only one contact, a distant cousin, in New Britain.

While New Britain may have been an improvement over Elida's impoverished girlhood in Skåne, the Harriander household of Frank's boyhood still knew deprivation. Ethel's childhood recollections always returned to an eternal, gnawing hunger.

"There was never enough food. I can't remember a time when I felt that I had enough to eat," she told Jean. "We got cocoa water and buttered bread for breakfast every day, and that was what we had to go to school on."

Living with Jean for the last eighteen years of her life, Ethel hoarded food. When Jean and Jerry built a home in 1980, Ethel's room included, at her request, a recessed alcove for a concealed refrigerator. She also crammed her drawers and cabinets with stacks of canned goods.

Ethel's memories of not getting enough to eat cast a sharper light on the question Grampa always posed to my father and his brothers after every meal: "Are you full up?"

Throughout her married life, hard-edged Elida also may have had the unenviable job of keeping Elof's drinking in check. Toward the end of his life, his alcohol abuse was imprinted in Jean's memories. If Elof had struggled with drinking while his children were growing up, this would explain why my grandfather Frank never drank and opposed all alcohol consumption.

"Frank always felt bad for Elida because her life was so difficult," Ethel used to say.

Jean, who had just escaped becoming another lost Harriander, accepted Elida's coldness toward her with grace.

"I don't fault Elida for how she was when I came into her life. She had a hard life. Mentally, emotionally, physically, she was an old and tired sixty," Jean said. "I had a great childhood, I had a really happy, loving environment. I could never say anything different."

Jean's brown eyes widened before she broke into laughter, grabbing my hand, when I told her my dad's story of how Ida was shocked to behold Elida's unsafe method for cutting bread, during a visit supposedly right after Frank and Ida's marriage. "That's how Elida used to cut bread!" Jean giggled. "She'd hold the loaf against her stomach and cut toward herself."

Grampa grew up in New Britain surrounded not only by his parents and numerous siblings but also among an extended family that included his paternal grandmother, aunts, and uncles, as well as numerous first and second cousins. Between 1880 and 1887, almost every member of the Harriander clan emigrated to New Britain from two small villages near Malmö in southern

Sweden's Skåne region. This included Frank's paternal grandparents, Per and Ingar Harriander, their eight children, Frank's bachelor great-uncle Olof Harriander, and his great-aunt Cecelia (Harriander) Selander and her husband and children. They all fled the poverty of those Swedish villages for jobs in the booming manufacturing city of New Britain.

Frank's paternal grandmother, Ingar Harriander, died a year after he left New Britain. Did Frank love his grandmother as I had loved him? I sometimes wonder. Did Ingar, like Ethel, miss and mourn Frank when he left?

In a photo studio portrait of Ingar taken around 1910, when she was in her midseventies, a full-length dress with long puffed sleeves drapes her thin frame as she poses, standing upright yet graceful, her right hand resting on the back of a chair, her left loosely holding a few flowers. She had scraped her straight dark hair back from a severe middle part into a bun, forming a smooth cap, still more brown than gray, that framed a face hollowed by time and the loss of teeth. Above a prominent nose, Ingar's brown eyes—Jean's eyes—gaze calmly at the camera.

"She was a kind woman," Ethel told Jean. "When we were kids, we always used to go over and play in her yard."

I can imagine a fall afternoon around 1909 at the house on South Main Street where Ingar, widowed in 1901, lived with Elof's brother August and his family. In the backyard, the shouts of Frank, Al, Ethel, Helen, and their cousin Walter would have pierced the brisk air. In the kitchen, as I envisioned at the start of this chapter, Ingar might have been making lace with a small shuttle, the craft known as tatting, while Swedish ginger cookies in the oven filled the kitchen with their sweet aroma.

During my years of looking for Frank Hanson and Ida Howe, my fate had been that of the hapless time traveler, forever condemned to be deposited by a malfunctioning time machine in the wrong place and time. Now, with the stories of Ethel and Jean to guide me, I nimbly leaped back and forth through the decades of a vanished century. Alighting as Elida tried to escape the pain of first-time childbirth by hiding in the closet, I then bounded forward to hover nearby as Elof thumped his fist on the dinner table before finally gliding back into the kitchen of my great-great-grandmother Ingar as the red-haired boy who would become my grandfather played outside.

CHAPTER 25:
I FEEL LIKE I'VE KNOWN YOU ALL MY LIFE

SEPTEMBER 15, 1918 *(Imagining the past)*

STRANDS OF GRAY-BLOND HAIR escaped the knot atop Elida's head and hung limply over her broad forehead as she slumped in a wooden chair near the kitchen stove. A faded cotton frock strained to encase her girth, the fabric's patterns indistinguishable after countless launderings. Elida stared straight ahead with vacant eyes, her lips clamped in a flat line that intersected at their chapped corners with deep grooves that continued up to her nostrils.

Near her mother, sixteen-year-old Ethel prepared supper, her shiny cropped dark hair pinned back as she bent over the stove. Elida took no notice of Ethel's light steps between pantry and stove, or the rapid chopping sound as her daughter sliced carrots and potatoes, which she deftly deposited into the family supper pot. Nor did Elida seem aware of the scrap of pale infant flopped loosely within her thick forearms.

Eight-month-old Florence squirmed and whimpered. Sensing her mother's apathy, the baby opened her tiny mouth wider to issue a mewling cry that began with a troubled bleat and accelerated an octave into a screeching staccato. Startled into awareness, Elida sat up and pulled the child close, slowly rocking forward and back.

"Åch *min babby*, no cry, no cry," she murmured, kissing Florence's forehead.

As the howls continued, Elida unbuttoned the top of her frock and chemise in a rapid, practiced movement, cradling her baby's downy head in the crook of her elbow. Latching onto Elida's breast, Florence sucked greedily.

"I not know what I do if I not have min babby hold. Not cry min babby girl." With her Swedish lilt, Elida whispered to her nursing child, as if chanting a somber nursery rhyme. "I not know what I do if I not have you hold, min lilla girl, min lilla girl."

Finally, with a grunt of satisfaction, Florence lolled back in her mother's arms, her blue eyes half-closed and her small stomach engorged with milk.

A rapid clomping of boots on the rickety wooden steps leading to the family's second-floor apartment signaled nineteen-year-old Frank's arrival home from his shift as a toolmaker at Rockwell Brake. Slow, heavy thuds, accompanied by wheezing grunts and groans, would have heralded the approach of Elof, father to a brood that until the day before, when five-year-old May died, had numbered nine.

With a squawk, the wooden door opened, and Frank's solid frame appeared.

"Hey, Ma, hi, Ethel." He hung his cap on a nail by the door, running one hand through his flattened gold-red hair.

Still stirring the stew, Ethel turned anxious brown eyes toward her eldest brother. Frank took off his jacket and moved quickly toward the stove, passing Elida, who had returned to her stupor, the satiated child seemingly forgotten on her lap.

"Any change?" Frank spoke to Ethel in an undertone.

"No. When I got home this afternoon she's sitting there lookin' at nothin', just like when I left this morning. When she's nursing the baby, she'll whisper those same words to her over and over, then she's like this again." Brother and sister heaved deep sighs, tears rolling silently down their cheeks.

"Only other time she's said a word was right before I left for work today. Ma was crying and moaning at Pa that it's his fault because, uh, because…" Ethel's quavering voice broke into sobs. "Because he didn't send for the doctor."

"Ma. Hey, Ma." Frank knelt in front of Elida, stroking the rough, red hands that loosely clasped Baby Florence. "Ma, it's me."

Elida looked dully into the sober blue-gray eyes of her firstborn and then turned away.

"Hi there, hi, my little girl."

Frank scooped Florence into his arms as he stood up, crooning softly and nuzzling the infant's head with his wet cheek. He swayed back and forth, holding the squirming baby close against the thick gray cotton work shirt that was buttoned up to his neck.

"How's Baby Florence tonight? How's my little girl?"

Florence grinned up at her big brother, her soft, plump legs vigorously churning the air. As he gently bounced the gurgling infant, Frank's pinched features slowly relaxed. Warm, salty tears dropped silently from his chin onto warm, wriggling Baby Florence.

"YEP, HE'S A HARRIANDER all right!"

Those were the first words of Jerry Czako, Jean's husband, upon meeting my dad at our inaugural Hanson and Harriander reunion in Connecticut in October of 2003. Marc and I came down from Boston, my dad and Carol drove up from Philadelphia, and a roomful of smiling Harriander cousins warmly greeted us. Although I had invited the entire extended Hanson family, a combination of busy schedules, the disinterest of some, and for a few, deep ambivalence, limited the Hanson turnout.

"I truly appreciate your inviting me, but I just can't do it," Aunt Virginia had said in declining my invitation. "I hope you'll understand."

At the time, I didn't. How could the grand dame of the Hanson family project, the one who started it all almost a half century ago, turn down the chance to meet Frank's real family and to see where he and Ida grew up?

I think I get it now. Learning the truth of Ida's and Frank's pasts shocked and distressed Virginia. When my dad called with the news, at first she refused to accept it. Most of all, like everyone who knew my grandmother, Aunt Virginia simply could not wrap her head around the idea that Ida abandoned her first son.

"I just cannot conceive that Mater would leave her child," she told me.

Although she subsequently acknowledged the truth of my findings, she never wanted to know the details. It hurt that Mater and Pater, whom she had loved so truly, had lied to her. Moreover, Virginia was reeling from the loss, three years earlier, of her beloved Harv, my father's twin, who had been at the center of her life. I suspect she couldn't bear to witness the disintegration of still more of her known universe.

The only feeling my dad admitted to prior to our first reunion was nervousness. Once there, he deeply appreciated his new family's sincere welcome.

"I never had any relatives. Now I have so many I can't keep track of them all," he said, then and many times to come. "And they're really nice."

His Christmas card that year was a group photograph of him with his new cousins, taken at that first reunion dinner in October of 2003.

Jean and I couldn't stop hugging as we all bade each other farewell in the parking lot at the close of that dinner.

"They can't get enough of each other." Jerry laughed.

For my birthday in February of 2004, Jean threw a little party at one of our Swedish Lasagna cousin get-togethers. Looking at the smiling faces of Jerry, Linda, and Diane as I blew out the candles of my chocolate cake, happiness and gratitude washed over me. What a precious and unexpected gift it was, to be taken in and accepted as one of the family.

As my relationships with my new cousins developed over time, Marc was with me every step of the way, accompanying me to reunions, dinners, and other get-togethers.

"He did what?" Jean chortled when I told her how Marc had spent a summer Saturday afternoon traipsing through Fairview Cemetery with me when I was hot on the trail of the Steeles in July 2003. "You hold on to him. He's a keeper!"

After I moved in with Marc in 2007, Jean observed, "You two are just right for each other. You're very high energy, and you get excited. Marc is calm. You balance each other out."

Once, at a reunion at Linda's house, a bunch of us were sitting around the dining room table, talking and joking. Between lamentations about the misguided redevelopment that had decimated downtown New Britain and lots of laughs over stories I cannot now recall, Jennifer, Linda's daughter, unexpectedly said, "Florence, my grandmother, told me she used to go down to visit an aunt who lived in Brooklyn, off Flatbush Avenue."

What? Flatbush Avenue in Brooklyn? The place where Grampa always claimed he grew up? Jen didn't know the aunt's name or other details.

"Oh, yes, yes," Jean exclaimed when I later asked about this mysterious Flatbush aunt. "I thought I told you. They had an aunt down in New York City who lived near Flatbush. I want to say her name was Sophie. I think she was related to Grandma Elida, because she had a different last name. They always went down in the summer to visit and they always got new clothes."

Beginning with Jen's chance recollection, the Hanson terra firma shifted yet again. This time, Dean Street, the site of so many pilgrimages, added its own twist to the ever-evolving tale. Did Frank tell his sons he grew up on Dean near Flatbush because that's where his aunt lived? Or maybe he and Ida themselves lived at that address in the summer of 1924, after leaving New Britain, choosing the neighborhood because of its familiarity and the proximity of Frank's aunt.

From my first meeting with Jean, I loved her warmth, her energy, and the heartfelt joy with which she welcomed me. Although our connection began with a shared, deep emotional involvement in our families' pasts, we built a relationship based on the here and now. With Swedish Lasagna Sundays, Hanson-Harriander reunions, birthday get-togethers, and phone calls just to catch up, Jean became a beloved cousin close to my heart. At the wedding of her son John, in 2005, my dad, my stepmom, Carol, Marc, and I were there, along with the rest of the family.

"Oh, I so much wish my mother could be here for this," Jean said often. "She would have loved you."

Although Ethel had her grandmother Ingar's dark hair and eyes while I am fair, I have Ethel's mouth and, in one of those genetic quirks, some of her mannerisms.

"I can't get over how much you remind me of Ethel," Jean and other family members said many times. "When you speak, your mouth moves like hers did, and your mannerisms are a lot like hers," Jean explained. "It's really strange."

For me, looking at photos of Grampa's sister Helen in her youth connects past and present most vividly. I see an earlier incarnation of my physical self in those dusty eighty-year-old images of young Helen, with her long face and chin, generous forehead, and pale skin.

However, I seem to pop up all over Harriander territory.

"You look a lot like Diane did when she was young," Kathy, Jean's daughter, commented once.

Although Diane and I both have blue-gray eyes and thin faces, I didn't see the resemblance until, one Sunday, Jean pulled out a photo from a 1969 summer pool party. Twenty-six-year-old Diane, her long wet hair slicked back from a wide forehead, cradles baby Jennifer Corazzo, her smiling face at a three-quarter profile to the camera. With minor tweaks, that photo could have been me at twenty-six.

When I was at Wesleyan University in Middletown, Connecticut, New Britain was just eleven miles away. Frank Harriander likely passed through Middletown during rides with his motorcycle gang around the rolling countryside of central Connecticut, because Middletown possesses one of the few bridges crossing the Connecticut River in that part of the state.

"How are you liking it up there with those Yankees?" he wrote me once.

Beyond that, Frank Hanson never dropped the slightest hint that he had more than a passing familiarity with Connecticut.

"I hope I see Frank again before I die," became Ethel's refrain in her final years.

What a difference it would have made for Ethel, and for me during those difficult college years, if only I could have bridged the chasm between us. A short bus ride down Route 9 and I could have been in New Britain, if only I had known. But during my time in Connecticut, those eleven miles might as well have been eleven thousand, so complete was the barrier between our worlds.

By the time David and Eliza Steele's headstone yielded its secret in 2003, it was too late for Ethel. When she died in 1981 at seventy-eight, her dream of reuniting with Frank remained unfulfilled. She never learned what became of her brother, and she never knew how hard Frank's family was looking for her.

I don't believe the dead look down on us from some faraway heaven. Yet I do feel that in finding Grampa's lost family and building relationships with them in the present, I am helping to mend a painfully torn family cosmos.

When I first met my new Steele and Harriander families, I was surprised to learn that many of them had not gone to college. So central is higher education to the Hanson identity that it simply hadn't occurred to me that this might not be true among the descendants of the families they left behind.

"I think Ida was the one behind the education," Jean said to me, seemingly out of the blue, during a phone conversation. "I don't see that push for it on our side."

With Ethel working ten hours a day, six days a week during Jean's childhood, as people did then, college had seemed beyond reach.

"It was impossible. It was just something you couldn't do," she told me. "About a third of the kids I grew up with didn't graduate from high school."

When I was growing up, the Hanson story I knew, featuring the carpenter and his ultra-educated sons, had seemed inevitable, its trajectory preordained. I don't see it that way now. Without Ida's insistent pushing, a college degree might easily have slipped beyond the reach of my father, who got mediocre grades in high school before finally buckling down to his studies at the University of Akron. The same was true of Uncle Al, whose boundless energy and curiosity did not prevent him from flunking out of the U a few times before finally getting his undergraduate degree. Akron's labor unions also played a key role in creating the University of Akron as a municipal school, with low tuition that made college possible for working-class kids.

"Educated," my father instantly responded upon being asked who the Hansons were. "Working-class. Blue-collar," he said firmly in the next breath, when asked where he came from.

Watching his parents' quiet fight to nurture him and his three brothers during the Great Depression formed my father's worldview. He saw the immensely positive impact of President Franklin D. Roosevelt's public works infrastructure projects, which during the 1930s gave meaningful work to his unemployed carpenter father and millions like him. Grampa and Dad loved

Roosevelt because he respected the dignity of working people and provided jobs to those who so badly needed them.

"Being educated is a way of thinking. It's a class in itself. It's not about money," my father had said. I took those words to heart.

For me, being educated, above all, means reading. Books open doors, transport one to unknown worlds, and bring new ideas into the palm of one's hand. Being educated also involves the ability to analyze information and think critically, and a willingness to question assumptions, as well as to continually seek out new information. Education opens up the world, not to mention professional opportunities, which, in turn, lead to money and a comfortable life. For the current generations of Hansons, education is the closest thing most of us have to religion, with everyone graduating from college and most of us going on to graduate school.

Many of our Harriander and Steele relatives back in Connecticut took a different path. Unlike Grampa, who refused to teach his sons carpentry and discouraged them from entering the building trades, Jean's husband, Jerry, believed that having a trade was critical for economic survival. It was his duty to pass on his trade of auto body work to his sons.

"My husband truly believed that he had to teach his sons body work," Jean told me. Jerry was distraught when one son elected to become an auto mechanic instead. "My husband was so upset," Jean recalled. "I told him, 'Mechanics can make money, too.'"

At first, this difference made me uncomfortable because I realized that many members of my new family held political, social, and religious views quite different than my own. My initial instinctive reaction was to quash my discomfort and focus on all we had in common. Since they were genuinely nice people, this was easy enough. Nonetheless, a few awkward conversations cropped up.

"Do you *believe* in God?" Jean's daughter Kathy, brow furrowed with concern, asked the question directly while we were out to lunch together.

I was telling Kathy, whose life revolves around her Bible-focused Christian faith, how Marc and I were going to incorporate the Jewish traditions of his background into the nonreligious ceremony we were planning for our upcoming wedding.

"I don't know," I replied after a pause, softening the truth in an attempt to lessen her discomfort, and by extension, mine. I should have just come out and said "No," since Kathy understood what my answer meant anyway. "I respect other people's beliefs, and I also expect mine to be respected," I told her. Kathy and her family do respect my views.

Although I continued to studiously avoid all political discussions, I concluded that it was better to be honest about my creed, which I characterize as secular humanism. Kathy told me she prays that I will come to believe as she does, yet we were able to agree to disagree.

We joke about our differences now.

"Sometimes you just get lucky," I posted on social media once, commenting on Marc's and my first wedding anniversary and our ten years as a couple.

"Sometimes you just get blessed," Kathy replied, the accompanying smiley face acknowledging our dissimilar views.

Despite our separate pasts and experiences, so completely did Jean embrace me that, for her, our histories merged and became one. At the end of one of our early Swedish Lasagna Sundays, Jean stood at the kitchen sink, her small hands a whirl of motion as she put away utensils and washed pans. Linda and Diane had already left, and I was gathering my things, preparing for the long drive back to Boston.

"You know, I feel like I've known you all my life." Hands still for a moment, Jean turned toward me. "Do you feel the same way?"

I hesitated.

"It's a yes-or-no question. Do you?"

The honest answer was no, but I didn't want to make Jean feel bad by admitting it. I can't recall the words I ended up stringing together. Speaking with Marc later that night, I fretted about whether I had hurt Jean's feelings or harmed our relationship.

"I don't think you have anything to worry about," Marc replied. "She's in it for the long haul. She'll do what it takes to make it work."

I never came to feel I had known Jean all my life, and I realized it didn't matter. Neither did the fact that we lived in very different worlds.

"Oh, I wish I could go with you!"

That's what Jean, who had never been in an airplane or traveled farther from Connecticut than Niagara Falls, always said when I told her about Marc's and my latest trip to Europe. Jean never asked me about my religious beliefs, even though, like Kathy, she was a committed Christian who worshipped at an evangelical church. I think she had figured out the answer and chose not to bring it up.

Although I didn't feel I had known Jean all my life, I do wish she could have entered it earlier. During my high school years, and then especially when I was at Wesleyan, Jean's warm, accepting love, combined with her insights and directness, would have made those hard times a little easier.

Marc and I got married in a restaurant near my dad's house in November of 2010, in a small ceremony with just family present. We had hoped Jean could make it, even though she was severely ill. After a diagnosis of late-stage liver cancer a few months earlier, her health had failed rapidly.

"If I have to drive her down there in a stretcher, I'll do it," Kathy said.

Jean didn't live long enough. The last time I saw her was in September of 2010, when Marc and I visited her at a nursing facility outside Hartford.

"It's kind of ironic, isn't it? Seven years ago you found Florence in the nursing home, and now here you are in the same situation with me," Jean said, looking up at me from her pillow as I sat at her bedside, touching her arm and trying not to cry. An enthusiastic contributor of material for this book, Jean had read a draft of the chapter in which I found Florence at the Brittany Farms nursing home.

Jean's generous spirit and insights into human nature made it easy to love her. She helped me understand and appreciate how the trajectory of the Harrianders' and Hansons' paths had diverged during our eighty years of separation. She was a beloved cousin, friend, and guide as I navigated the new landscape of my grandparents' past and my transformed present. How lucky I was to have her in my life.

Anne and Harley, December 1999.

Karen, Carol, Alex, Anne (standing, left to
right), Harley seated, December 2003.

Anne and Harley at Frank and Ida's grave in Akron, 2008.

Anne and Marc, wedding day, 2010.

Joyce and Anne, 2016.

CHAPTER 26:

AN IRISH DIVORCE

MARCH 12, 1924 *(Imagining the past)*

"LOOK AT THE CAMERA, SWEETHEART," Ida said. Tom Jr., who was turning six in a month, stood in his winter coat and hat on the wooden porch, blinking in the bright sun that reflected off piles of snow deposited by last night's storm. Ida peered through the viewfinder and pressed the shutter. "That's good, Tommy. Let's take a few more."

Accustomed to posing for Mama's many photos, Tom Jr. cheerfully trotted about the porch, oblivious to the tears that were rolling silently down his mother's cheeks. He plopped backside-first into a wooden barrel, his boot-clad feet sticking out.

"Mama, look at me!" Forcing a smile, Ida snapped another picture.

"These are real good," she said. Walking over to the boy, she pulled him out of the barrel and kissed his cheek while stroking those impossibly narrow, defenseless shoulders. This was the last shot in the roll.

The photo that would haunt her, Ida thought, was the one she took from outside the house, at the window, while Junior stood at the window inside, looking out at her. The sweet expression in those brown eyes, the innocence of his face, framed by the window, was a memory she wanted to keep forever.

She wiped her wet cheeks with her sleeve and took several big gulps of the cold, fresh air. "You're always my good boy," she said, taking Tommy's small hand and leading him inside. She pulled off his coat and hat and hung them on a nail.

"Mama has some things to do now." She retrieved a toy truck from a box and handed it to him. "Here, sweetie, you can play with your truck."

Ida entered the cramped bedroom she shared with Tom Sr., making sure to keep Junior, who was running his truck up and down the hallway, within view. Although this North Street rental was peaceful now, as it always was when her husband was out, it didn't feel like home any more than the other rooms and houses they had inhabited during the almost seven long years of their marriage.

Her photo collection and warm weather wardrobe were already in Frank's valise, having been smuggled out of the house bit by bit. When she left tomorrow, she'd wear her big overcoat with the bell sleeves, with extra layers of clothing beneath.

Ida opened her jewelry box and carefully picked out a pair of earrings that had a pearl within a turquoise horseshoe. This was the only keepsake from poor Mama that she was bringing. The horseshoe symbolized the fine stallions that Mama's father, Ida's English grandfather, Frederick Howe, had raised and sold before he went back to Sheffield, before Ida was born.

She couldn't wear the earrings because they required pierced ears, which might be all right for Italians, but not for Steeles. Mama had boldly pierced hers at sixteen, when she was still a Howe, right before she married Papa. After wrapping the earrings and a few other pieces of jewelry in a handkerchief, Ida tucked the bundle into a small drawstring pouch, which she placed in her purse, along with the camera.

Ida pulled a folded piece of paper from her purse to check, yet again, the schedule she and Frank had planned so carefully. 7:34 NB WB, 11:44

WB NH NY, she had written in her neat cursive. First thing tomorrow morning, she'd take Tommy to Cousin Minnie's, and then she'd catch the 7:34 a.m. train for Waterbury, a nearby town that also happened to be a railroad hub. She was bound to run into someone she knew, so she'd say she was taking her husband's broken dollar watch to the Waterbury Clock Company for repairs.

After performing her errand for all the world to see, Ida then would return to the train station. There, instead of boarding the train back to New Britain, she would catch the 11:44 to New Haven and New York City. Ready or not, a new life was about to begin.

A quick glance down the narrow hallway showed that Tommy was still absorbed in his truck. Ida's stomach churned. She felt as if she was going to vomit. Until she looked into Frank's eyes again, until they were on that train together, headed for New York, she wasn't going to be able to breathe.

THE DAY BEFORE SHE LEFT New Britain, Ida snapped the last photos she would ever take of Tom Jr., as he played on the porch of their North Street rental in the late winter sun. Bringing the undeveloped film with her when she left the next day, Ida would later write the date March 12 '24 on the back of one of the prints.

In that same roll of film, Tom Jr. stands inside a house, looking out at Ida through a closed window, his dark, glossy hair and straight bangs forming a smooth cap atop his head. Ida photographed him from outside the house, looking in as her son gazes through the glass at his mother. Above a blouse with a dark floppy collar laced up to the neck, Tom Jr.'s expression is serene, his luminous eyes resting on his mother in an expression of perfect trust.

"Nice photo, artsy," I had mused when I first viewed this image in 2002. At the time, I had no way to know of the pain and heartache behind this picture.

More than eighty years later, that photo of a calm-faced boy gazing out at his mother through the glass panes of a closed window foreshadows the devastating loss this innocent child is about to experience. It also offers an eerie preview to a bright September day, thirty-one years in the future, when Ida will drive by the house of this child, now a grown man, and photograph it through a closed car window.

In June of 2019 I was seated at a big, brown wood table at the Connecticut State Library, reviewing the complete case files of my grandmother's siblings' divorces. What exactly was I looking for? I wasn't sure. Maybe some detail in these documents would provide insight into the lives of Ida's siblings and, by extension, into hers.

In a 1917 pleading in Elsie's divorce, I saw that her attorney was M. D. Saxe. His firm also represented Ida's youngest sister, Edith, in her 1929 divorce from William Skene.

Something clicked in my brain. I was pretty sure "Saxe" was a Jewish surname, whose variants include Sacks and Sachs. It derives from "Isaac," who was one of the patriarchs of Israel in the Bible's Old Testament.

Although laptops were forbidden in the reading area, a quick Google search on my smartphone confirmed my hunch: New Britain attorney Morris D. Saxe had belonged to a New Britain synagogue and was active in Jewish philanthropic causes during the early decades of the twentieth century. After practicing law for about twenty years, he became a judge.

Finally. At long last, the source of Ida's mythological Jewish guardian had surfaced. In her fictional account, this lawyer looked after Ida following her parents' deaths and ensured she continued to have a Catholic upbringing. Supposedly, when Ida turned twenty-one, she and Frank went to his office, and he gave them his blessing to marry.

The reality was a lot more complicated.

When Elsie was getting divorced in 1917 and 1918, she probably told Ida a great deal about her lawyer, Morris D. Saxe. During these years, Saxe practiced law in the heart of New Britain's busy, bustling downtown, in an office near the train station, then a splendid edifice with an adjoining shopping arcade. He was too young to have been an old friend of Willard Steele Sr., although as a young lawyer just starting his practice, he might have exchanged pleasantries with Mr. Steele when the big man drove his team into town to conduct his business.

After Ida and Frank fell in love, Elsie might have recommended that they seek the advice of Morris Saxe. Perhaps the pair even visited Saxe's office together. The counsel they sought would have been whether and how Ida could divorce her husband, Thomas F. Keevers Sr.

Following some initial questions about Ida's marriage and why she wanted a divorce, Saxe likely would have inquired as to whether her husband was willing to cooperate. During the early 1920s, divorce was an adversarial procedure in Connecticut and most US states. The plaintiff—the person seeking the divorce—had to prove that the defendant was at fault, meeting a limited set of criteria such as desertion or adultery. During this era, sometimes an unhappy wife claimed desertion, and her equally miserable husband admitted to the claim, regardless of actual events, just so the divorce could proceed.

Most critically, in light of Ida's circumstances, the prevailing "clean hands doctrine" required that the plaintiff be free of fault. Saxe would have explained to Ida and Frank the painful fact that, because Ida was engaged in an extramarital affair with Frank, she would not be free of fault in the eyes of the law.

If Ida had mentioned divorce to Tom Sr., he most certainly would have refused to cooperate. He was an observant Catholic whose religion forbade divorce. He might have been prepared to live with Ida unhappily ever after.

Tom Sr. could have threatened to expose Ida's adultery to the world if she dared sue for divorce. Reporters at the *New Britain Herald* and neighboring

BURIED SECRETS

publications would have diligently reported the details of Ida's extramarital affair, because scandal sold newspapers, and the more salacious, the better. As the party at fault, not only could Ida have lost custody of Tom Jr., but she would have been subject to agonizing disgrace and public censure.

After spelling out her limited legal remedies and their consequences, Saxe, feeling pity for Ida and sympathy for the young couple, might have spoken informally about other available options—one of which was to simply leave New Britain and start a new life far away. To Ida, at the time, this might have felt like permission to pursue a path she and Frank were already considering.

When she later wove scraps of her real history into the fable of the Jewish lawyer guardian, perhaps Ida created this role for Saxe because, at an emotional level, she felt that he had in fact acted as her guardian when he provided his informal advice on a way out of her dangerous quagmire. From there, it is a short hop to the make-believe scene in her Jewish guardian's office, where this kind gentleman gave Ida his blessing to marry Frank when she turned twen-ty-one. Her lies always included a healthy dose of repurposed truth.

In 1930, thirty-two-year-old Myron Steele, one of my grandmother's brothers, and his then-wife, Bernice, engaged in a dramatic, and very public, marital dispute that resulted in their troubles being splashed across the front pages of the *New Britain Herald* for a week. The bullet lodged in his body that Myron later refused to discuss was in reality a self-inflicted wound, occurring when his wife threatened to leave him.

In one of the newspaper stories, twenty-year-old Bernice Steele, by all news accounts a lively and outgoing young woman, minced no words in stating her opinion of her husband's family.

"The whole Steele family is queer," Bernice said. "Myron has four sisters and two brothers, and one of the sisters, Ida, while traveling from this city to Waterbury six or seven years ago, on a train, disappeared and has never been seen or heard of since. A brother, Willard, walked away from his home seven years ago, and nobody has seen or heard of him since. He [Myron] has three sisters in this city, but they had nothing to do with him, nor he with them. He could not get along with his own family, and they did not want him to visit them."[8]

Ida, while traveling from this city to Waterbury six or seven years ago, on a train, disappeared and has never been seen or heard of since.

Chatty Bernice Steele, in her 1930 comments to a *New Britain Herald* reporter, provided the only near-contemporaneous account of Ida's departure from New Britain that I have discovered to date. A 1923 train timetable indicates that twelve trains a day ran from New Britain to nearby Waterbury, the latter a hub from which one could transfer to trains traveling to New York City, elsewhere in New England, and to destinations across the United States.

As for the fairness or accuracy of Bernice's assessment of Steele family dynamics, I cannot say. Myron and Elsie threatened legal action against Bernice for her statements, although they don't appear to have pursued the matter. Following her 1936 divorce from Myron, Bernice went on to marry and divorce at least two more times.

Unsurprisingly, given the Catholic Church's prohibition of divorce, in the early 1920s, divorce was rare among observant Catholics in the United States. In predominantly Catholic Ireland, not only were divorce rates extremely low, but the constitution of Ireland (Eire) actually banned divorce in 1937, the year Ireland became a country, following the secession of the former Irish Free State from the United Kingdom. Divorce remained illegal in Ireland until a 1995 referendum brought about final removal of the ban in 1996.

One occasionally hears stories of married Catholic couples of the early and mid-twentieth century who lived apart for decades without divorcing, while one of them, usually the man, engaged in relationships with other partners. In Ida's case, if she had set up house with Frank in New Britain while remaining married to Tom Keevers, she would have lost custody of Tom Jr. and endured public excoriation, because the robust double standard of the time would have labeled her a shameless sinner. Moreover, everything I know about my grandfather tells me that he wanted to have children and live with Ida as if married. This was impossible in the New Britain of 1924.

Any way you look at it, if Ida played by the rules, she was trapped. By circumstances, by the time she lived in, and by her gender.

In the nineteenth and early twentieth centuries, a phenomenon known colloquially as the "Irish divorce" sometimes occurred among unhappily married Irish Catholics on both sides of the Atlantic. The husband simply disappeared and began a new life in parts unknown, leaving behind his wife, children, and questions forever unanswered. In Ireland, he might depart for England or America, while in the United States, he often headed west.

In New Britain, Connecticut, Ida Steele Keevers, a Yankee convert to Catholicism, boarded a train bound for Waterbury. Turning the gender tables, she went and got herself an Irish divorce.

CHAPTER 27:
DEEPLY BURIED

When I am in bed there is so many things I would like to write
and tell you, then next morning I can't remember them. Cracking
up gal, or getting old... I won't say that I don't miss you because I
do, it is just as tho someone was kicking me in the stomach.

~ Ida Hanson, letter to Harley, September 1952

"SO, WHAT DO YOU MAKE of all this? How do you feel about what your parents did?"

In the years after I first discovered his parents' true identities, I asked my father versions of this question multiple times. He, in turn, provided a variety of answers.

"Growing up, I never had any relatives. Now, I have loads of them."

That was his reply in late 2003, a time we came to call the "year of the discoveries." He made similar comments many times thereafter. "I never had any relatives before. Now, I have so many cousins that I can't keep track of them."

Unaware of their existence until he was seventy-two, my father did indeed have a large extended family, many of whom he met personally in the years after I cracked the case. Not only did he and Carol visit our Harriander and Steele cousins in Connecticut multiple times, but the two of them also traveled with me to Sweden to reunite with descendants of the few Harrianders who had remained in the old country.

"My parents were the world's best secret keepers. They should have been spies or something—maybe they were," my dad said numerous times, regarding his parents' ability to maintain their subterfuge. "I'm just surprised they did as well as they did with their stories, for as long as they did. It was essentially seamless, weather-tight seamless. And you know, my mother was a spinner of tales if there ever was one, more than my father."

When Aunt Virginia sat her in-laws down for that genealogical interview in 1953, I can imagine Ida seated at the dining room table, outwardly unruffled, yet her pulse racing and heart pounding. Did she whip up her creative tale of rearranged facts on the fly? Or, suspecting that her gentle, beloved Virginia would at some point ask family history questions that required answers, did Ida concoct her fabulous family tree in advance? Its limbs, richly laden with their patchwork cornucopia of fictitious fruit, possessed the outward trappings of truth.

Frank would have had an easier time with the interview than Ida. During my father's childhood, for the most part, Frank chose to remain silent if he could not speak honestly. In the information he gave Virginia, he either hewed close to the truth or omitted people altogether. He simply changed all the Harriander surnames to Hanson, and, with the exception of his paternal grandparents, an aunt, and an uncle, he entirely failed to mention his extended family in New Britain.

For the first few years after my discoveries, my dad claimed that learning his parents' secret had not significantly affected him emotionally. The most he would admit to was confusion.

"How did learning the truth about your parents affect you? Did it change you in any way?" I asked.

"No, I don't think so," he said.

"How do you feel about it?"

"Nonplussed," he replied. "It's very hard to understand."

Over time, however, as I continued to ask about his reactions and feelings, my father began admitting to more complex emotions.

"It's difficult. I'm bewildered. I still don't know what to think about it," he said later.

"I thought you said before that it hadn't really affected you. Now it sounds like you're saying it did."

"Well, what if you found out I wasn't who I said I was? How would you like to know that your father isn't named Harley and isn't named Hanson? How would you like that? Your parents don't lie to you, right? Mine did. They lied about everything."

That's about the closest my dad ever came to directly expressing his distress to me. One day, however, I accidentally unearthed a far deeper layer of emotions.

It all started during a visit to Philadelphia, when, as usual, I stayed first with my mom and then with my dad and Carol. For months, I had been prodding my dad to let me search his private study, the "junk room," for the collection of bread recipes that Grampa had recorded on the back of old timecards in the 1970s. Although my dad had stated several times that he wanted me to have these recipes, the obstacle, as always, was his dread of confronting the memorabilia of his past.

"I don't feel like getting them," he groaned in response to my request.

It felt as if I were trying to persuade him to let me see his parents' photo collection, all over again. Finally, on one of my visits, at long last, he gave me permission to search his private room for the recipes.

Prior to that day, I had never spent more than a few seconds in this tiny eight-by-ten-foot chamber. Boxes, bags, and random objects were piled everywhere. In contrast to the tidiness that prevailed in the rest of my dad and Carol's home, this room looked as if a tornado had just blasted through it.

I began sorting through the containers, which were crammed full of papers of every conceivable description. Interspersed among utility bills dating from the 1970s and equally ancient bank statements were postcards, letters, greeting cards, and other mementos. These boxes seemed to contain every single item that the US Postal Service had ever delivered to my dad. Never before had I realized what a packrat he was.

"You know, you're in the inner sanctum. I've never been in there." Eyes wide, Carol stopped at the door of the little room as I dug through the chaos. "Good for you, finally getting some of this stuff cleaned up."

I carefully sorted through box after box. At first, although I didn't find Grampa's recipes, I unearthed lots of unexpected items, including my parents' wedding album, a box of photos from my father's and my childhoods, and a small book, *The History of My Life*, which his brother Al had created at age thirteen. One box contained a cardboard Santa Claus my dad had made as a child, with a suit of red paper, a cotton-wool beard, and moving limbs attached by small round brass joints.

I was a woman on a mission. *If I just keep looking through every single box, I'll find the recipes*, I told myself. *Be methodical, systematic, thorough. That was how I had finally uncovered my grandparents' secret. Just do the same thing now.* Grampa's recipes, precious remnants of his indefatigable creativity, had to be here somewhere.

"Who needs this stuff?" That was my dad's terse comment during his occasional passes up and down the hallway outside the room. "Take it back with you. If you don't, I'm going to throw it all out."

So absorbed was I in discovering these treasures that I barely registered the tension underlying my father's brusque statements. I thought it unlikely that he would make good on his threat to toss these irreplaceable items, yet I wasn't taking any chances. I began stacking boxes in the hallway outside the junk room, to come back with me to Boston for safekeeping.

After my excavation of the junk room failed to unearth the recipes, my dad directed me to the basement storage area, a dark alcove next to the laundry room. Until that moment, I had never even known it existed.

"Go through anything you want," he said, turning on a bright light that revealed a hodgepodge brigade of stacked boxes and bags.

Sitting on the floor in front of the boxes, I got to work. Stashed in these containers were my dad's elementary school report cards, spelling exercise books, and early book reports. I also unearthed his short-lived childhood diary and the first pages of a memoir he had begun in the 1980s. My search even turned up correspondence with B. F. Skinner, one of the founders of modern behavioral psychology. After meeting Skinner during graduate school at Duke, my dad remained friendly with him for decades. Skinner is perhaps best known for his operant conditioning enclosure, the "Skinner box," which is used to study the behavioral response of laboratory animals to positive reinforcement.

Buried deep in the storage area, beneath an untidy pile of bags, I found boxes stuffed with letters from my grandmother to my dad, all neatly tucked in their original envelopes. Between September of 1952, when he left for graduate school, and March of 1960, when cancer robbed her of the ability to correspond, Ida wrote literally hundreds of letters to her beloved Harley.

"Dad, there's tons of letters from your mother," I said, when he poked his head in the storage area. "Can I read them?"

"Read anything you want," he said. "Take anything you want. I'm going to throw it all out." He kept repeating those phrases: *Read it. Take it. I'm throwing it out.*

During my dad's first year of grad school, Ida's letters reflected the profound loss she felt after his departure. *"It is just as tho [sic] someone was kicking me in the stomach,*" she wrote in September of 1952. Ida was forever asking what she could get or do for him, or requesting that he send his footlocker of dirty clothes to her so she could quickly wash and mend them and send it all back.

"Please don't hesitate to ask for anything that you need," she wrote. "I hope you know I would do anything I can for you."

In 1953, with all of her sons out of the house, Ida found new purpose when she enrolled at the Akron School of Practical Nursing to become a Licensed Practical Nurse (LPN). Thereafter, her letters were filled with stories about nursing and about the profound satisfaction she derived from working as a practical nurse at Akron's St. Thomas Hospital, where she began as a student nurse and continued after receiving her degree in 1955.

"I am having fun even if it is hard work," she wrote. She excelled in her chosen profession, with patients frequently asking that Mrs. Hanson be the one to care for them. Speaking of patient Mother Roselia, a nun and Catholic school teacher, Ida wrote, "She paid me a very nice compliment, she had to have a Scultetus binder put on, other nurses had her on my days off, she told them that I was the only one that made her feel comfortable and would they get me to put it on her again." (A Scultetus binder is a large abdominal bandage with many tails that are wrapped in overlapping fashion.)

Patients frequently called Ida at home, too. "Just had another telephone call from patients, that is three tonight," she wrote Harley.

"Listen to this. It is so funny," I called out to my father from my seat on the basement floor as I skimmed a 1956 letter. Ida was describing how much she enjoyed it when the registered nurses were out, because then she got to perform tasks, such as catheterizations or changing dressings, which usually were the province of the RNs.

"I like it very much, just think no baths or pulling sheets or turning over baby elephants that don't try to help themselves," she wrote. "Wonderful work. It is too bad some of the RNs can't stay off more."

When my grandmother began the LPN program and started working as a nurse, the anxiety and depression that had intermittently plagued her throughout my father's childhood disappeared.

"I feel better now than I have for a long time and sleep much better," she wrote Harley. "I am better off working. I don't have a chance to have any aches or pains."

While heartache and guilt over leaving her first son undoubtedly haunted Ida for the rest of her life, ministering to others through nursing seemed to have brought deep relief and satisfaction. Although it is only speculation, perhaps, each time Ida eased a patient's suffering, she also was decreasing her own and exonerating herself of the pain she had caused in her earlier incarnation.

However, I also think that my grandmother, a talented and energetic woman, simply needed a purpose, an outlet for her passion and intelligence, beyond the confines of home and family. She found it through nursing.

"I sure do enjoy doing it," she wrote. "I like to make a patient as comfortable as possible especially if they have some incurable disease, or cancer."

Although the concept of feminism was virtually unknown in public discourse during the 1950s, Ida's pursuit of her nursing career strikes a surprisingly modern note.

Of the nun who supervised her at St. Joseph's, Ida wrote, "She thinks it is remarkable that I work when I don't have to work for a living."

Employed full-time at the hospital, Ida faced issues that many women still encounter today. Even when working, she was responsible for maintaining her and Frank's home.

"I'm 'dog tired' after 8 hours on the hard floors, we are not permitted to sit down while on duty," she wrote of nursing. "It certainly keeps me busy, plus caring for the house, washing, ironing and cleaning my floors."

Out of everything I learned about my grandmother during my investigations, the profound satisfaction she derived from her nursing career, begun in her fifties after her children had left home, is one of my favorites. Ida, who in her twenties found the courage to start over and paid an enormous price, later in life possessed the strength, yet again, to begin a new and fulfilling chapter that added yet another layer to her story.

Midafternoon, my dad again appeared in the basement storage area.

"Annie, you wanted to go to the gym, didn't you?" His steady tone was as close to plaintive as I had ever heard it. "If we're going to go, we should go now."

Although our dad-and-daughter gym excursions were a treasured ritual of my visits, today I had more pressing tasks. I didn't know if my dad would ever let me go through these boxes again. I needed to find and preserve as many significant items as possible.

When I finally finished burrowing through the basement, it was eight p.m. Some ten hours after beginning my dive into the receptacles of my father's past, I had finally unearthed Grampa's bread recipes, tucked in a manila envelope at the bottom of a box. So eventful had my day's explorations been that I scarcely remembered that finding the recipes had been my initial goal.

"I think I can do without hearing any more from my mother's letters," my dad said.

Carol had prepared a dinner of quiche and braised squash, which, as usual, we consumed in the keeping room.

"This is great," I said and went back for seconds. I hadn't eaten since breakfast, a frequent occurrence when I'm totally absorbed in a project.

Before dinner, my father had gulped down a few glasses of his favorite drink, iced tea with vodka. Now, as we sat at the dinner table, he mostly rearranged the food on his plate.

"It's good, it's really good," he kept saying, yet he ate almost nothing, and the words tumbled out almost as a chant, in a key just higher than his usual tone.

While Carol and I chatted amiably, he didn't join in.

As we were concluding the meal, my dad abruptly stood up from the table and sat on the keeping room couch.

"It's OK, it's all right," he repeated over and over, the words coming out in a breathy rush. He leaned forward from his perch on the edge of the couch, staring at his feet. Although he clearly had drunk too much, too fast, which I had seen before, this was different.

It finally hit me: He was trying to reassure himself.

"It's all right, it's all right," he kept saying, in spasmodic, short phrases. Always outwardly calm and in control of his emotions, this was my dad's version of a meltdown.

A sick feeling twisted the pit of my stomach. What had I done? I had been so determined to find Grampa's recipes, so proud that I could ferret out anything. Had my relentless search through the artifacts of my father's past been reckless? Selfish?

He lurched up from the couch. "Is Sox out?" He was referring to the much-loved cat that he and Carol had adopted as a feral runt kitten.

"Don't worry, I'll let him back in," Carol said now, putting her hand on his arm.

"I'm going to bed."

It was nine p.m. This was unheard of. My father never went to bed before midnight. Without further comment, he slowly walked down the hall to his and Carol's bedroom.

Carol and I stood in the kitchen. I couldn't stand this sinking feeling. "Oh my god, is he OK?"

"He'll be all right," Carol said. Her tone was confident.

"I feel so bad, I didn't realize what the impact on him was going to be."

"You did a good thing. He'll be fine in the morning," Carol continued. "He wanted you to do this. It'll be a huge weight off him to have that stuff out of here."

"I just had no idea he was going to react this way." I couldn't shake the worry that I had harmed my father.

"You know, he's a total softie," Carol said. "He misses his brothers so much. He feels a lot, but he doesn't show it," she added, echoing Joy Medvec's description of the Steeles.

I remember how my dad comforted me when Uncle Harvey died. After seeing my uncle take his last breath on June 17, 2000, I had sat in my rental car in the hospice parking lot as night fell, screaming and crying. Later, while dozing on my hotel room bed with the lights on, in a fog of sadness, I had been awakened by the phone ringing. It was my dad, calm and reassuring as always, making sure I was OK, even though his twin brother had just died.

"I think your father was his mother's favorite," Carol mused now, as we stood in the kitchen. "He always paid attention to what she was doing. He always worried about her and wanted to take care of her. He knew something was wrong, but he didn't know what it was."

This reminded me of a comment my father made a few times: "I was the sweet one." When I asked him why he said that, he couldn't answer me.

Now, I think I know why. Of the four brothers, my dad was the observant and sensitive one, the child who noticed the feelings of others and tried to understand them. He was the twelve-year-old who kept his mom company in the kitchen as she cooked, listening to her stories as he chopped onions and potatoes. He paid attention to her moods, noting them in his short-lived diary: "Momee [sic] isn't feeling well," "Momee is sick today," "Momee is better."

When I walked down the hall toward the guest room in my father and Carol's home later in the evening, the door to their bedroom was open. My dad was lying on his back on the bed, fully dressed, asleep. I had never seen that before.

The next morning, he was fine, just as Carol had predicted. After grabbing a quick breakfast at a local diner, we cheerfully chatted about the sunny weather, perfect for the long drive back to Boston.

"I bet Marc's really gonna love all this stuff you're bringing back," he joked as we hauled the boxes out to my car.

Yet another piece of my dad's life was coming home with me—for safe-keeping, for remembering, for telling his story. I was keeper not only of the archives, but of my dad's past.

"You should put the photos and letters in a safe," he said. "Buy a safe, and I'll pay for it."

Typically for him, he expressed his deepest feelings indirectly, in this case through an offer of material support.

When I later asked my dad about his distress that evening, he didn't remember it. His short-term memory wasn't what it used to be, especially after a few drinks. Nonetheless, he did his best to answer my questions.

"Why do you hate looking through the boxes so much?" I asked.

"It's painful," he said.

"Why?"

"I find it enormously anxiety-producing."

"What do you mean?" I prodded.

"It just stirs up old things, things long gone and handled."

"Can you give me some examples?" I persisted.

"No."

However, another time, when I asked him why going through the boxes of mementos was so painful, he did provide an example.

"My mother, for one. Her dying the way she did."

When the cancer was metastasizing throughout Ida's body, the pain was unbearable, yet her doctor refused to prescribe medication sufficient to relieve her agony. His rationale was that he didn't want her to become addicted, so they needed to hold off on the painkillers as long as possible.

"She's dying, and you're worrying about her getting addicted?" My dad's anger remained visceral. "That was unforgivable."

Horrified by his mother's suffering, twenty-nine-year-old Harley had taken matters into his own hands. He got hold of some codeine, spent a few sessions with a buddy packing it into capsules, and drove to Akron with a big batch of pills. Frank administered the codeine to Ida, so her final months of life were comfortable and peaceful.

Among all the discoveries of my Hanson family investigation, for me, the surprise occurring closest to home was the discovery that emotions ran strongly beneath the surface of the calm, steady father I had always known and counted on. Especially for men of my dad's generation, quashing or denying feelings is not unusual, but nonetheless, discovery of the "total softie," as Carol put it, was a revelation.

"One thing I've learned in the last few years is that you do have strong emotions, but you always keep calm, you keep things under control," I said to my dad.

"That would be a correct statement," he replied evenly, before heading back to his comfort zone. "In the laboratory, you have to keep everything at arm's length, not become involved. If you get overinvolved, people start making up data."

One Christmas, when I gave my dad a University of Akron T-shirt to wear at the gym, I again saw, for a brief moment, the emotions he always suppressed. When he opened the gift, his head jerked up ever so slightly and a tear came to his eye, which he quickly blinked away. I had never seen this before. I realized that for my dad, this wasn't just a T-shirt. The University of Akron represented his mom's insistence on education, the love and sacrifice of his parents, and their wholehearted support of him during college and graduate school. It was a piece of his past that had shaped the course of his life.

He hadn't actually started his psychology career as a scientist, my dad told me. When he first began studying psychology at the University of Akron, the department was strictly Freudian, and so he had focused on people and therapy.

"There was definitely an element of trying to understand my parents," he said. "I wanted to understand where I was and where I was coming from, and at the time, clinical psychology seemed to offer this."

However, once my father got to graduate school and discovered behavioral psychology, a scientist was born, and touchy-feely went out the window. Nonetheless, his profound desire to understand his parents remained. His preferred way of expressing this sentiment is not necessarily comprehensible to the ordinary person.

"Why were you so interested in your parents' pasts? Why did you encourage all of us to do the research?" I asked him.

"Well, I am a psychologist," my dad replied. "People of my ilk are interested in the controls of other peoples' behavior, as well as in their own."

"Dad, you've gotta say it in plain English!" I laughed.

And he did.

"There were a number of things about my parents that were not understandable. Why wasn't there a clear track of their past, a clear history? Why did they act in this way?" He added, "Now I know, this was not random behavior. People do things for reasons."

As for that family trip to New York City in December of 1949, when Harley had been so baffled by Frank and Ida's refusal to show the twins the supposed Brooklyn neighborhoods of their youth? When Frank subsequently disappeared for an afternoon and upon his return said that he had seen his mother's grave, he had, indeed, gone to New Britain. Photos from my grandparents' collection of New Britain's Winged Victory Soldiers' Monument and the World War I monument in Walnut Hill Park turned out to be from the same roll of film as Hanson family snapshots from that New York excursion.

Some have asked whether, after learning the truth, my father felt he had been shortchanged during his childhood or harmed by his parents' lies and contradictory tales. Always, his answer was an emphatic, "No."

"I can't speak for my brothers, but that is absolutely not true for me. My parents were very good parents," he said. "I think kids are capable of handling all sorts of diametrically opposed ideas. What do they call that, cognitive dissonance? That's just the way things were."

He had always wanted the truth, and now, at long last, he had it. After a lifetime of trying to understand his parents, their behavior finally made sense.

"When you broke the case, this was my first opportunity in seventy years for the possibility of clarity," he said firmly. "Now, I know why they did what they did. I don't feel angry, not at all. Since you found out about my parents, I have a whole lot of answers."

CHAPTER 28:
HAVE I EVER LIED TO YOU?

1960 *(Imagining the past)*

"I SHOULDN'T HAVE LEFT HIM," Ida murmured, staring straight up at the ceiling from the hospital bed Frank had set up in the living room. "I'm sure he hates me."

"You know he's all right. We saw him at his house," Frank replied quietly. That was the sort of thing he would say to comfort her, without lying. Sometimes, he simply held her hand.

"You mustn't tell the boys." Ida turned her head toward him. Her voice, now a hollow echo of her former decisive tones, contained more plea than command. "They can never know."

"I won't tell them."

Ida sighed and closed her eyes.

Sitting by the bed as Ida rested, Frank's thoughts traveled back to that fateful encounter in New Britain, when their lives first began to intertwine. He saw the long-legged, forceful, tantalizing young woman with whom he had fallen in love. Her skin shimmered in the sunlight, and her clear, expressive eyes spoke to his mind and heart. This woman, a force to be reckoned with, had become his.

Ida, forever, was the strong, supple creature ready to plunge into the waves as she gazed out into the ocean in the summer of 1924. Frank's life had never been the same after Ida entered it. And he didn't regret any of it, not one bit.

IN THE MID-1950S, when Ida found the lump in her breast, she didn't tell her sons and she didn't get treatment. She just kept on working as a nurse at St. Thomas Hospital.

Ida finally underwent a radical mastectomy at St. Thomas in September of 1956. "I received the 'Devil' from both Doctors for putting it off so long when I knew what I had and being a nurse," she wrote Harley. "I just couldn't let anything stand in my way of seeing both twins receive their PhD Degrees and taking my State [nursing] examination." Among the many secrets Ida kept from her sons was that breast cancer had killed her own mother at forty-three and her maternal grandmother, Ellen Howe of Sheffield, at fifty.

Even by the standards of the 1950s, Ida's mastectomy was performed poorly, resulting, among other things, in hemorrhaging of the forty-square-inch graft that the surgeon had carved from her right leg up to her neck. Nonetheless, despite the opposition of Frank and her sons, Ida insisted upon returning to nursing part-time after an arduous six-month recuperation.

"It is such a healthy tiredness to work and have the satisfaction of doing some good to others," Ida wrote Harley when she was longing to return to nursing. She had to buy new uniforms with a high neck and wide sleeves to hide the disfigurements resulting from her mastectomy.

By 1959, Ida's cancer had returned, with the deadly cells spreading through her body at a lethal pace. In early 1960, Ida and Frank bought a hospital bed for the living room, because she wanted to die at home. "I won't see my grandchildren grow up," she sobbed to my dad.

Frank quit working so he could take care of Ida himself.

"I am now a Cook, Dishwasher, Laundryman, Nurse and think I am doing alright so far," Frank wrote Harley in May 1960.

Employed steadily as a construction site boss for the past fifteen years, he, along with Ida, had saved enough so he could be there for her when she needed him most. Neither of them ever relinquished their Depression-era frugality. "If you make a dollar, you save a dime," Frank always said.

In those last weeks and days, when Frank fed Ida, bathed her, and administered her medications as she lay in her living room hospital bed, I wonder if the pair ever talked about the past they had so thoroughly buried. Did they discuss the people they had once been or family members they missed? Did they speak of Ida's first son?

Frank called my dad at 12:15 a.m. on Thursday, November 17, 1960. My dad and mom were in bed.

"Your mother just died," Frank said. "I'm standing by her, and she died a minute ago."

"Oh, not good, not good." Recalling that moment for me many years later, my dad still held his emotions at bay. "He loved my mother. He took care of her all through her life. He stuck with her through thick and thin. He took care of her up to the bloody end."

Ida was buried in her nurse's uniform. The first two paragraphs of her obituary in the *Akron Beacon Journal* focused on her nursing career accomplishments.

Late in Frank's life, he told my dad how sad he was that he no longer had anyone to take care of.

"I've always taken care of somebody," he said. "My sisters, my brothers, your mother, you, and your brothers. Now I have no one to take care of."

"That was the purpose of the man—to take care of people," my dad told me.

⁂

"Show me where you used to wave to your mother when you walked to school," I said to my father. In March of 2008, on a cloudy day following a snowstorm, we were standing in front of his childhood home at 1160 Clifton Avenue, in Akron. My cousin Frank—Frank Elmer Hanson III—was ferrying my father, Carol, Marc, and me around Akron on a tour of Hanson family landmarks during a visit with him, my father's surviving brother, Frank Jr., and Frank III's sister Tracy and her family.

"It's this way," my dad said. We strolled together down the sidewalk, past well-tended bungalows and two-story wood houses, in the same direction he and his brothers used to walk on their way to the Andrew Jackson Elementary School. "Right here."

"Why don't you turn and wave like you used to, and I'll take a picture."

My dad turned and waved back at the house, just as he had twice every school day as a child, once on his way in the morning and again when heading back to school after lunch. More than sixty years had passed since Ida stood outside the front door, waving her sons off to school, keeping them in sight as long as possible.

"That's how we did it," he said.

We strolled back toward the house. When my father had walked here on a warm July evening in 1943, the dark street, punctuated with house lights every few feet, had echoed with the sound of President Franklin D. Roosevelt's voice. The radio in every modest home was tuned to Roosevelt's "Fireside Chat," the series of enormously popular radio talks he gave between 1933 and 1944. In the era before air-conditioning, with all windows flung open in hope of a breeze to relieve the stifling heat, the radio waves carrying Roosevelt's assured tones emanated from each house, reverberating up and down humble Clifton Avenue.

In March of 2008, windows were shut tightly, and inside every dwelling each TV was no doubt tuned to a different cable channel. My father's childhood home, however, looked much as he remembered it. The shingles that Frank had painstakingly applied and painted gray retained their color, and the two second-story dormer windows still poked up through the long, sloping front roof. One of the windows had been the boys' bedroom, the other Frank and Ida's.

"Look at that," my dad said. "See those storm sashes? My father made them. How about that? They're still here."

Framing almost all of the windows, the red of the storm sashes Frank built in the 1940s from salvaged redwood was clear and dark in the flat white light reflecting up from the snow-covered ground.

For almost two years prior to this Akron pilgrimage, my dad drove around with a paper coffee cup half-filled with dirt, which he stashed in the glove compartment of his silver Toyota Highlander. He had collected this soil during a summer 2006 visit to the New Britain grave of his grandparents, Elof and Elida Harriander. Using his windshield ice scraper, he had dug up enough soil from the front of their gravestone to half fill the empty cup, which happened to be rolling around the Highlander at the time. After he had scraped up the dirt, my dad and I posed for a photo at Elof and Elida's grave. With his left hand clutching the scraper and coffee cup of New Britain earth and his right on my shoulder, my dad wore a satisfied grin beneath his floppy light-green hat. Here was a man who felt he was about to set things right.

At Akron's Mount Peace Cemetery in March of 2008, where the chilly grays, whites, and muted browns of winter had displaced the sun-dappled greens of summer, my father finally completed his mission. He, Frank III, Marc, and I trudged through the snow to Frank and Ida's grave, a reddish-gray marble tombstone with HANSON inscribed in large letters, with my grandparents' first names, birth and death years, and a large cross. The cross had been Ida's choice.

Grasping the top of the stone for support, coffee cup in hand, my dad leaned over and sprinkled the soil in a neat row across the front length of the gravestone, mingling New Britain earth with a few dried brown leaves curled up on the frozen white crust. He had wanted to erect a small sign stating that this was the grave of Frank Harriander and Ida Steele, but his surviving brother, Frank Jr., had vetoed that plan. Never much interested in his parents' past, and a stickler for propriety, Frank preferred the old version of the Hanson family story.

In what seemed to have become a Hanson family tradition, we took group photos at the gravesite. In all of them, my hand, clad in a brown leather glove acquired in Argentina, rested on top of my grandparents' gravestone—sometimes just two or three fingers, sometimes my whole hand, but always touching. Beginning with my first excursion to New Britain's Fairview Cemetery with Marc in July of 2003, I had become a regular at graveyards, ironic for one who previously had avoided them so assiduously. When Marc and I first encountered the tombstone of my great-great-grandparents David and Eliza Steele, which had whispered the clue that opened the door to the past, I had placed my hand on their gravestone with just a trace of uncertainty.

Five years later, during that chilly March afternoon in Akron, I felt no such trepidation. For me, it had all started with Grampa. I just wanted to be close to him.

When I "broke the case," as my dad always referred to my July 2003 discoveries, he was the first to say that I should write a book. In the years that followed, we engaged in a never-ending dialogue about his parents' past, his childhood, and mine as well. During visits, informal conversations had a way of turning into family history dialogues.

"What were you telling me about the soot from the power plant on the Cuyahoga River?" I asked one evening.

"Let's see," my dad said, leaning back in his chair and looking up, as he often did while plucking yet another vivid sixty-year-old nugget from his memories.

"If I stood under a tree when the wind was blowing from the power plant, the soot sounded like rain when it landed on the tree leaves," he said. "On the rare occasions I was forced to wear a collared white dress shirt, after a few hours the collar would be stained gray with soot."

And off we went on another time travel session, my gear the nearest pen and paper I could grab. Marc and Carol slipped out of the room, leaving my father and me to our shared journey. After responding to each question, my dad paused, patiently waiting for me to finish scribbling before he continued his reply.

Other times, back home outside Boston, I'd call him with more questions or to check details.

"Hi, Dad, got a minute for a couple questions?"

"I don't know if I can answer them, but I'll try."

Sitting at Marc's desk in the condominium we now shared, I'd talk into the speakerphone, typing my father's comments as quickly as I could.

"What color was that Studebaker your parents drove in the 1950s?" I asked once. "I see it in the background of a lot of those photos they took in Fairview Cemetery."

"It was dark green. We used to call it the Green Monster."

After responding to each question, he always waited patiently for me to finish typing before he continued.

Occasionally, my father called to make sure I understood the significance of a detail we had previously discussed.

"I was just thinking about it, and those redwood window storm sashes that my father made, they're still on the house sixty years later, still functioning well," he said once in a typical voice mail message. "Yeah, he built them to last."

My dad's surviving brother, Frank Jr., always the least involved of the siblings in the family project, initially refused, as had Virginia, to accept my discoveries. While he ultimately admitted their truth, he never had any interest in the details, although he did speak on the phone several times with cousin Jean Czako.

"My feelings on this are rather mixed. I acknowledge the fact that it is true, but it hasn't changed my life very much," he said once via email, in a typical comment. "The fact that my parents were able to lie to us kids is a little disappointing, but they certainly did a great job at it."

Uncle Frank committed to attending the 2004 Hanson-Harriander reunion, only to back out the day before I was to pick him up at the Hartford, Connecticut, airport. Although I cannot recall his excuse, I believe the real reason was that his increasing frailty, along with his preference for the old version of his parents' past, rendered him unable to face the emotions of such a reunion.

By contrast, my dad always embraced the new experiences that my discoveries brought, no matter how difficult the emotions. For years I had no idea how profoundly he struggled with the revelations of his parents' pasts. Indeed, it was Carol and not he who later told me how agitated he was before our first Harriander-Hanson family reunion in the fall of 2003.

"When we were going to that reunion, we were meeting these people, but he wasn't completely understanding why these people were relatives," she said. "He kept saying, 'I can't believe it, I just can't believe it.' This was the last thing he ever expected to know about his parents. He was so totally blindsided."

At the time, I just saw the same calm and steady dad I had always known. I hadn't understood that he, always so fiercely protective and supportive, felt it was his duty to shield me from his pain.

"He didn't want to burden you," Carol said.

During our conversations in the keeping room, usually later in the evening, I also learned the extent to which my dad had endeavored to protect me during my parents' divorce. Through his quiet comments, I learned, for the first time, that my mom was the one who had wanted out of the marriage into which these freshly minted University of Akron graduates had entered, at what now seem the impossibly unprepared, tender ages of twenty-one and twenty-two.

When my dad, twenty-one and already engaged to my mother, left home to attend Duke University in September of 1952, he entered an exciting universe of new ideas. He was fortunate to learn from some of the leading intellectuals in the field of behavioral psychology, such as Norman Guttman, and he began thinking in an entirely different way.

"It was a whole new world," my dad told me. He began having second thoughts about his upcoming marriage to Joyce in December of that year.

"I knew it was a mistake, but it was too late to do anything about it," he said, in a gentle tone.

Prevailing norms were different in the 1950s, my dad added. "The informal law of the land was that you married in your early twenties, you had the first child two years later, and a second one two years after that. For your mother and I, it worked pretty well, I think, for a number of years."

"I married your father because I wanted to get away from home, to get out of Akron," my mother later said, in confirming my dad's account of their split.

I suspect my parents were in love, once. Buried deep in my dad's papers was a love poem my mom wrote to him shortly after their marriage. I, their third child, resulted from a romantic evening with a bottle of wine that my parents had enjoyed after moving to Pennsylvania for my dad's job at Merck. Thinking about my conversations with both of them, I believe that part of their undoing may have been that the more the young scientist Harley embraced the concepts of behaviorism, the less he was able to meet the emotional needs of Joyce, a talented, strong woman whose father had let his family down badly.

Talking about their relationship with my dad, and then my mom, gave me a sense of closure I hadn't known was missing. Although I had long since made peace with the pain I suffered during and after my parents' divorce, their split made more sense now. With a better understanding of their earlier lives, all the more deeply do I appreciate now the foundational love they gave me during my childhood, as well as how hard they worked to support and nurture my sisters and me.

"Truth is best," my dad said, when my discovery of his parents' real past was just beginning. That goes for me, too. I wonder how often people go through life with mistaken narratives of the past that could be corrected through loving, honest conversation.

Aunt Virginia preferred to keep her distance from the new version of the Hanson family history. She never asked questions and, despite having patiently answered a host of questions for this book, she did not want me to write it.

"Your grandparents didn't want anyone to know," she said. "You should respect their wishes. It's fine if it's just for the family, but not for other people."

When I told my dad Virginia's views, his response was immediate and unequivocal.

"I think it's wonderful you're writing this. I'd like to send copies as Christmas presents," he said. "It's all part of the public record when you think about it. Everything you found, it's all there for anyone to see. As far as I'm concerned, we don't have any deep, dark secrets."

Ironically, given my father's belief in behavioral psychology, speaking with me at length about his childhood, his past, and his parents served as a type of talk therapy that helped him work through the pain of learning his parents' true past and the extent of their lies.

"It's not difficult now," he said during one of our later conversations. "Talking with you, and your working on this book, has helped me get a lot of closure. My appreciation of the past, of my parents, has been helped by your research."

Near the small keeping room sofa where he read during the day, my dad kept a draft of this book, which he read and reread, sometimes making small comments in the margins or noting questions that he wanted to ask me. Through reading my book and thinking about its contents, my dad, a deeply emotional yet controlled man, got the answers he needed via a medium that he could digest at his own pace.

It could not have been easy for him to read the scene in which I depict his distress after I found the bundles of letters that Ida wrote him in the 1950s. His only comment, directed toward the book as a whole, was, "It's a little more about me than I expected."

Although my dad understood why his father maintained his silence while Ida was living, he thought Frank should have told his sons the truth after she died.

"That's the time he should have come clean," he said. "Especially when you were up in Connecticut in college. But he elected not to do that."

Ida's flair for spinning fibs about the past, based on skillful recycling of real elements from her history, may have been a source of courage that helped her persevere and overcome obstacles in the new life and family she built with Frank. The alternate past that Ida created and nurtured, featuring the wealthy English gentleman father living on the Prospect Park farm, might have provided comfort and inspiration. In this brighter, happier universe, made real through ongoing repetition, Ida didn't drop out of school to go to work after her parents died. She didn't make the biggest mistake of her life, her marriage to Tom Keevers, the day after her eighteenth birthday. She had been educated, gone to normal school, and waited until she was twenty-one to marry Frank, the love of her life. Ida's fantasy of the past became the very real future—of education, of success, of secure, productive lives—into which she propelled my father, his brothers, and future generations.

Ultimately, for my dad, the moral of the story is that you should endeavor to tell your children the truth.

"Have I ever lied to you?" he asked me. "I hope I haven't. I try not to. It's hard to avoid with little kids, but it's very easy with adult children."

Some have said to me that, at some level, Frank wanted us to find the truth after he was gone. If he really wanted to make sure no one would ever discover his and Ida's real past, wouldn't he have destroyed every single one of the telltale photos and negatives?

I tend to think not. Living in an era before the internet, not to mention the twenty-first century's ubiquitous social media and advances in genetic genealogy, Frank simply could not anticipate how technology would transform our ability to uncover secrets of the past. He could not foresee that in the early twenty-first century, a curious and determined grandchild would have the ability, using an invention called the personal computer, to connect to a global network of information residing on a network of linked, massively powerful computers, commonly referred to as the internet. He could not have predicted that I, by researching nineteenth-century US Census records available via this internet, could discover the link to Ida's real family via the blurry inscription on the crooked David and Eliza Steele tombstone photo. Without the internet, it would have been exceedingly difficult—although, freed of time and money constraints, not strictly impossible—to connect Agnes Ida Howe, supposedly of Brooklyn, New York, with Ida Agnes Steele, granddaughter of David and Eliza Steele of New Britain, Connecticut.

Frank's failure to destroy the telltale photos does, however, testify to his love for Ida. I think of the time I visited him during college, and he remarked that he couldn't bring himself to throw away the jars of tomatoes she had preserved twenty years earlier. His attachment to her, and his inability to discard artifacts of her past, trumped his resolve to keep their secret.

In 2008, Harley waved at 1160 Clifton Avenue (middle house) from the same spot where he waved to his mother on the way to school every day during childhood.

EPILOGUE

MY DAD DIED OF CARDIAC ARREST on May 18, 2016. Coming with no prior warning, it was a horrible shock. During our last phone conversation two days earlier, I had grumbled about having to leave for another business trip to Utah that afternoon, while he told me about his workout with his trainer at the gym a few days earlier.

"Talk to you soon, byeeee!" Those were his last words to me, uttered in his usual affectionate, singsong tone, stretching out the final syllables.

I was devastated by my dad's death. Paralyzed by pain, for three years I spent my free time in front of the TV, catching up on shows such as *Mad Men* and *Downton Abby*, which I had never had time to watch before.

I have learned that the price of a deep and profound love is an equally deep pain upon its loss. My bond with my dad, always strong, strengthened in ways I never could have anticipated in the years after my discoveries. When I found the truth about his parents, I gave my father something he had yearned for his entire life.

"People spend years in therapy trying to understand their parents," a friend said. "In discovering the truth about your dad's parents, you gave him something most people never get to have. It was a gift of love."

During our years of family history conversations, I also became the repository of my dad's memories. Through his stories, I traveled through his past with him and became part of it. Sharing it with me, he was no longer alone. He, in turn, told me many times how proud he was of me and my research.

"You can run from Annie, but you can't hide," he joked. "She'll find it out."

How my dad would have loved the remarkable gift that David and Mark Roden, Marty and Hilda's sons, gave me in June of 2022—a tour inside the Steele farmhouse at 771 Farmington Avenue, which was uninhabited and had been boarded up. I stood on worn floorboards in the dining room where young Ida had unknowingly eaten her pet pig, Tug-Tug, for supper. Here, too, was the spacious front parlor, the original dark wood frame occasionally visible behind mid-century wallpaper, where Ida had accidentally barged in when poor Mama was being embalmed. The clamor and footsteps of the seven Steele siblings as they raced up and down the steep second-floor stairway echoed across a vanished century. My father didn't get to visit his mom's childhood home, but I saw it for him.

As we left the house, Mark plucked a long old-fashioned housekey that was hanging on a nail high by the door and placed it in my hand with a grin. With his gesture I came to possess, literally, a key to my grandmother's past. I hope I have brought her home to New Britain, reuniting her with the life she could never entirely leave behind.

Above all, my dad wanted this book to be published. Despite his parents' unique history, he saw his family as representing working class people in mid-twentieth century America who used education to get ahead. He wanted told this story of ordinary people who struggled and overcame tremendous obstacles, some posed by society and others stemming from their own actions. It is about a woman, my grandmother, who silently bore the burden of a terrible secret, yet found a way to love, nurture, and educate her four sons during the Great Depression. And it is about Frank Harriander, my grandfather, who gave up everything to love and protect Ida Steele Keevers in the new life they created together.

I am forever grateful for the journey my dad and I took together. He was the first love of my life. He laid the foundation for my relationship with my husband, Marc, who is the love of the rest of my life.

In 2019, I got back to work on the book, finished the last bits of research, and revised a final time. This book is my gift of love to my dad, Harley Hanson.

ACKNOWLEDGMENTS

I AM DEEPLY GRATEFUL to the many people who helped me on the long and winding road I traveled with this book. Special thanks to Joy Medvec, Jennifer Nichols, and Bonnie Hearn Hill. Above all, I thank my husband, Marc Springer, for his love and support. I probably could have done this without him, but it wouldn't have been nearly as much fun. The center holds, now and always.

ABOUT THE AUTHOR

ANNE HANSON, an inveterate explorer of the unknown, has always followed when her curiosity beckoned. She crossed the ocean for her African Studies degree, and as a reporter would drive endless miles across town to get the story. Finally, when investigating her grandparents' secrets, she journeyed into a bygone century, her vehicle painstaking and detailed research.

Anne has written for the *Boston Globe* and numerous newspapers, as well as for corporate publications and the New England Historic Genealogical Society's *American Ancestors* magazine. Although she loathes first drafts, Anne loves whipping unfinished writing into shape.

When she is not sleuthing or writing, Anne, a lover of food, foreign languages, and local history, can often be found photographing plants and trees during open-air exercise sessions, or creating art with repurposed objects. During the day, she works for a software company. Her favorite authors include English novelists of the nineteenth and twentieth centuries such as Jane Austen, Anthony Trollope, and Barbara Pym.

A Wesleyan University graduate, Anne grew up in suburban Philadelphia, where she attended Quaker schools. She now lives with her husband just outside Boston, Massachusetts.

BOOK CLUB QUESTIONS

SPOILER ALERT

Beginning with Section II (The Past Revealed) on the next page, these questions refer to specific details of Frank and Ida's secret past. The author suggests that you hold off on reviewing them until you have finished the book.

I. BEFORE THE BREAKTHROUGH

What did you think the secrets were going to be at the beginning of the book?

Why do you think Harley so dreaded facing the box that contained his parents' photo collection? Have you had a similar experience?

Unlike Harley, his twin brother, Harvey, never wondered about his parents' inexplicably missing past. "I have all the family I want and need," Harvey said. Are you more like Harley or Harvey?

When reading the "Gun by the Bed" chapter, what did you think was Frank's reason for having the gun?

What drove Anne's intense determination to discover the truth of her grandparents' past?

II. THE PAST REVEALED

Do you think Tom Keevers Sr. physically abused Ida during their marriage? Does the imagined scene of Tom Keevers assaulting Ida ring true to you?

Only intense fear could have made a devoted mother like Ida leave her child. Agree or disagree?

Short of vanishing from New Britain and leaving her child, what other route, if any, did Ida have out of her troubles in the New Britain of 1924? What role did Ida's gender play in limiting her options?

Ida's failure to tell her younger sister Edith about her plans to leave New Britain caused Edith lifelong pain, just as Frank's failure to contact his sister Ethel caused her great anguish. Why did they cut these ties so thoroughly? Was it hard-hearted, or something they had to do to prevent discovery?

With Jean as her guide, Anne traveled back in time into the world of the Harrianders, the family Frank left behind. In the same way, through her dad's stories, she traveled with him into his childhood. Why do some people possess the gift of remembering and bringing the past to life, while others have little interest?

Did the "Education Above All" chapter, with its discussion of how Frank and Ida nurtured their boys during the Great Depression and after, add to your understanding of life in the US during the mid-twentieth century? Do the family's experiences have parallels in your own family's history?

"We always knew you had to be out there, but you didn't know about us." This comment from Jean captures her wistfulness as well as her joy when Anne found the Harrianders. Why did Frank's granddaughter finding her mean so much to Jean?

III. IS THE PAST EVER REALLY OVER?

Looking back at the big picture, did Frank and Ida succeed in leaving their past behind? Does anyone ever succeed completely in leaving the past behind?

What obstacles would a young couple trying to disappear today face that Frank and Ida did not in 1924?

Harley thought Frank should have come clean about the past after Ida's death. Why do you think he didn't? Should he have? Do you think he ever considered doing so?

Frank could have destroyed the pictures after Ida died, but he chose to leave them. Do you think he wanted us to discover the truth after he was gone? Were the photos his way of providing clues, or simply a testament to his love for Ida?

All families have "founding stories" that mix truth and wishful thinking. Agree or disagree?

Does this book remind you of stories or secrets from your own family's past?

Does this book make you want to research your own family history?

IV. THEMES AND CHARACTERS

Did your opinion of Frank change over the course of reading the book? If so, how and why?

What is your opinion of Ida? Did your views change over the course of the book? If so, how and why?

Truth is best, Harley said, as Anne uncovered more and more seemingly inconceivable facts about his parents' past. Do you think truth is always best?

When Harley learned the realities of his parents' past lives, he accepted them without judgment or anger, despite the pain he experienced. What does this say about his character?

"That's the beauty of children. They take love where they find it." Do you agree with this quote from Jean, in which she refers to her childhood among loving aunts and uncles, and her cold grandmother?

The author rethought her ideas about class as she came to know the families her grandparents left behind. Did this cause you to think about your own ideas about class, and where you fit in?

Ida chose a highly non-traditional path in the 1920s when she left New Britain with Frank. Thirty years later, in the 1950s, she pursued a career in nursing.

Do you think she was, in her own way, an early feminist? Why or why not?

Anne, Harley, Frank, and Ida are the lead protagonists of Buried Secrets, but the story depends on numerous supporting characters, too. Who stands out in your mind, and why?

Do you like the imagined scenes with which several of the chapters commence? What do they add to the narrative? If you could add another imagined scene to the book, what would it be?

According to the author, Buried Secrets is a love story, on multiple levels. What are some of the ways love is expressed in Buried Secrets?

If you could travel into the past and interview one person in this book, who would it be? What would you ask him or her?

Ultimately, what do you think Buried Secrets is about?

ENDNOTES

1   Ruth Schell, "'Swamp Yankee.'" *American Speech* 38, no. 2 (1963): 121–23.

2   Patrick Thibodeau, *New Britain: The City of Invention* (Chatsworth, CA: Windsor Publications, 1989), 43.

3   "KEEVERS, Thomas F.," *Hartford Courant*, August 17, 1999.

4   "Judge Discharges Conductor Keevers," *New Britain Herald*, March 25, 1916.

5   Arlene C. Palmer, *Images of America: New Britain Volume III* (Charleston, SC: Arcadia Publishing, 1999), 123.

6   Milt Berkowitz, "Memories May Outlast Sarsfield Hotel," *Hartford Courant*, January 1, 1972.

7   Per Clemensson & Kjell Andersson, *Your Swedish Roots: A Step by Step Handbook* (Provo, UT: Ancestry, a division of MyFamily.com, Inc., 2004), 17.

8   "Suicide Attempt Blamed on Wife's Farewell Letter," *New Britain Herald*, September 4, 1930.

Printed in Great Britain
by Amazon